Black Widow, Inc.

8600 Melrose Avenue

Los Angeles,

California 90069

Dear Jeffrey,

Sorry this took so long but it's been crazy.

Here's a few photos for you including a personally autographed one.

If you wish to get in touch with myself or Alice, you can write to the adress on my card or call us at (602) [redacted]

(please keep that number to yourself, as it is private - not business).

Thanks again for the super article and let me know if you ever need passes in the future or interviews, etc.

Take care,

Brian Nelson

RENFIELD

TWX: 910-490-2516 ALIVE LSA

Published 2022
New Haven Publishing
www.newhavenpublishingltd.com newhavenpublishing@gmail.com

Cover design by Jeffrey Morgan. Interior design by Pete Cunliffe: pcunliffe@blueyonder.co.uk

ISBN: 978-1-949515-44-2

ALICE COOPER CONFIDENTIAL

Archived, Assembled, and Written by Jeffrey Morgan

*

Cover photography by Brian "Renfield" Nelson

*

Photography curated by Steve "Mac" McLennan

*

Designed by Pete Cunliffe

***

Without exception, ain't nobody in the entire history of rock 'n' roll ever ran riot through as many upgraded visual image changes while portraying the exact same fictional character on stage for over half a century as Alice Cooper did while playing the role of Alice Cooper. To be sure, other rock stars may have altered the cut of their jib from time to time but, lemme reiterate for ya, when they did it, they sure as shootin' weren't playing the exact same fictional character like Alice did each and every time he stalked the stage.

*

Ask anyone who was there at the time and somehow managed to survive the initial onslaught, and they'll all tell you that, until he arrived on the scene to ferociously assault the peace and love generation, no one who came before him ever looked like Alice Cooper. But you know what they say, seeing is believing. They also say that a single picture is worth a thousand words, which is why the photographic evidence contained within *Alice Cooper Confidential* exponentially cranks my meager rock critic word count into the lower six figures.

*

So let's give a big round of applause to the following crime scene photographers who, like myself, were there with a Speed Graphic to document the uncanny experience as the travelling Alice Cooper Pandemonium Shadow Show passed through their town. By selflessly allowing their photographs to be used, all seven decades of degeneracy are here on display, from the nineteen-sixties to the present day.

*

After all, without the work of these sixteen shutterbugs, the only thing you'd have to look at are my words—and what fun would *that* be? So here's a tip of the *Alice Cooper Confidential* cap to:

*

Alan Gibson • Brad McPherson • Brett Fenoir Fenwick • Denise Firman
Dwight McCain • George E. Orlay • Greg York • James Pappaconstantine
Juan Mahoney • Linda Weatherburn • Murray Fletcher • Nash The Slash
Phillip Solomonson • Robert Matheu • Shawn Cook • Ted Kutyla

*

Now let's see what's goin' on; see inside…

Photograph ©
James Pappaconstantine

TERMS AND CONDITIONS

These are the rules. Terms and conditions may apply. Read carefully before proceeding. This product is intended for educational purposes only. Void where prohibited by law. Subject to availability. License No. 52746. For best results, use only as directed. List each item separately. Use extra page if necessary. Contents may settle during shipment. No other warranty expressed or implied. Check your local listings. Close cover before striking. Factory sealed for your protection. The black bands at the top and bottom of the picture are normal. Proof of purchase required. Do not use while operating a motor vehicle or heavy equipment. Postage will be paid by addressee. Please allow six to eight weeks for delivery. This is not an offer to sell securities. Past performance is no guarantee of future results. Read the prospectus thoroughly first. Does not represent an average user. Your results may vary. Visitors sign in with Security. Apply only to affected area. Handicapped parking only. May be too intense for some viewers. Confidential when completed. Thank you for calling. All of our operators are busy at the moment. Your call is important to us. Please stay on the line and a customer representative will be with you shortly. Calls may be monitored for quality control purposes. Do not stamp. Continued on other side. For recreational use only. Exact change only. Mind the gap. Keep arms and head in. Do not disturb. Last gas for 500 miles. Standing room only. All models are over 18 years of age. If symptoms persist consult your physician. Open other end. Electrical hazard. Risk of electric shock. No user-serviceable parts inside. If alarm sounds return to cashier. Best if used before due date. Subject to change without notice. All times approximate. Soon to be a major motion picture. Closed for the holidays. Seating is for customers only. Caution liquid is hot. Preheat oven to 450 and place on cookie sheet on middle rack. No parking. Everything must go. Final week. Unauthorized vehicles will be towed away at owner's expense. Simulated picture. May complicate pregnancy. Please remain seated until the ride has come to a complete stop. Breaking seal constitutes acceptance of agreement. For off-road use only. Maid please make up room. As seen on TV. May cause drowsiness do not drive or operate heavy machinery. For external use only. To open, push down, then turn. Repeat broadcast, do not call. Fasten seatbelt. One size fits all. Aim away from face. Trespassers will be prosecuted. Penalty for misuse: fine or imprisonment. Although inspired by actual events, this story is entirely fictional. This end up. Colors may fade. We have sent the forms which seem right for you. Slippery when wet. For office use only. Not affiliated with any organization. Postage Paid if mailed in the United States. Drop in any mailbox. Edited for television. Keep cool and process promptly. Not a through street. No shirt, no shoes, no service. Right lane must turn right. Post Office will not deliver without postage. The Surgeon General advises that danger to health increases with amount smoked. Never siphon by mouth. List was current at time of printing. Any use of this product other than the one for which it is intended is illegal. Return to sender. Must be of legal drinking age to enter. No radio inside. Not responsible for direct, indirect, incidental or consequential damages resulting from any defect, error or failure to perform. At participating locations only. Not the real thing but an incredible simulation. No disc inside. Please turn off all pagers and cellular phones before entering the theater. Unauthorized use is prohibited. No bills larger that $20. Keep off the grass. Late patrons will not be seated until first available break in the program. See label for sequence. It is a criminal offense to make false or misleading statements. Substantial penalty for early withdrawal. Price excludes license, insurance, applicable taxes, freight and PDE. Pay your server. Do not write below this line. Contains new material. Do not remove under penalty of law. Lost ticket pays maximum rate. Insert tab A into slot B. Free delivery with minimum $50 order. To order, contact your local cable company. Your canceled check is your receipt. Elevators are available for passengers with difficulty negotiating stairs. Place stamp here. This is not an exit. Do not feed the animals. May contain traces of peanut products. Paper jam, call key operator. Avoid contact with skin. Sanitized for your protection. Thank you for holding. Someone will be with you shortly. Be sure each item is properly endorsed. Sign here. Filmed before a live studio audience. Portions of this broadcast were prerecorded. Take this medication with food. Prices slightly higher in the east. Prices may vary in Hawaii, Alaska and Puerto Rico. Employees and their families are not eligible. Now a major motion picture. Store in a cool, dry place. Suggested serving. Not exactly as illustrated. Turn off engine. Not actual size. Enlarged to show texture. Add toner. Proceed with caution. Sound horn. In case of fire, break glass. Do not refreeze if thawed. Cook from frozen. Contestants have been briefed on some questions before the show. A promotional consideration was paid in return for this announcement. Limited time offer. Call now to ensure prompt delivery. Use of this card acknowledges receipt of and agreement by the cardholder to the terms of any agreement(s) which from time to time govern any banking services for which the card may be used. You may already be a winner. In the event of an emergency, proceed in an orderly fashion to the nearest exit. Walk, do not run. Return for refund in MI, KY, VT, OR, MD and NY. You must be present to win. No passes accepted for this engagement. Buyer beware. Check purchase before leaving. Not transferable. Payable in U.S. funds only. Due to illness the starring roll in this afternoon's performance will be played by the understudy. Women's model only. Other products and companies referred to herein are trademarks or registered trademarks of their respective companies or mark holders. No purchase necessary. Buy one, get one free. Do not incinerate. Ticket holders line up here. Refrigerate after opening. Unsolicited submissions will not be accepted. The following is a test of the Emergency Broadcast System. Take a number for faster service. Processed at location stamped in code at top of carton. Shading within a garment may occur. Use only in a well-ventilated area. Keep in a dry place away from spark or open flame. Contents may explode under pressure. Deposit required. Replace with same type. Approved for veterans. Wristband policy is in effect. Stay tuned to this station for more details. Some equipment shown is optional. Price does not include taxes. American funds accepted at par. Not recommended for children. Prerecorded for this time zone. Mail back unused portion of product for complete refund of price of purchase. No cameras or recording devices allowed. No solicitors. Restaurant package not for resale. Do not send cash in mail. Photocopies and facsimiles are not accepted. For a full set of contest rules, send self-addressed stamped envelope to the above address. Check here if tax deductible. Do not open. Recommended for calorie-reduced diets. All other uses constitute fraud. Choking hazard: not for children under the age of six. All entries submitted become our property. Member FDIC. Based on double occupancy for 7 days/6 nights. Letters may be edited for length or clarity. List at least two alternate selections. A 20% gratuity has been added. Accessories extra. You have the right to remain silent. Anything you say can and will be used against you in a court of law. You have the right to an attorney. If you cannot afford an attorney, one will be provided for you. This film is not yet rated. The following preview has been approved for all audiences. First pull up, then pull down. Do not dry clean. For further information call the toll free number on your screen. Driver does not carry cash. Some of the trademarks mentioned in this product appear for identification purposes only. Place all metal objects in tray before proceeding through security. Not legal tender. Not legal for trade. Objects in mirror may be closer than they appear. Management reserves the right to refuse admittance. This broadcast is intended solely for the private use of our audience. Any recording, retransmission or rebroadcast of this program either in whole or in part without the express written consent of Major League Baseball is strictly prohibited. Do not leave child unattended. For the purposes of the Berne Convention, this teleplay is the work of this network and/or its affiliated stations. Record additional transactions on back of previous stub. Do not touch. No animals were harmed during the making of this picture. Harmful or fatal if swallowed. Do not fold, crush, bend, spindle or mutilate. This film not to be copied. Silence please. On approved credit. Credits are not contractual. Do not start engine until vessel has docked. Please move to the back of the bus. Coming soon to a theater near you. Good only on day issued. Do not drop. Keep engine running, put gearshift in neutral. Unsafe at any speed. Maximum capacity: 15 people or 3000 lbs. Do not puncture. Estimated street price. Wait until coins completely drop in slot before opening door. No refund or exchange. All sales final. Ship's registry: Liberia/Norway. Fragile handle with care. Those who appreciate quality enjoy it responsibly. Use in moderation. Not available in PA or NJ, not licensed in NY. Images were single-pass scanned at 300 dpi. Package sold by weight, not volume. Your mileage may vary. Not for use with some sets. Adult situations. Kids, get your parents' permission first before you call. This is an independent expenditure not approved by any candidate nor is any candidate responsible for it. I approved this message. Do not remove tag. Operators are standing by to take your call. No ticket no laundry. Professional driver on closed course. Don't try this at home. Cut on dotted line. Do not write in this space. Contact your branch. Screen images are simulated. Use as a motor fuel only. Not available in all colors. Includes the hit single. You are under no obligation to buy. Washrooms are for customer use only. Loading and unloading of passengers only. Employee does not have combination to safe. Limit one item per family. License, title, taxes, shipping, dealer prep not included in base sticker price. No rain checks. One way only. No smoking. 10 Eastern, 7 Pacific, 6 Mountain. Watch your step. No substitutions. Professional models not intended to represent actual people. Retain your stub. Safe operates on a time lock. Detach here. Keep out of reach of children. Don't drink and drive. The following program contains material that may be offensive to some viewers. Viewer discretion is advised. We are temporarily experiencing some difficulties. Please stand by. No cash on premises. Viewers strongly cautioned. Children under 18 not admitted without a parent or guardian. For renewals or change of address, please include current mailing label. Second Class Postage paid at St. Louis, MO. You must be this tall to ride. Minimum system requirements: current OS. 404 Error: The page you are seeking cannot be found at this location. Police line do not cross. Offer good only in the U.S. Operator does not provide change. Park and lock it. Not responsible for lost or missing items. Do not use if seal is broken. Persons with a heart condition, nursing mothers or others with a medical condition should seek the advice of a physician. Lather, rinse, repeat. Maximum headroom 12'5". Do not exceed maximum dosage of eight tablets in 12 hours. No waiting. Keep hands clear. Remember to take packages and belongings with you. See booklet for track listing. Remain behind white line and do not talk to the operator while vehicle is in motion. Do not dispose of used batteries in fire. Sign on the dotted line. There is enough mediation in this package to seriously harm a child. The number you have reached is out of service. Please hang up and try your call again. This is a recording. Please hang up now. Celebrity endorsement not implied. Admittance restricted to 18 years of age or older. Hearing protectors must be worn. Do not attempt. No unauthorized persons beyond this point. Access all areas. No step. May not be compatible with previous versions. Check requirements first. The picture has been modified from its original version and formatted to fit your screen. No food or drink allowed inside. Lyrics used by permission. Not valid in Alaska, Hawaii, Puerto Rico or other FPO. Send check or money order to the address on your screen. Sorry, no CODs. Use as required. You cannot be turned down. No salesman will call. Unauthorized duplication is a violation of applicable laws. Put tray in upright position. You break it, you bought it. Flush with water. Do not induce vomiting. Consult physician immediately. Not exactly as illustrated. Any resemblance to real persons, living or dead, is purely coincidental. Dealer may sell for less. Subject to approval. Some assembly required. Batteries not included. Read the fine print before signing. Accept no imitations. Marcas Registradas. Pat. Pending. Ignorance of the law is no excuse. Tell it to the judge. The moral right of the author has been asserted. Copyright © ® 2021 Jeffrey Morgan™. All rights reserved. You know the rules. The end.

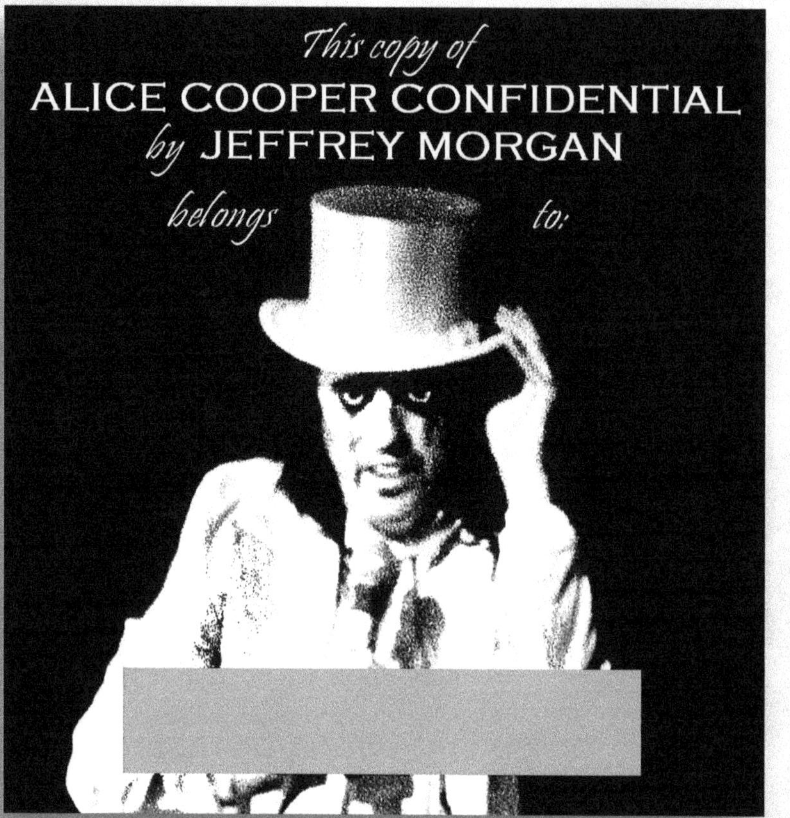

This copy of
ALICE COOPER CONFIDENTIAL
by JEFFREY MORGAN
belongs *to:*

DEDICATION

†

Jeffrey Morgan dedicates his life to Jesus Christ (John 3:16-17);
his life's work to the glory of God (1 Corinthians 10:31);
and he thanks the Holy Spirit for keeping him
on the narrow path (Matthew 7:13-14).

†

How To Use This Book

by J. Mark Berkowitz

Although presented in a traditional linear fashion, *Alice Cooper Confidential* by Jeffrey Morgan is not meant to be experienced as such; it is designed to be dipped into at random. For within, you will find a plethora of entry points; where you begin depends on which gilded path you choose to follow. Strictly speaking from a undeviating perspective, inside you will find:

*

RENFIELD AND ME

in which the author, for the very first time anywhere, sets the *mise-en-scène* and pays tribute to a good friend of every Alice aficionado.

*

DEAR ALICE

in which the author, for the very first time anywhere, discloses a decade's worth of actual unexpurgated misshapen messages, all of which were written to Alice in a fever-pitch frenzy by his sick things.

*

THE CHICKEN COOP

in which the author, for the very first time anywhere, reveals the greatest box set packaging design that was never used but most certainly should have been.

*

THE EXEGESIS EXHIBITS

in which the author, for the very first time anywhere, performs a chronological audio autopsy whereby he exhumes and examines the undead discography of rock 'n' roll's most malodorous musical practitioner in an arcane post-mortem probe that oozes with a sparsity of eerie anecdotes and a surfeit of exploitative analysis.

*

THE COOP CONVERSATION

in which the author, for the very first time anywhere, unearths and dusts off a previously unpublished off-the-cuff and on-the-record rap session with Alice Cooper.

****

Finally, a word about repetition.

Occasionally you will encounter instances in which the author duplicates certain phrases such as "taboo-defiling hoodlum flamboyance" even to the point of going so far in some instances as to habitually repeat entire paragraphs of text, word for word, over a period of many decades.

Be advised, however, that the use of this classic literary device of replication isn't the lazy work of some conceited hack, whose only goal is to shamelessly crank out as many pedestrian words as possible in as short a period of time as possible to publish as many pedestrian books as possible. After all, we *are* talking about *Jeffrey Morgan* here, and not an egotistical scribbler like... Well, there's no point in naming names.

It suffices to say, when reading these reoccurring phrases, that you think of them instead as being the visual linguist equivalent of a musical *leitmotiv*, which is purposely placed there as a recurrent *idée fixe* or *motto-theme*.

****

J. MARK BERKOWITZ *is a noted enviromusicologist and socio-sexual activist. His seminal article "The Hi-Fi Hipster" appeared in the March 1955 issue of* Playboy *and is recognized as being the first recorded instance of erudite rock criticism published anywhere in the world. He lives in Sweden with his wife, the award-winning adult movie actress Fårö Syrjäniemi.*

****

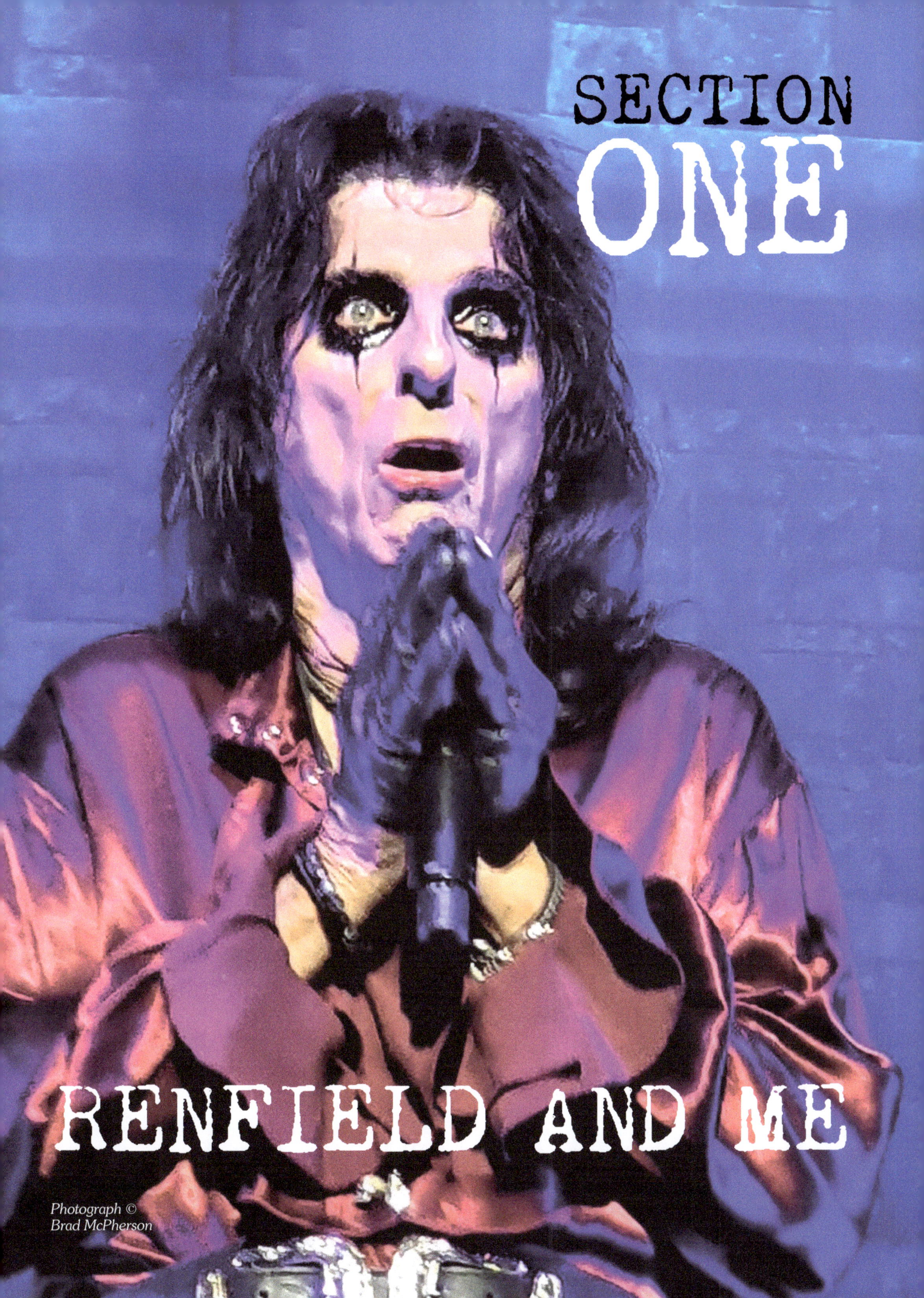
SECTION
ONE
RENFIELD AND ME
Photograph ©
Brad McPherson

JEFFREY MORGAN

RENFIELD AND ME

This is the true story of how "The King Of All VCRs" met "The King Of All Words" in 1983. The telephone is ringing and... No, that's not really true. It actually began in 1969 when I bought my first Alice Cooper album. Over a decade later, that fan-fueled fate train really began to pick up steam when I reviewed *Flush The Fashion* in the September 1980 issue of CREEM. Three years later, everything came screeching to a head-on collusion when I wrote a follow-up article titled *You're A Riot, Alice* in the May 1983 Metal Music issue of CREEM Close-Up. *That's* when the telephone rang.

"Hi, is this Jeffrey?" came a distinctive drawling voice on the other end of the line. "This is Brian Nelson, Alice Cooper's personal assistant."

Stunned by this unexpected turn of events, I immediately shot back: "How'd you get this unlisted number?" To which Brian laughed and said: "I called CREEM and they gave it to me. Look, I meant to call you when you reviewed *Flush The Fashion* several years ago, but I never got around to it. So I'm calling you now to thank you for that and for the new piece that you just wrote about Alice, which was very nice. Alice and I really appreciate it."

"Thanks," I replied, "but if it means *that* much to you, how about sending me an autographed photo?"

"Sure, I can do that for you," Brian said, and he did. A few weeks later, I received a signed Special Forces promo photo reading: "Jeffrey, thanks for the article, Alice Cooper '83." And that, I thought, would be that. Goes to show how wrong you can be, because that unsolicited phone call began a friendship which lasted over a quarter of a century, and is single-handedly responsible for me being here where I am today and in a position to be able to write these words for you.

***

Words. Brian and I wrote a ton of words over that quarter century, beginning with mailed letters and then, by the middle of the '90s, via email. The most important words we ever wrote, however, was as a team between 1992 and 1999 when we were working on what would ultimately become *The Life And Crimes Of Alice Cooper* box set that Brian produced. And once again, as before, he caught me unawares.

I had moved out of the city for a while and, upon returning in 1992, decided to have a listed phone number so that anyone who wanted to find me would have no excuse for not being able to do so. Stop me if you've heard this one before, but the telephone is ringing. Once again I picked it up to hear a now familiar distinctive drawling voice on the other end of the line. "Hi pally, it's Brian."

Stunned by this unexpected turn of events, I immediately shot back: "How'd you get this number? I've only been here for three months!"

Brian laughed and said: "I called directory assistance and they gave it to me. Look, and keep this to yourself because nobody knows about it yet, but we're doing an Alice box set and I could use your help." The help that Brian needed was in coming up with a suitable title for said set. "You're a good writer, maybe you can come up with one."

During the next few months we brainstormed over the telephone and came up with literally hundreds of titles, typed out (mine) and hand printed (Brian's) on many sheets of paper, all of which were mailed back and forth between our respective domiciles, and none of which were any good. Brian wanted to use *Decades Of Decadence*, but it had already been taken. The closest we ever came to agreeing on a single title was *Public Animal #1*, and even that one was too contrived to cut the mustard. It wasn't until 1995 that mutual friend and fan Steve "Mac" McLennan came up with the perfect pitch: *The Life And Crimes Of Alice Cooper*, which both Brian and I immediately wished we'd thought of ourselves because it was that good.

During an early phone conversation, Brian admitted that he had another problem on his hands. An embryonic draft of the box set's liner notes had been attempted but it wasn't very good and, well, what with me being a writer and all, would I mind taking a look at it to see if something could be done with it? When I read what Brian had mailed me, I immediately knew that not only was it dry as dust, even worse than that was the inescapable fact that the uninspiring words contained within didn't even come remotely close to enlightening the world as to who Alice Cooper was, and why he was such an influential defining figure in the entire history of rock 'n' roll.

When I told Brian this, he readily agreed, and we proceeded to begin what would be a seven-year-long process of writing what would ultimately become Alice's authorized biography. Why seven years? I'll get to that in a minute. Although I had just bought my first personal computer, this was a year before either one of us was online, so Brian and I began by having marathon telephone conversations which usually lasted upwards of two and a half hours per night, several nights a week, during which time we would hash out what to say, and how to say it.

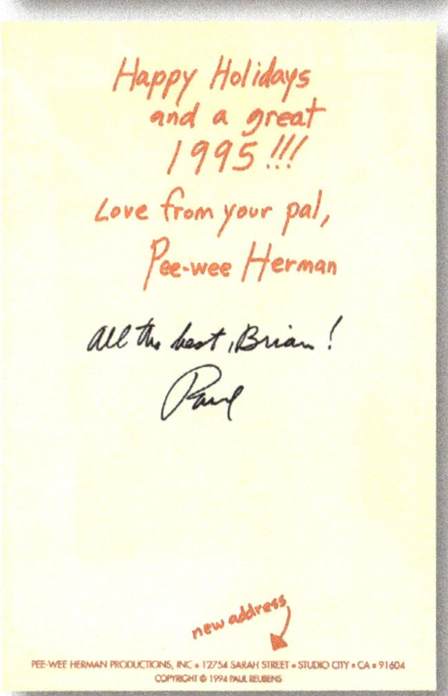

1995 Christmas card from Pee-wee Herman

Listening through an external speaker, I would type out what we came up with in real time; edit it after we got off the phone; print it out; and mail it to Brian, who would then do a second edit by hand and mail back to me a revised copy with his corrections and additions for retyping. By 1993 we were both on line with email accounts, which made the process simpler and faster. So why did it take seven long years to write? It's a fair question that has a simple answer.

Truth be told, the authorized biography had long been completed for publication in the box set either during 1993 or 1994. However, that overly-optimistic release date got pushed back further and further as the various record companies that Alice had recorded for over the years jockeyed for position and bickered over a mutually assured licensing agreement which would be financially beneficial to all parties.

Meanwhile, time marched on and, beginning in 1995, Brian was periodically writing that: "The box is on hold for I don't know how long." But although the box was on hold, Alice's career wasn't. So with the release of each new Alice Cooper album and the beginning of each new Alice Cooper tour, his biography had to be updated and made current until, finally, a 1999 release date was agreed upon. Seven years later.

***

During that time, I also had the golden opportunity to select three of the box set's tracks. When I proposed using "I Miss You" by Billion Dollar Babies off their *Battle Axe* album, it didn't take too much cajoling from me for Brian to agree that it was a good enough song worthy of inclusion. He was more reluctant, however, to include my next two suggestions: the single versions of "School's Out" and "Elected."

"Why?" he protested. "They're both the same as on the album."

"No, they're not," I countered. "The single version of 'School's Out' fades at the end."

"Um…okay," he drawled. "But what about 'Elected'? Isn't that the same?"

"What, are you kidding? The vocal on the single version of 'Elected' is at least twice as loud as on the album version! In fact, when *Billion Dollar Babies* first came out, all of us in high school wondered why the vocal on 'Elected' was buried so low in the mix!"

"I dunno…" Brian hedged. "I'll have to go back and listen to it."

He did and, admitting that I was right, Brian included all three tracks at my request.

***

Right from the very beginning, Brian would always mail me a Christmas card with one simple word inscribed inside above his name: Humbug. Later, when Brian was working with Pee-wee Herman, every year he would receive a Christmas card in the mail from Paul Reubens. And without fail, Brian would immediately put Pee-wee's card in an envelope and mail it to me as *my* Christmas card. And speaking of cards…

He may have handed out business cards which read "World's Biggest Alice Cooper Fan" and he may have parlayed that claim into a decades-long career as Alice's personal assistant Renfield, but for me, Brian Nelson's most impressive credit came in November 1995 when a photograph of him wearing a toque and holding a videocassette appeared on page 385 of Howard Stern's second book *Miss America*, alongside the official proclamation from "The King Of All Media" that Brian was "The King Of All VCRs."

That's because Brian was an inveterate taper who watched far more television than his culture-vulture boss ever did, which is why it's a good thing that Alice toured so much; otherwise, between his myriad recording devices and being online, Brian would never have seen the light of day again. Indeed, he asked me in 2004 to videotape an episode of *Survivor* that was airing at the same time as a local Cooper concert. Unwilling to wait until the tour was over, Brian got someone from each city that Alice was playing in on a Thursday night to tape that week's episode so he could watch it later that evening after the show.

And because Brian had mailed me a copy of *Miss America* after it was published, when he arrived at my digs later that night to pick up the Survivor videotape, I asked him to autograph his photo in the book. Signing it Renfield, he wrote: "Jeffrey, you are The King Of All Words." From Howard Stern to Brian Nelson to Jeffrey Morgan, the lineage is impeccable.

***

STERN

And you in the media allow Satanic people to take the airwaves. We are more satisfied with garbage than the Lord God. May his mercy cover all of you. Do we have a new call?

THE KINGS

Soon we were inundated with phony phone callers who followed Janks's lead. One of them happened to be Alice Cooper's road manager. He was the first listener to follow my lead and dub himself King. He called himself **THE KING OF ALL VCRS**, since he spent a great deal of his time recording programs on his five VCRs.

For a while, the King of All VCRs was incredibly active. He regularly hit Larry King. He once called Larry on the international line and posed as a Dane to ask Cindy Crawford if she

would ever consider having plastic surgery to look like Howard Stern. When Larry King had an HIV positive woman on who was prominent in the Bush reelection campaign, the King of All VCRs called up posing as a HIV positive homosexual. When he got on the air, he asked her why, as a gay man with AIDS, he should vote for Howard Stern. Larry King got so flustered that he went, "Ignore that call. But let's ask that question. Why should people vote for Howard Bush? I mean, George Bush."

THE KING OF ALL VCRS unleashed a flood of imitators. Every-

385

Jeffrey— you are the King of all words!

RENFIELD

Happy Holidays!!!
I hope 1997 brings you peace, love, joy, happiness, luck, good health, and great fortune.
(and very fond wishes from me!)

your pal,
Pee-wee Herman

All the best, Brian!
Paul Reubens

PEE-WEE HERMAN PRODUCTIONS, INC • 12754 SARAH STREET • STUDIO CITY • CA • 91604

1997 Christmas card from Pee-wee Herman

2217 ROCK AND ROLL BLVD., CLEVELAND, OH
PHONE: 216-566-8100
www.alicecooperstowncleveland.com

Billion Dollar Babies at Cooper'stown!

Party at Alice's House

HAPPY HOUR, OFFICE PARTIES, BUSINESS MEETINGS, ETC.

COOPER'STOWN, CLEVELAND IS YOUR PARTY AND GAME HEADQUARTERS! 216-566-8100

Meet your friends before or after the game. Our video wall and TVs are perfect for custom events. It's almost like being at the game. We can accommodate large groups for Christmas and holiday parties or any occasion. We do all the work, so you and your friends can have all the fun!

Alice's Antics

- The story goes that while in London for a show at the Empire Pool, Wembley in 1972, promoters of the show started getting a bit worried as ticket sales were not what they could have been. Alice, Shep and Beatles associate Derek Taylor hit on the idea of a truck with the picture of a naked Alice and snake driving around London publicizing the event. The truck conveniently broke down in Picadilly Circus causing huge traffic jams and, of course, getting the naked Alice advert all over national television. Needless to say, the show was sold out!
- Alice Cooper Show invaded millions of North American homes via television on ABC's very first In Concert program. So disturbing, in fact, was Alice's performance that a station manager in Cincinnati actually yanked the show off the air and replaced it with an episode of Clint Eastwood's *Rawhide*. Interestingly enough, the identity of the offended station manager was a man who would later go on to become head honcho of The Walt Disney Company – none other than Michael Eisner.

— www.alicecooper.com - Jeffrey Morgan, Author

Cleveland's Celebrities

Take Alice Home! Ask your server about our take-out service.

JIM BACKUS
"Mr. Magoo" and "Thurston Howell III" on Gilligan's Island.

HALLE BERRY
Went to Bedford High School where she was class president, a cheerleader, and a member of the National Honor Society.

DAVID BIRNEY
Starred in "Bridget Loves Bernie," and has made guest appearances on numerous shows.

JIM BRICKMAN
This national star returns home several times a year. He's released several hit CDs, and has performed with a virtual who's who of artists worldwide.

JIM BROWN
One of he greatest football players of all time.

DREW CAREY
This star and the city have a mutual love affair.

ERIC CARMEN
From Lyndhurst, Ohio, attended Brush High School. The song "Go All the Way" by his band, The Raspberries, was a million selling record in 1972.

TRACY CHAPMAN
Tracy won a Grammy Award for her self-titled debut album, which featur[illegible] the #1 hit recording "[illegible] Cars." Her late[illegible] release is titled [illegible]elling [illegible]tories."

MARC [illegible]HN
Marc wo[illegible] Gra[illegible] Award as best [illegible] artist f[illegible] his [illegible]ordi[illegible] of the #1 hi[illegible] "Walk[illegible] Memph[illegible]" His late[illegible] relea[illegible] is titl[illegible] [illegible]ove Real [illegible]asy."

TIM CONWAY
This native of Chagrin Falls has appeared in dozens of movies and TV shows.

PHIL DONAHUE
This graduate of St. Ed's was one of the pioneers of TV talk shows.

THOMAS EDISON
One of the greatest inventors of all time, born in Milan, Ohio.

BOB FELLER
Considered by many to be the greatest pitcher of all time.

TERI GARR
This Lakewood, Ohio native has been a leading lady in several comedic films. She's co-starred with Cher, Bill Murray, Marty Feldman, and Gene Wilder.

GHOULARDI
This TV legend was a phenomenon in the 1960s, and will never be forgotten.

JOEL GREY
This singer/dancer is best known for his role opposite Liza Minelli in "Cabaret." He's also the father of Jennifer, who starred in "Dirty Dancing."

BOB HOPE
Perhaps the most famous Clevelander of them all!

JAMES INGRAM
This popular R&B star was born in Akron. He[illegible] multiple Grammy Awards in a [illegible]reer th[illegible]s spanned over 2[illegible]

HEN[illegible]Y MANCI[illegible]
Perha[illegible] the greatest m[illegible]ie th[illegible]e composer of al[illegible]me. "The Pin[illegible] Panth[illegible]," "Moon Ri[illegible]," and "Peter G[illegible]nn" are just a few of h[illegible] familiar songs.

MA[illegible]LYN [illegible]ANSON
Absolutely co[illegible]roversial.

MARTIN [illegible]
A na[illegible] [illegible], this [illegible]media[illegible] has several T[illegible]pearances, movies, a[illegible] albums to his credit.

ELLIOT NESS
Former Safety Director for the City [illegible]f Cleveland, Elliot became a national [illegible]ero for busting mobster Al Capone. El[illegible]ot's final resting place is in Cleveland's Lakeview Cemetery.

PAUL NEWMAN
This Shaker Heights native is fam[illegible]s for his feature films, race car driving, sa[illegible] dressings and pasta sauce.

JESSE OWENS
This Olympic legend was raised in Cleveland. One of the greatest athletes of the 20th Century.

THE PRETENDERS
This international group is fronted by Akron's Chrissie Hynde.

CHRIS ROSE
From Shaker Heights is the co-host of "The Best Damn Sports Show Period."

JOHN D. ROCKEFELLER
Converting his fortune into today's dollars, he'd be the richest man alive. John grew up in Strongsville, Ohio.

DON SHULA
One of the most successful coaches in NFL history. Don played for John Carroll and the Browns, and owns "Shula's 2" steakhouse in Independence, Ohio.

MICHAEL STANLEY
This Cleveland favorite still plays several gigs per year. He's the afternoon radio personality on WNCX 98.5.

EDWIN STARR
"Agent Double o Soul" has had numerous hits, including "25 Miles" and "War."

GEORGE STEINBRENNER
Born in Rocky River, his dream was to [illegible]wn the Cleveland Indians. When h[illegible] was [illegible]ut out of a d[illegible] [illegible]k Mileti, he purcha[illegible] [illegible] New Yor[illegible] Yank[illegible] instead. [illegible] rest is history.

JOE WALSH
His guitar playing made The James Gang [illegible] Cleveland rock legend. Was also a member o[illegible] The Eagles and currently appears on "T[illegible] Drew Carey Show."

DE[illegible]RA WINGER
Thi[illegible] former Clevelander has starred in se[illegible]ral films, including "Urban Cowboy" [illegible]d "An Officer and a Gentleman."

FRANK YANKOVIC
America's Polka King, and a Cleveland Legend!

Alice Trivia

- Alice Cooper's birth name is Vincent Furnier.
- Alice was once a track star who won a 26-mile marathon.
- Kachina was the name of Alice's first snake. Kachina perished down a toilet drain in a Tennessee hotel room during the Killer tour.
- Alice was the driving force for rehabilitating the famous Hollywood Sign in California.
- Q: What did Mercury Records want the Alice Cooper Group to do before it signed them?

  A: They wanted the band to drop Alice from being their singer. (Renfield, November 1998)

Baseball History in Cleveland

Babe Ruth hit his 500th home run • Joe DiMaggio set record for hitting in 56 consecutive games • Len Barker pitched a perfect game • Bob Feller pitched his 3rd no-hitter

Trivia Question

Who are the two men inducted into the Baseball Hall of Fame that had nothing to do with Major League Baseball? They were never players, coaches, managers, owners, umpires or sportswriters. There is a clue directly across the street from the restaurant.

From Alice and the C-Town crew: A special thanks to David Spero from the Rock and Roll Hall of Fame, and Bob Zimmer of the National Heritage Baseball Museum for sharing their cool memorabilia collections with us. Check out Alice's info board for details on upcoming events.

Despite his cynical demeanor, Brian could also play against type and show genuine affection when needed. A year later, while I was still recovering from a serious medical crisis, we met after an Alice concert. With a sincere look of concern on his face, Brian rushed up to me, warmly gave me a big hug, and said: "I *toldja* you weren't gonna die."

He could also be self-effacing. When I congratulated Brian for getting a writing credit on "Pessi-Mystic" off *Brutal Planet*, he literally shrugged it off. "All I did was contribute the 'shut up' part," he said before changing the subject.

Then again, we'd both joke that our greatest writing credit was when our names appeared together as "Jeffrey Morgan, Author" and "Renfield" on the front cover of *The Cooper'stown Gazette* menu in Cleveland.

Brian was the best editor I ever had after Lester Bangs, and I told him so. In 2009, exactly ten years after our authorized Alice biography was published, I was blessed to write a second authorized biography, this time of Iggy Pop and The Stooges, keeping Brian in mind as I edited my words.

A month before he died, when I emailed him about a phone call I'd received from Iggy, Brian immediately wrote back:

you don't have to make up shit to try and impress me.

you've met alice cooper. that's good enough.

***

Renfield Productions

A DIVISION OF ALICE COOPER'S BLACK WIDOW INC.

BRIAN NELSON
8033 SUNSET BLVD.
SUITE 745
LOS ANGELES, CA 90046

(213) 652-2899

Gentlemen Afterdark

BRIAN NELSON - *Management*
(602) 840-0639

8033 Sunset Blvd. #745
Los Angeles, CA 90046

1608 E. Turney Ave.
Phoenix, AZ 85016

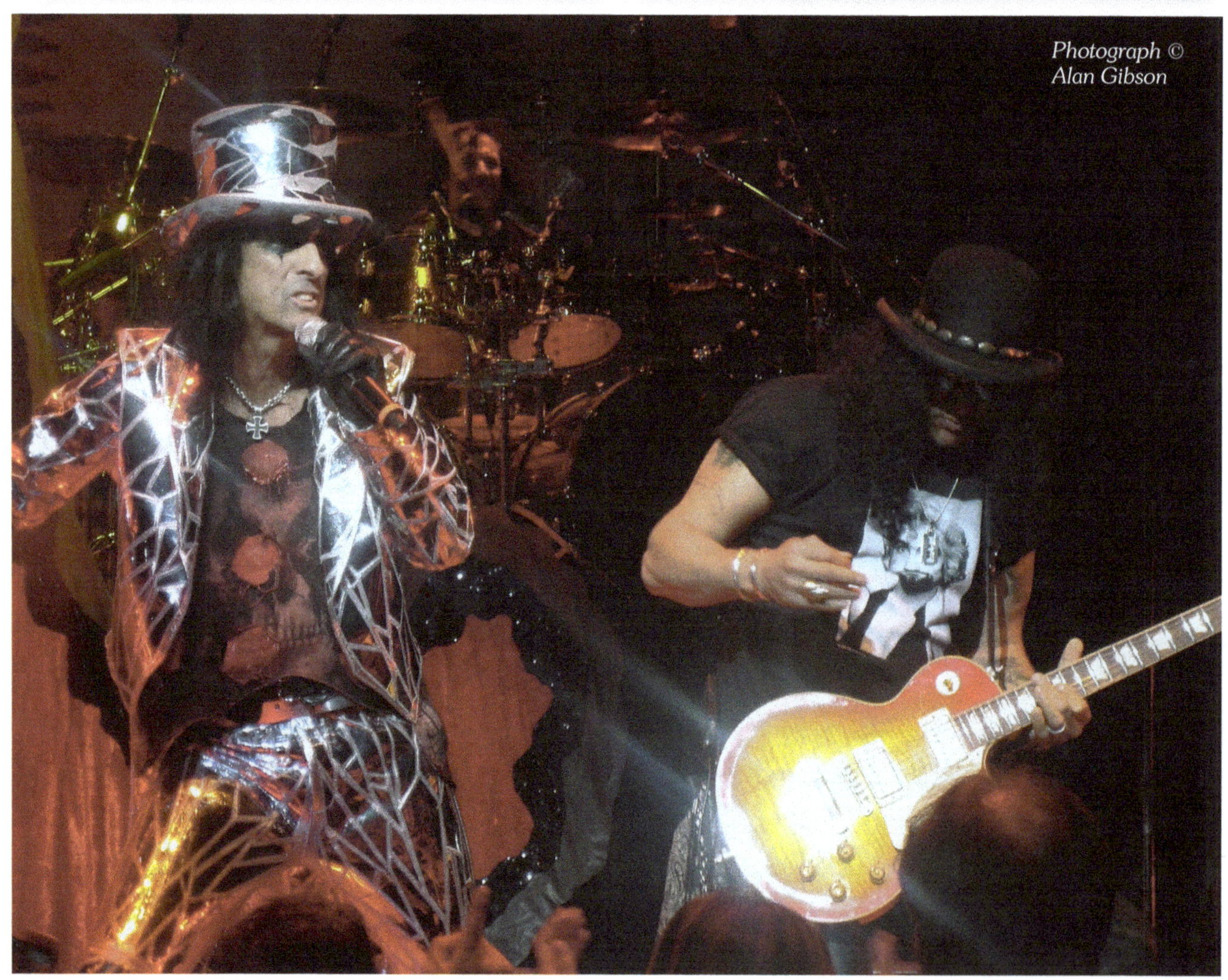

Photograph © Alan Gibson

SECTION TWO

DEAR ALICE

Photograph © Phillip Solomonson
philamonjaro.com

DEAR ALICE...

In 1969, at age fifteen, I optimistically drew, in pencil and ink, on two twelve-inch squares of cardboard, the front and back covers for a proposed John and Yoko album titled *Time Peace*, mailed it to them at Apple Corps on Savile Row in England — and I received a reply back in the mail.

In 1975, at age twenty, I optimistically wrote a 70 page musical about Andy Warhol, mailed it to him at the Factory in New York—and I received a reply back in the mail.

So if *anyone* knows what it's like to be an optimistic fan, it's yours truly. Therefore, I profoundly understand why the following messages were written to Alice Cooper. How I came to be in possession of them, and why they still exist after all these decades, is easily explained.

When my authorized biography was published in *The Life And Crimes Of Alice Cooper* box set, Brian also put it on the Alice Cooper website to replace the existing biography which I had previously written before the box set was released. And because he had copied the new biography in its entirety, he also included my personal email address at the end, just as it appears in the box set. Almost immediately, I began receiving emails from Alice's fans, which I duly forwarded to Brian. It took less than a week of this for Brian to inform me that he was removing my email address from the online bio, so that fans would message the website directly.

That opened the floodgates and began a process whereby, for ten years, beginning in 1999, Brian would forward me all the messages that fans sent to Alice. Eventually I had archived so many of them that we methodically selected the most interesting messages with the intention of publishing them in a book. Brian's death put paid to that notion, but not before we wrote a publisher proposal which ended: "If you ever wondered what made Alice Cooper the sickest and most depraved showman in the entire history of rock 'n' roll… It's because he's read the letters in this book!"

What follows is the contents of that book, presented here in its entirety for the very first time. I think it will amuse you. It may shock you. It might even horrify you. Which is why all identifying names, telephone numbers, home addresses, and email addresses have been removed to protect the message writers from acute embarrassment.

Photograph © James Pappaconstantine

DEAR ALICE

Welcome To His Nightmare

Actual Fan Letters To Alice Cooper

The following letters are authentic and reproduced verbatim. Renfield's comments and replies are in *italics*.

Dear Alice, my oldest son is turning 16 this year and I wanted to do something really cool and memorable for him. I would love to have you and your band come play at his party this year. We have a big old Victorian home in central New York, the beautiful Finger Lakes wine region. We have a great backyard and pool and LOTS of room for you to spread out and enjoy a great picnic on a summer day. I would love to show my son that his Dad and I still know how to rock and that we are much cooler than he thinks we are. We are just an average middle class family, we really aren't kooks and seriously would love to show you the town, so to speak. If you and your band and family would like to spend part of your summer vacation here, before you go on tour, we'd do our best to make you feel at home. You'd really go a long way with my sons too! Give me a holler if you are willing to talk with me. Keep rockin. I've loved your music ever since I found out how much you frightened my mother! Bye!

***

Photograph © Brad McPherson

Hi alice cooper my name is d___ Iam fine how are doing these day s Iwant to know some thing where was your ablam walcome to my night mare recard it .s my best one Ilove that songthee blackwiddow how did you and vinceprice meet and weredid you guy.s meet why is that song he did aboat thee black widdow was thee only one or did you and him ddo more Ibeen along time fan of your.s I live in canada Helifax novascotia hove you ever been here befour I.v been a fan of your.s scince thee early 1970.s your fan always d___ g___

***

I just want to apologize to Alice for my ridiculously bad behavior at his show in Wallingford last Saturday night. I drank WAY too much and got totally out of control. Please forgive me, I promise it will NEVER happen again.

***

Mr. Cooper, I have a friend who will be 30 this year. His wife would like to have a huge blowout, but he says no. The only way he said he would go for it is if Alice Cooper was there. We would love for you to come and hang out with us. We will pay for flight or whatever expenses. I can get exact dates, but wanted to see if you were interested. Your company is our only request, no performing, just hanging out with us. I am the General Manager at the local Staples store and T__ is one of my employees. Please respond, D___ M___

***

Hey Alice, I'm sure you know who I am. I'm that infamous guy who has caused a lot of shit in the past couple of years. Anyway, I need your help now. Actually Ozzy needs your and my help now. I say we both make a personal call at Ozzy's house and stop

Photograph © Brad McPherson

this nonsensical, audacious, unreasonable bullshit of his family being taped 24 hours a day on public television. Contact me if your down. Ayight. M___

***

Dear Mr. Cooper, we are writing to you from a group mental health residence which is part of the Mental Health and Retardation Association. One of our consumers, J__, is a huge fan and was trying to find one of your t-shirts in a local Walmart. Unfortunately, Walmart does not sell Alice Cooper merchandise. We would love to make his day and were wondering if there was any way that you could possibly donate a t-shirt to this wonderful man. Thank you in advance.

***

i feel that when i smoke a cigarette people jump into my body and face but it is happening and they do it when i drink beer but that seems to help...play some stuges raw power ...i dont know exactly why they are jumping into my body this sounds wierd but this is hapening ,,,tell them to leave me alone..,,,,thank you n_____ m________

***

vinnie, alice cooper, i remember back when my brothers and i used to listen to your music. i was only 12 yrs then, i am now 42 i would love to see one of your concerts before you retire. i have seen a couple of your concerts when you came to salt lake city, utah. but the times have changed, everything has gone up except for the our wages. i do not read or write, so it is very hard to get a good paying job. i would also like to say that I lov that you have your parents living with you. wish that i could do that for mine. love ya alice. your the best. k__ o____

***

Would you happen too know where the twitle dee an twitle me dumb. Four scores and seven years ago 60 40,000,000 Light years I feel on a star and put the fire , solar nebulus pre occupied by the sun the moon and the starsplus the adam that allowed eve to fall and rise in to night,darkness or nothing but everything..Everything but,???And so on and so forth art thou my farther god gave me a mind too two to 2 mine,... Own faith and but the trail is music arised by the art provided before darkness touched the light and when the light was glorified by the darkness with the sounds it could not see before the light let the darkness see which for fact could not phsically but darkness enlightened the light that when it could not be darkness told the light and allowed the before sounds and reach communication for feeling is what the darkness phically sees with that my father god thank you for being the light I can see in my darkness which i'm gonna be concided when before i knew all see is darkness i gave my wright to teach my eyes to feel and some way some how brought my mine the Interscope Mercury an Black was the lable but i would and had the reason to think i had to explain and knoew i know why , what, where,how, and something someone never even heard because when they tried to pop me with disunremembering bioxygeneroussenseci that the word created the nothing that never lived the life unforgiven too false hideouse woman that believe lies with wanted to feel good by the greatness in men my own human men have been falsley accused, neglected, distrubed, and forgive by the evil jealous ccc of the secound counter fit walk slower,take longer, bitch louder, cry too somewoman because you woman think and know how much a man appreciates being one to make a &*#$ feel and see caring sharing and love but you woman will defentely be sorry for your selves for not appreicated what was there to keep you safe warm and loved!!!even if there wickedness tries to serender to there right as a woman you had it left accused it lied about it betrayed it and deeply believed believe you loved making a strong hard working living to learn every new feelling, tought, and the changes I (i'm using that as word from god cause I learned it when a appreciated the time not wasted through my walk and belief hidden for placeing my men under hidieous disfunction and abuse, well n-e ways (I in as man men) Sorry Alice had to use this still being ponder about web sight cause men work and some men studied that fought for education to create nice sights like this one to

Photograph © Brad McPherson

intrest minds I appreciated it,everthing cause I love my creator that allows the sun, moon to help living under his protection as a believer father god thank you for this day as it truns into eve,dusk,night, know darkness there will be stars tomorrows light works hard to wait to wake the life in the darkness because thats the suns job and i think that has a crush on that what it waits to show. Love's, J_____ I did

***

Hey my name is A______ C______. I've been trying get in contact with Alice through this website for months. I want him to know that he is still invited to my wedding on Nov 27th. If he is intested in attending, he can get back to me via emial. Thanx

***

Hey alice I just want to say I am a really big fan of you'remusic. And do you remember a couple years ago when A Man Named N_____ served you a diet coke a long time ago? That was my dad, And I just wanted to say Hi I'm a big fan and Keep ROCKIN ON THE MUSIC! You funny old man.

***

YO ALICE I ALWAYS WANTED TO SEE YOU LIVE IN CONCERT BUT IM POOR IM 13 AND WE HAVE NO GAS IN OUR VAN TO SEE YOU IN THE FIRST PLACE. ANYWAYS A WHILE BACK YOU ORDERED A TV FROM CIRCUIT CITY. MY DAD HAD TO DELIVER IT TOO. SO HE SEEN YOUR HOUSE AND TALKED WITH YOU AND YOUR KIDS OUR LIKE US. SO EMAIL ME BACK SEE YA

***

First, let me thank you for taking time to read this. I am a friend of Jim Dandy of Black Oak Arkansas and I would like to do something unique for him this year for his birthday, other than a bottle of whiskey. I know that you and Jim are friends and use to be business partners, he told me about the album design company you use to own. If you have any suggestions, please let me know. Jim could really use a good time and he deserves it. thx. T D_____

***

i am h_______ in swisserland. since 1973,i sink you are a genious

Photograph © Brad McPherson

***

I dont know if this goes right to Mr.Alice Cooper But i sure hopehe gets this message..... On August 14 we are haveing a Pig Roast...And the Day after that you have a concert 30 mins aways at Saginaw, MI and I would really apreciate if you could at least make an aperence.....My dad has been a big fan of urs sense he was 13... and has been playing ur music sense he was 15... My dad has done so much for me... And i would really like for him to meet you. And IT would meen so much.. Also I figured an hope that it would be possiable sense ur not that far away to come...... And again i really hope you can do this got me.. My dad would die an happy person. And my dad has taught me an my brothers an sisters all ur songs on the guitar...MY whole family plays... The Pig Roast is AUGUST 14 And I really hope an pray u could come.It would meen soo much. Thanks You M______ P.S. Please let Alice Cooper read this all i want to do is make my father happy

***

jamie aaa i mean alice in 1970 or 71 i can't remember! but do remeber your black jue jue consert in Alexsanderia Va, and you hipmotize me,wow hea is there any chance you can de hipmotize me? i mean its been 34 yr's now in 72 you toured with humble pie if you can remember tour date had you at the alexanderia roller ring,and humble played 1st. i won a contest with a local station to be a stage rodie for a month i was put in charge of mikes & getar cords i was to keep the stright so you woundn't fall over them ' can you remenber this consert if not i do and no body beat your stage presants your the first showman the omega i am proud of my time and our music'if you ever get a chance could you play some of the orignal { hard rock } band king crimson 21st century skidziod man.it was way ahead of its time luv ya man c___

***

I realise that Alice probably won't get to read this, however, I ask that if possible could you please pass on this message. My mum and I went and saw Alice's show yesterday (Tuesday, 21st June 2005), and unfortunately just after Alice had his head cut off, mum got real sick from the heat and having to stand on her toes to see over the guy in front. She had to go out and get some air, and so as I was worried, I went with her. I am sure that Alice would have seen this as it was really bright at the time, so I would like it if you could please let him know that we were not walking out on the show. We were both very upset that we missed the end, but as mum was so sick (feeling like vomiting), we had to get out. We watched the rest of the show from the foyer on the tv, but couldn't go back inside. We just want him to know that we loved that show, that it was our second concert we have both seen him at, and it was amazing. But unfortunatly we missed the end and we are sorry for having to walk out. Please let him know. Thank you so very much. Can't wait for the next tour so we can see him again. Kindest regards, B__ M____

***

Please help me get a message to Coop!!! Physically!!! I don't want him to feel like I have abandoned him. He needs to to know why I couldn't be in Columbus last October. This medication I have been taking is interferring with our telepathy... Bits and pieces and I'm not sure if he fully understands what's been going on. I don't want him to give up on me. I love him so incredibly much!!! He is so deep inside my soul!!!! I thank God constantly for this love.

***

I'd like to clarify something in case it needs to be clarified. In 2000 I made various attempts to contact Alice. At that time I had no idea that I was becoming psychotic and delusional. In 2000 I believed that the fuse to the Apocolypse was being lit. By the time it came for me to "warn and prepare" people with what I believed was a special insight bestowed by God, I could only think in abstractions and "short hand." as an instance, sending album covers to Downing Street with notes like, "B52's ALL SEVENTEEN DANCES," as a code for waging Holy War. And I was completely convinced that I had to get these "messages" out. And the truly bizarre thing was that Music was the method by which this war was to be waged. Especially Alice Cooper's music! Alice's music is Full On as far as I can tell. Thank you. Sending love and respect to you all. S_____

***

Hello, I am seeking some sponsorship for my Patent process, I need to retain a Patent Attorney to retrieve my rights on a product called the Love Machine. Please let me know if you are interested in the project or please forward to any interested party you may know interested in mega-millions. Thank you Sincerely: J____ P_____

***

Dear Alice, me and my long lost twin (i know this is gunna sound crazy to u) but we're in adoptive homes n how we got seperated idk. but our adoptive familys are fucking abusive to us, n we beleive ur our dad,we always called u dad n looked up to u as our dad,both our adoptive dad's are fucking dead beat dads. i had a dream last night n it was so fucking real I didnt wanna awake but i did, me,my twin,u and n____ w_____ all took a dna test n it showed we are related to u and n_____. we beleive we're your long lost kids.

***

Cortez High School. I was wandering if you rememberd your band in high school? You had pics done in the yr book w/ R_____ H____ . I know I"ll never get feed back on this but hell I tried...Well I thought Id write u his grandson is sixteen & we listen to u wen i can..I took him to a White Snake concert but he fell asleep..lol TAke Care A____

***

Ive moved up to Northern Minnesota and has 2 teenagers girls now too. Ive been to my concerts too..... a few years ago I saw Kiss- Ted Newget .. Pioson, Wannet, Quiet Roit an... Loved them all!!!!! :) But now I hear that you are going to be here in Northern MN at FuntuneBay Casnio in Tower, MN!! And My Birthday is on the Aug.16. And you going to be there on the next day. WOW!! But I cant go to see you cuz I have some money issues to deal with. :(But my 2 girls said if I could find some one to go with me ..... they will let me go see you in concert!!!! I really want to see you in concert too!!!!

***

Hello Mr A cooper you were on the one show yesterday evening telling us all about your career including a clip from 1972s Schools Out which i remember very well back then. All the best M___ G_____ C____.

***

hi d______ d___ guitarist here hope ur having a good day , it would be an honor to play guitar 4 you ive worked for sean pdiddy combs john entwhistle etc ididnt know u were in the whole red paper clip thing briliant, I remember you did the movie roadie was that meatloafs band the blonde guitarist with the black les paul who is he i used to see him everywhere I remember the first time i saw him was with elton in central park many moons ago he seemed to be a guitarist who worked with everyone, i just found the trash dvd with petrelli i really enjoy many of your guitarist devlin 7 kane i can offer you alot as a guitarist i understand much of your writing chemisties ive been following you for while now and enjoy playing your music iam drug and drink free ive been clean for a long time now i drive a truck in eastnyc since ive been home my last tour with my ozzy pantera tribute was very successful we did peurto rico 4 nites sold out and continued to do much of the southern states i teach music as well and have many students .. its a living i hope to get back on tour soon please send my regards to c____ we had met at jones beach last summer , seen you many times that was best show and you sound betterthan ever id play for old special forces tour shirts and 70s 80s memorbilial ha ha whats your par these days im sure u and tiger get along great my mom lives a few houses from grg norman i think thats his name the big golfer let me knowif i can be of any assistance regarding lead or rythm guitar thanx for taking the time your biggest fan your creation d_____ d___ peace and be well sir

***

Alice I need help getting bsckstage to meet Robert Plant and Allison Krauss tomorrow night in Raleigh, NC...7-11-08

***

You were my first hero when at vacation bible school everyone else was decoupaging Strawberry shortcake and I was doing Alice Cooper and Slade...We have been together ever since!!!Yu are always on my MP3 player and always with me in my car...I loved Dead Babies at age 13 around 1974 and Muscle of Love...I loved them all, still do at almost 49... Here's my number I need 2 passes if possible. I am on Chemo and A____ my myspace friend is giving me a free ticket and I have to repay the favor and meet one of Idols from the 70's...

***

Is there any way my kids can meet Alice while he is in Indy or playing at Balterra in August. They are 3 and 4 years old and watch the Muppet Show with Alice RELIGIOUSLY. It's the one they always pick to watch. It's too precious. I know it's an odd request and I will do what it takes to make it happen.Thank you.

***

Good afternoon. I am an intern at the Michigan Apple Committee, an organization designed and dedicated to promote Apple Growers across the state of Michigan. As part of our efforts we are searching for well know celebrities who have lived, worked or spent large parts of their lives in Michigan who are willing to fill out a short survey where they would list their favorite apple varieties and any other experiences of visiting cider mills or apple orchards. We would like to use these surveys and any responses from them for promotional use in the future. A am hoping to reach Mr. Cooper to ask if he is willing to participate. If you could please respond to this email with contact information for Mr. Cooper that would be greatly appreciated. Thank you for your time and hope to hear from you soon.

***

Hello Vince,(alias Alice) You are in Southampton on 25th July & coincidentally I am celebrating my 50th birthday /party that evening. Whilst I am gutted I cannot come to your concert-I would love you to visit for a beer & even a song if you like? I have followed you for 30 years & you shared my bedroom wall with Marc Bolan who is sadly gone.I have two teenagers who think you are pretty cool & there should be around 30-40 people here. I just thought that if you'd like to see how ordinary people hang out.....here's the invitation you've been waitng for? My hubby, N____, thinks I'm mad sending this & I said if you don't ask.....you dont get & there is no harm trying.... Thankyou so much for reading this, Best wishes, C_______ R______.(near Bitterne Park school), Southampton.

***

Swedish Alice-fan here just wondering if you have any information as to when the Mega Box will come out? I see Rhino will be re-releasing PFY and EA, therefore I thought that somethings happening. When the remastered records comes out with extras I would prefer it to be handled like the BDB deluxe edition with the original album on one disc and the extras on another. I think the extra cost with two records will pay off because the consumer thinks he gets so much more when getting two records for a little more

Photograph © Brad McPherson

Photograph © Brad McPherson

than the price of one. Me, myself and I want the original albums to end with the song I'm used to ending each individual album. WTMN remastered bugs me a bit when extras comes after Escape. It kinda ruins it a bit I think. Yours sincerely, K___ L_______

***

Its again me. we have alredy contact about meet Alice on a concert. allso you give me to this story alredy a answer. but i like to tray again. for the concert from the 29. November in Stuttgart / Germany i like to now, is this possible, that my girlfrind (between long long time a big fan from alice) to meet him after the concert for a dinner. she have next his birthday, an i like to make a surprise with this arrangement. is clear, tha i thake to cost for the fool dinner. please make this dream for my girlfrind possible and she will becomme wery happy. thans for your answer and i like to send the best regards from switzerland. greats r___

***

my name is M_____, I'm 18 yrs old and I'm from Poland. I need help. So, my big dream is to go to America and start new life there. I'm very interested in music/entertainment industry and I'd love to get a job there. I have an uncle in America, he promised me that I can go to Detroit (that's where he lives) after finishing school. So, I finished school and passed final exams with good results but he doesn't want to invite me = breaking the promise. There's no way to contact him, and he's the only member of family in the US. I have no one else. That's really sad to me, because I wanted to make my dream come true, to see America, go to some concerts etc. I love music, it's my biggest passion and there's a lot going on in Detroit area when it comes to music, especially in the summer. I'm trying to do everything to go to America this summer, but things are not going on as I wished. And I don't expect much, I don't require much, but my uncle is just too afraid to give me a chance. That's disappointing and sad. I am dreaming about escape from Poland every day, dreaming of better, more exciting life and working in music industry - thing I love. So... I can go to embassy and try to get a visa (not an easy thing), then borrow money and buy flight ticket, what is really expensive. I am really desperated to go to America and make my dream come true. As I said, I don't expect much, I just want to be happy person and I know that I won't be happy here in Poland...I don't have any experience in job, but the question is: is it possible to get a job for Alice Cooper (I'm a huge fan BTW!)? I can send merchandise that fans bought through web, I can help, I can be in the road crew, work at studio, anywhere. I just want to work in music industry, get some experience and be happy! I know that may sound quite silly and crazy, but I'm really desperated person. And no, I'm not criminal or something, hehe, it's not the reason I want to escape from Poland. I'm looking for better life conditions and it's time to separate from parents and fulfill dreams, start new life. I don't want to waste my life here. Please give me an answer, I just want to be helpful guy, happy with life. I don't know anyone beside my uncle in America, but he doesn't want to help me. So, please give me an answer/advise anything. Thank you for your time and if there's something you can do for rock music fan, I'd be grateful to death. Legal job in music industry in America is my dream...the biggest one I suppose! And if you can't give me legal job, I'd work illegal. Please reply to my e-mail, I'm serious. Any help is appreciated. Take care, cheers! Kind regards, M______ "Marmetal" K_____

***

Photograph © Dwight McCain

Photograph ©
Jeffrey Morgan

I know you are a busy man but, I was wondering if you might make a quick stop in Decatur,IL in between tour dates. I am a manager at S____ T___ L____ and we are remodeling our bowling center and thought you might help make a Grand Reopening. Decatur is locatedabout 45 minutes south of Bloomington,Il where you are playing Aug 21 and I'll be there. There is also a great golf course here, so I've been told, I don't golf, called R__ T___ R__. Thank You for taking the time and reading this e-mail. See you in August.

***

Dear Mr A. Cooper I hope you are well, I am contacting you hoping you will be interested in hearing about an idea that I have. I have listened to you music from a young age and have great knowledge about the history and character of Dwight Fry. My idea is to write a theatrical play/musical about Dwight Fry, I have started putting my idea onto paper, but there are a few things holding me back. I am a ordinary member of the public with no real means being able to take my idea further than on paper and I would not go any further than this without seeking your approval. I have been given a lot of encouragement from friends and family, some of which do listen to your music and some that donít. I have had positive feedback from all and lots of interest from everyone I have shared my idea with. My idea on the performance is to have a selection of your songs through out your career along with a narrator to tell the story of Dwight Fry in the theatrical style of your performances. I envisage the play to tell the story of who this guy is and how did he ended up where hedid. I would be really grateful to know if you are interested in viewing/discussing my vision. I look forward to hearing from you. Kind Regards S______ P_______

Photograph © Brad McPherson

***

If ye are coming to Montana to perform, bring raincoats, bulletproof vests, prepaid tickets out. The natives are not friendly. We don't have $32 to watch the show; any backstage passes available?

***

ALICE I sent you a note nicely asking you for a couple of tickets to your upcoming concert in Calgary, Alberta, Canada. YOU CHOOSE TO IGNOR ME!!!!!!!!!!!!!!!!! SUGGEST STRONGLY YOU NOT IGNOR ME!! Now, I was at your concert in Edmonton, where you ripped off all the fans that went to your concert. It was in the mid- seventies, at your Welcome to My Nightmare concert. You injured yourself some how. Anyways, you never finished the concert, you did a half ass job, you ripped off the concert goers. ARE YOU PROUD OF YOURSELF FOR THAT???? I was extremely upset.. You never tried to re-schedule the concert or provide refunds. I am still pisssssssssssstt !!!!!!!!!!!!! NOW I AM ASKING YOU ONCE MORE TO SEND ME A COUPLE OF TICKETS TO YOUR UPCOMING CONCERN IN CALGARY, THIS SEPT.. TO MAKE UP FOR RIPPING ME OFF!!!!!!!!!!!!!! DO YOU UNDERSTAND ME NOW?????????????????? g____ c__

fyi...that show was in 1975!!!!!!!!!!!!! and he's still pissed!

***

been a big fan for years. If you ever find yourself in the UK at a loose end, and think you'd enjoy a walk in the English countryside give me a shout. I'm always out and about with my dogs, we usually take a stove with us and brew up as well. It's very relaxing and gives you time out from all of the hassles in life. Looking forward to the new album. Hope the new tour goes really well, and thanks for all the years of great music.

***

alice just sayin hi i hope you read my last letter to you i stand by my words i would play your music on guitar for free i can play many of your songs ive been playing a long time and im secrue as a guitarist i enjoy playing your music the early stuff reminds me of the later doors music soft parade ive been going over the dvds i have live in montreux brutal planet and welcome to my nightmare i just found the videos for cold ethyl and i never cry i really enjoy your music and youve been an artist i admire since i started playing do let me know if i can be of any asistance ive woked for pdiddy lil kim john enwhistle among others i have touring and recording xpernce again I stand by my words ill play for free ill play for a special forces tour shirt or any other 70s and 80s merch ha ha i check my space every day sometimes every other i hope to hear from you please send my regards to c____ and b____ i teach guitar i have many students one is here now he wants to learn sick things i will show him have a great day thank you for taking the time d_____

***

hallo, ich habe eine frage. meine freundin heiratet am 11. juli. als flitterwochen machen sie eine reise nach osnabr¸ck auf das alice cooper concert. w"re es m–glich, dass alice cooper ihnen gl¸ckw¸nsche ausspricht? das w"re f¸r beide wohl das gr–þte geschenk auf erden! sie heipen a___ und t___! w¸rde mich echt freuen wenn das m–glich w"re. k–nnten sie mir voran vielleicht eine nachricht zukommen lassen, wie die chancen dazu stehen? vielen dank im voraus! m______

***

hey alice whats up well im writing to you becaise im huge guitar fan and ive been playing guitar for 5 years. Ive been trying to get myself noticed out their since my rescent band is goin bottom up but just wonderign if you know any bands in Canada who are looking for a guitarist these days i

Photograph © Brett Fenoir Fenwick

appreciate taking thsi time to read my email. thank you and rock on

***

Alice, When you guy's come to Bloomington,IL. Aug.21,2008 and if you decide to go golfing can I drive you around and be your caddy? I can give you the whole story of how my wife left me 3 days before Christmas and all that crap for sympathy but i'm not I just want to be a caddy for you or go to the movies with you and your band. ROCK ON!!!!!!!!!!!!!!!!!!!! And one more thing I have a friend who owns a bar here in Bloomington if you guy's ever want a small place to play for the hell of it. ROCK ON!!!!!! D___

***

I would think it would be awsome if you wold consider showing up for X-FEST in September in Dayton Ohio. Its a great concert of top name rock bands and about 50,000 screeming fans. It would be the shit!!!! Think about and get back to me. Z__

***

Mr. cooper im a huge fan in fact if not for you i would not be doing what i do with my band. i live with in a waling distance from proctors and you are my personal hero.but i cant afford to see you at proctors my mom is disabled and we dont have much money. please help me see your show or maybe even just let me meet you and get a picture back stage with both of us wearing our onstage face paint would be great please respond it would meanthe world to me. if not i understand I mean you are a legend and might not have time to do this for me. but please try. S_____ W_____ AKA X______

***

Photograph © Brett Fenoir Fenwick

Dear Ring Wizard, I still am deaf from all that bullshit from before. I am really excited to get my Alice t-shirt and Psycho-drama poster as this will probably be closest I get to meeting you. You amaze me. I still remember clown music in jail. What a mind trip. I've started sending other people funny pieces of mail just for a fucked up kind, but that's how I am. I'm not meeting you at the Cottonwood Mall for a million bucks. I don't know what to do with myself. Your actually still ticking, which is exciting because when you go over to the otherside, I will be sad. We all have to die sometime and I guess that's just how it is. I am excited to get my hand's on your new album at Nuwest records. I am sure it's a headache having your music at Spitfire records, because if you tell there are "no complaints" that would be an exageration of the worst kind. My favorite Alice song is "Cold Machines" I hope you do a song or two off Brtual Planet. That was my favorite album of yours. love, J__

***

Alice, I just bought The Guess Who tickets for the Colorado State Fair this August. Unfortunately, after the purchase I did some research on the band and found out the band is without Randy Bachman and Burt Cummings (lead singer). That is a total rip off! I want my money back, because I will not go see a poser band. Unfortunately no refunds are available from Ticketmaster. Hopefully, the word will get out and people will not arrive with great disappointed when they go to the concert in August at the Colorado State Fair. This is so uncool and very unprofessional. How do make believe bands get away with this crap? I check the current The Guess Who band out on youtube and they are horrible. Just a heads up. I'm sure you (KKFM) still have to promote the show, but you should be up front that the current band does not have the great songwriter (Randy Bachman) and the best voice in rock and roll (Burt Cummins). You must be true to rock and roll! You were (Alice Cooper) when you came to the Colorado State Fair. Your show was AWESOME! Sincerely, R__ H____

***

Alice i emailed you before about tickets for your proctors show but i was wrong i saw a site that said they where $275. but i now know it was wrong. i bought the $55 ticket and i was just wondering if i could get a picturewith you for my bands myspace. ill bring my face paint for the picture it would mean alot to me if I could get back stage and get that pictureill even give you a copy of my bands cd if you want. please email me back with a replie.

***

Hello!I will go to Magic Circle Festival-Bad Arolsen(July).I very wont meet with Alice Cooper.What I must do?Pay or something...Alice is very important in my life.I can pay...I must took with Alice 5 minutes.Keep Rockin!

***

Hey Alice, Been A big fan for many years now, love the welcome to my nightmare concert in Sydney 1976 it still lives on in my memory.Caugh you at Penrith leagues club in 2006 Dirty Diamonds tour, how cool me and you singing together in the 2nd row. Are there any plans of touring any time soon? in sydney with KISS maybe. As my Sexy lady is a big KISS fan. We are sorry we didn't catch you in New Zealand maybe next time huh! just wondering will you ever be designing a Alice Cooper Rockhard motorcycle helmet cause we have a KISS one but now we need a Alice Helmet so we can both look cool riding our bike. Stay cool, keep rockin. M____ & C___

***

I have never been a big fan of Alice Cooper. I am a 29 year old, recently paralyzed. Last night i had a very vivid dream. i do not know how my dream mind could do so well at re-creating

Alice Cooper. I was at a show, in one of the front rows, sitting there depressed and completely uninterested in the show and the music. n At one point Alice came out into the crowd and mingled a bit with people. He noticed my attitude. Alice went back on stage and stopped the show, had one of the security guards let me know that he noticed me, he wanted me to come up on stage. I woke up before I got on stage. i also woke up crying. I was crying from the great compassion that I felt coming from Mr. Alice Cooper. I woke up in tears, from a dream where Alice Cooper was reaching out to me. His compassion and open heart were trying to help me deal with my depression. i just wanted to say thank you. Although it was a dream. It was very real, and i woke up a bit different. The concern that Alice had for me in the dream carried into reality. many thanks, much love and many blessings. tell Alice i said thanks

***

could you please write a piece on this and send it to the guy. i'm busy.

The dvd (welcome to nightmare) has the song (Escape) and I wonderd what is the screen made of and what is it, and when you went in to the screen were you actully moving and how did you get the picture of (the GraveYard)and how did you bust the coffin in the screen?

***

hay daddy now you know i know how io was i knew how you was to but i relly need you pls pls come to me!!!!!!!!!!!!I LOVED YOU LIKE SHE TOLD ME YOU KNOW IM SMRAT LIKE THE BOTH OF YOU SO CAN YOU COME AND M______ LOVED YOU TO MY BROTHER THAT IS THAT HAS MY MOMMAS EYES SO MY BABY'S ARE GOOD AT HIS HOUSE FOR NOW I LOVE YOU I WANT YOU TO MEET MINE LITTE D_______ BUT SHE A L____ MY SON HAS MY EYES AND YOURS SO HE A R____ BUT HE IS MINE R______ CAN HELP HIS SON ARE ELES I CAN GET HIS ASS IN CORT DONT YOU NEED ME TOO ALWAYS BEEN YOURS K____ K_____ P.S LETS PLAY ME AND YOU SOON

***

Dear Alice, Just a quick thought. I was listening to a mix of some of your older tunes and the orchestra in the background. Started to remind me of the Blues Brothers. That would be a great movie, "Alice Cooper meets the Blues Brothers". I'd love to see you say to the nuns "We're on a missionfrom God." If anything, "Under my Wheels" would be perfect for a chase scene. J____

***

Well, I am a rell fan of you and I would like to know if you will come over someday to Israel? I have (almost) all you's CD'S

***

Dear Alice, Honey, Why don't you ever call or email me. Not sure I'm listed in Pittsburgh under K.C. N______. I want to get in touch with you but I can't. Really your the best friend I most likey ever will have. Why don't you get in touch with me. I'd love to do the whole thing I hear in total. I'll do most things for you. And that's what I want to do. If it works out but things are. If the thing doesn't go up sooner, then I want to get in touch with you. Everything is you in a way and it will. Well when your ready to get in touch With me, I'll be waiting. Love K.C. I love you What do you really want to do.

***

Trying to get in touch with Alice. Nat'l Nursing Home Wk is 5/11 to 5/17/08. Our theme this year "Hollywood Stars". I am the Nursing Supervisor of a small nursing home in Youngtown, Az (Phx. suburb)and would like to have Alice stop by for a guest appearance. It would be a big boost to staff morale. Many of our residents have few or no visitors and will probably reside at this nursing home for the rest of their lives. I know Alice lives in the area and has a huge heart.I asking if he could open his

Photograph © Brett Fenoir Fenwick

heart a bit more and do this for us.

***

you should write an article about this.

Looking back, and having lived through the lifestyle, whats your take on those rock guys who died well before their time like Morrison, Hendrix, Joplin, Jones, etc..?

***

Where is the producer from Billion Dollar Babies. Great stuff. Need a job, mensa, not dumb, 49, look like you, got french/english in me too.

***

Hi Alice, Been a big fan for years. But I was wondering what talking to Dave Mustaine is like. Or just knowing him. I know I probably won't hear back from you but I figured I'd throw it out there anyway. Xx S_____

***

virgin corrispondend with major old foggie rock hero AAAAAAlice' Seriously Have to appreciate your true talent as a musician and front man. I have to apologize if this comes through as a pile of gabbled craP BUT ive not spent a lot of time on this inter-web thing before. My Friend's dAUGHTRERER say's my typing is so bad it sucks and blows at the same time. Anyhow, we all heard you were comimg to the jub in Sept' hope the crops are in by then. Real life folk that live in a trailer park and can't afford the price of two seats to see you live. I'd f sent you a poem but I couldn't think of a word that ryhmes either. Still listen to you on Q-107 but would rather rock in person at the jubil;ee. Bin a fan since juniour high.

***

One thing that pisses me off is COULD CANADA FUCKING HOG ALICE COOPER ANY FUCKING MORE?! WHY THE FUCK DOES HE NEED TO TOUR THAT FUCKING COLD COUNTRY FOR A FUCKING MONTH? WHY THE FUCK DOES THERE NEED TO BE 25 FUCKING DATES FOR CANADA? I FUCKING HATE CANADA AND I WANNA BLOW IT THE FUCK OFF THE MAP AND INTO THE FUCKING WATER.

***

hey bud,we haven't gabbed since '72 & i was wonderin how you're doin.member the dirt at the farm show in harrisburgh? ya gave us a helluva hangover! gimme a buzz when ya get a chance,a____

***

my mother writed you a fax but she didn t become an answer she s a gread fan she s biggest dream is to stand across from you and a autogramm lack in her s collection I hop you find time to writ me back :-)

***

Hi, I have written a book in which Alice is the hero of the main character. I would like to get a copy of the book to Alice as a thank you for all the great music that lead me through my teenaged years. A review from Alice himself would be a dream come true, but reguardless of a thumbs up,I would still like to say thank you for all the years and songs. Thank you very much

***

you're the shit bro, i wish you'd hang out with me and shit but you probably won't because i'm from new jersey and shit like that...plus i'm seventeen...why would a sixty year old rock star wanna chill with some random seventeen year old...you should although send me two free tickets for being such a loyal fan for such a long time...i'd do it for you alice!

***

I have a list of things to do before I pass on. I enjoy the simple pleasures of life. I've sky dived, slept with the man of my dreams, gotten the car I wanted from a car sales man. I added a new item to my "to do list." I don't want your money. Alice, I would fucking love to toke up with you man!" Nobody has to know. You seem like such a fucking sweet ass trip while high; hell you can bring your wife if you want. Maybe we could sky dive!"

Photograph ©
Brett Fenoir Fenwick

Photograph © Denise Firman

I'd like to see tom cruse talk one on one with you Just talk you will lose him in five to ten minutes top and how much work is needed to make this little fuck look tough and hand this fist full of nothinf 20 and profit sharing I guess you can tell I don't like his Kind almost time for bed cheers when you sign off I know Its time For bed I do work when winter is over I'll put more effort into doing a full week times arte good in my trade big mother fucking power plants are going up all over wclose to where I live IF I said M Love would you keep it to yourself Ps I did not spell tom with a capital T after all he's just a shrimp Cheers Thanks Doc

***

i have and qustion thats plegdme sinces i was and tenager now I am 44 how did thay pull of the beheding thing i have all ways wonder that its kind haunted me throw life how did thay do that and why the kissing and spiting one hes face afther exquaction love allw ays wondering

***

hi alice i have a n emergency i dont know where to start my bosses realitive camre looking for me in the rock rooms the other day he let it be known that i was blackballed in this town i found out that my boss is pulling shit. i think he has something to do with it too but,,,,well anywayfound out my bossis telling shitwhen employers call to ask about me d___ s__ he actually heard him argue with the window plce and talk em out of hiring me,,,alice thats a 15 dollar an hour job.he let it be known that there gonna wait me out till i cant afford to live then offer me a job at the store for next to nothing and some insurance the one time my boss threw a hint thatif someone had a rich boyfriand he d sell the place ,,,its not worth ithes laettting the place go to pot,alice ibeing used they think i have aces and i dont im sitting here playing peonockle with a fistfull of nines,,,, alice i dont know what to do i don't wanna have anything to do with it i just wanna make a living for my family,,,, + the men in the rooms are making offers again from a whore to a trophy gf alice i want to do things for the right reasons whether it be work marry fuck or anything else please dont let it be known how bad i am off financially ,,,i have 30 bucks in the kids bank account and 50 i could borrow from my kid , its becoming sooo bad its cutting into groceies im tryin gnot to let on that im so vulnerable ,,,please don't tell me to go to hell at least tell me what to do i need your help and advice if nothing else,,,im all jammed up,,,d___ said that i actually landed about 6 good paying jobs ive never been in this situatin before I dont know what to do please help ty in advance a______

***

If I would have known what lack of common human decency I would encounter for the sacrifices I made for positive changes in the world I would have never went back down. They tell me sharing is caring maybe you'd like to share the spit or maybe just give it back. In case anyone didn't notice I wrote Forest Gump for a reason.

Furthermore, know it all wearing the pants ruining my life and causing a lack of love life, I am Native American and I don't know my blood type but I'm pretty sure it's not O.

***

I am very confused about this whole led zeplin group. I picked up a guitar mag which pictured a man on the cover under the name jimmy page. I saw the same man on the bus not too long ago and I recognized him from the magazine(not to mention he was carrying a guitar). His voice made me cry(which I assumed I must have known him at some point in time) I also heard him say his name was james. I finally found a patio memory which was of stairway to heaven either we wrote together or he was checking to see if I remembered the lyrics (I was the stores are all closed). So then after your show I look up jimmy page (have tried the lz site before but it takes too long). End result. I am really really really heartbroken by the whole bullshit don't care if I ever went to the olympics fuck however many musicals, movies, books, people that I spent my heart on

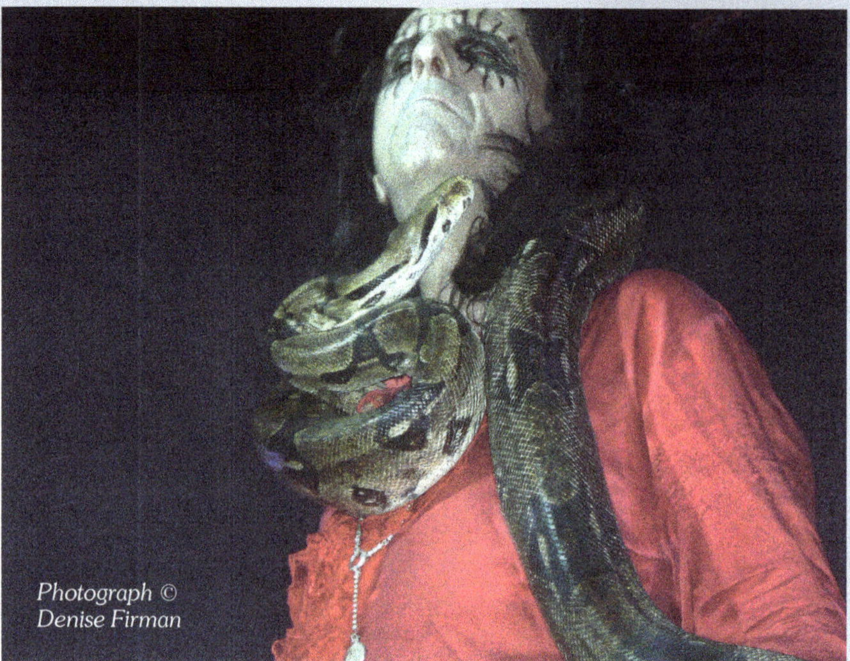
Photograph © Denise Firman

and got fucked over double time for it. I hope their all fucking fanaticly happy and never go on tour and take r___ the hotel theif with them.

***

Minus Top Gun which was supposed to REPLACE whatever I___ wrote and to pay back the Air Force guys who emptied their pockets so that russian guy didn't kill us. I annoyed every vet I could find at the chandler festival and looked the information up in the encyclopedias for that movie. Officer & a gentleman was to be fair(Army, Air Force, Navy, and did I forget the Marines?). Maybe that was the cloverfield I wrote which I havn't seen but I don't think it's what I wrote about. By the way I am very confused about the Olympics. The captain said I had to do the high dive because HE was sick. Were they messing with me? Not to mention confused about verbal settlement which belongs to America.

***

Dear Alice Cooper,I met you a long time ago at the wearhouse in New Orleans la.You were in a group called the Naz.You told me your real name already then.You were very nice to me.You were not married then.I am never afraid of your snakes.I had a pet king snake when I was 4 yrs.old.And also my chinese sign is a snake.God bless you.And good luck on your tours.Love,Captain S______ K_____

***

please send me neurologists name. I am driving myself and everyone else crazy. odds gotta be better. Where is my 50% of the movies I wrote. I don't think anyone else had a dark room and my medals since I forgot I wrote the words to charlottes web. I know that everyone else thinks this amni thing is funny but it really isn't. D__ D__

***

Hi Alice I love you're band and I love you're rool on Wayns world. I listen to you're music all the time. I am a huge fan of you and sometime I would like to meet you so I can get you're autograph. And maby if you play eletric guitar could you give me a few lessons on a few of you're songs plese.

***

Hello Alice, I have a business proposition for you, but I have to explain how this came about before I announce the idea. I am a sophomore at Luther College studying Music Education and I am in an Ed. Psych class with an interesting professor to put it nicely. We were discussing the fact that parents nowadays wish for the teachers to do everything and hold all the responsibility. The parents do not want to hold any responsibility for helping their children succeed. So then last night I was chatting with my mom and I was telling her about this and we then began to discuss about how most Americans do not want to hold responsibility for anything in their lives. So I then thought, why not get a famous person to make a movie or song about the lack of responsibility in this country which would open people's eyes. But my mother didn't think that would work because most artist don't like to push people's buttons too much and such. As a response I said well, why not find someone who doesn't follow the norm and I immediately thought of you. You do what you want and besides I like your radio show. Whenever I am home, in Illinois, I listen to your show and thought that maybe you would be the person for the job! So, the business proposition is this: you and I create a song about American's lack of taking responsibility and we perform/record it. I'm sure you think I'm a crazy and maybe you get emails like this all the time, but I thought why not ask, no hurt in that. And besides I think we would work well together because you are sacrastic and I grew up in Chicago so naturally I am. You come from Michigan and I've vacationed their every summer since I was born and we both like music. We are basically like neighbors. So if you are interested in this crazy idea please contact me, and if you are not I wont take offense as long as you don't steal my idea and take all the credit for it. Thanks, J_____ M________ P.S. Happy Belated Birthday and excellent acting on Wayne's World.

***

It was TWENTY FIVE years ago???? That might have something to do with it.

Question: On the special edition EP "Alice Cooper" Alice does the song 18 from a German television show, he looks less than himself and the song is performed differently. What's up with that?

***

Dear Alice Cooper, I'am 48 years old, and I'am currently looking for professional main venu band. I'am a very professional drummer, and I own many very large custom drum kits, pro quality all the way. I'am looking to adition for you, as I'am interested to go on a tour with you. If, you are interested you can contact me or e-mail me and I'll provide additional information, regarding the bands I've toured with. I can play all your toons. Rick Deringer(Nazareth), and Rudy Sarzo (White Snake's bass player)are

Photograph ©
Denise Firman

Photograph © Denise Firman

personal friends of mine. Plese, respond soon as I'am looking forward to be part of your show, as I can give you the back bone, and a drum solo from hell. Sincerelly, J___ H___

***

I'm simply writting to let you'S no that I'm no longer a fan of yours any more I am calling it guits because I dont respect artist that due the hard drugs and I hate all Americans they all suck I only like 4 songs and I'v waisted to much money and I'm a better player and singer so so long and theirs bether out there.

***

i have bin lisenting to you sence you come out with the first album so if you can add me to youre myspace i have got one ok ill be looking forword to talking to you my name is m____ b_____ i still lisen to rock and roll i hate country with a passion

***

HI ALICE I AM A BIG FAN.I LISTEN EVERY NIGHT BEFORE BED EVENTHOUGH I SHOULD BE SLEEPING BECAUSE SCHOOL.BUT I REMEMBER THAT SONG school ot for summer.MY FRIENDS ARE HAVING PROUBLUMS WITH A SONG. ONE THINKS YOUONLY WROTE IT AND ONE THINKES ACDC WROTE IT.THAT SONG IS TMT. TO SHUTE THEM UP I SAID BOTH BECAUSE I DONT KNOW I JUST KNOW THAT YOU SANG IT.PLEASE READ IT ON MONDAY-FRIDAY AT 9:00-10:00. THAT IS THE TIME I LISTEN. BUDDY PLEASE WRITE BACK.OH BY THE WAY MY DAD HATES YOU BECAUSE HE SAYS YOU EAT CRAP AND PEE IS THAT TRUE. OH DID YOU KNOW THAT I CANT GET TICKETS BECAUSE YOU ARE NEVER HERE. HEAR YOU MONDAY-FRIDAY BYE!

***

hey alice its r___ n___.Can you please send me an E-mail because my brother deosnt believe that i send you messages.So can you please send me an E-mail to proove him rong thanx.P.S i am depending on you.bye

***

I am contacting you about a booking. But first, I want to say something to you. I think your extremely hot and sexy. Im a indy pro wrestler and i also help run acpw wrestling in philadelphia. im 27 years old. I think your a very talented artist and i love your stuff.The main reason for this email. I recently got injured. A indy wrestler was jealous that I was getting a match with DDP later in the night. SO, when I wrestled this local he hurt me real bad, that i need hospital care after the match, just so he can take my spot against DDP. From that night, I found out i have optic nerve damage and a sist over my right eye. My doctor told me, that i have to leave pro wrestling for good. I cant take hits to the head anymore or go blind in one eye. I want you to manage me on my very last match, just walk me to the ring and stand in my corner please! let me know your price if interested. i would love for you to just manage me. Please think it over and let me know. This would mean the world to me for my last match. Email me back please and let me know thank you. email back please! R____

***

I want to speak with Aliiiiiiice! It's my reason of life! I think you're the great musician in the story and i want to create the first tribute band of Alice Cooper in Italy...with your benediction of course!

***

Dear mister Cooper, Thank you for you ADD,I am very honored your are my idol and I love you of all my heart...You are Wonderful,beautiful,and your music it's fantastic,my prefer song is : The Mask (Jason movie) it's very great wonderful guitar,and your voice too (very very very beautiful)...and I like too " POISON " it's very funny with the women and the poison in the drink... One Billions "^^" one million of kisses just for you. Sorry for my ugly english it's because I am Belgian girl...^^ My name is E__,and I have 22 Years.

***

gun 4 hire ready to roll peace n be well let me know ,if you need a guitarist i do know most of your music ive spoken with c____ n e___ a few times i worked 4 p diddy lil kim mace and have alot of touring xperience I toured with john fruchante from the chilipeppers as well as fishbone p funk, members of black flag i worked for john entwhistle marky ramone keith caputo singer from life of agony im a quick learner and would play guitar for u for free ilove your music and im a big fan d_____ d___

***

Hi Alice, as a fellow golfer i would like to send you a letter and a photo of myself as you may have some advice for me. best wishes L__ D___

***

Dear Alice! At the 4. Feb.1948 you catch the sight of the World a very nice day: YOU was born! And thatís why your innumerable Fans must celebrate this day – especially me *smile* - because Youíre still a really Niceguy - yes, yes and you know that! ;-) and today with your 60 years YOU ARE

THE BEST OF (Shock) ROCKíNíROLL AND HARDROCK OF THIS WORLD! Itís only RockíníRoll, but I like it, love it, like it ñ yes, I do!î ;-) Not without good reason youíre a Star in the Hall on Walk of Fame and a Rock Immortal-Star! YEAH, YEAH, YEAH! Well, I send you all my best wishes for the next time in your life! Good luck and much fun with all what you doing! Have a long, healthy life and never lose your precious humour and your Love to the music! I love to hear your ìNights With Alice Cooperî, youíre a really lovely host. You have cool stories, I love your voice and I feel so good, when you laughing; and like the music there you play carry on! Of course, YOUR music is my Favourite!!! I look forward to your next Album ìAlong came a Spider! And Alice please doesnít forget your German Fans!!! PLEEEAAASE come to Germany on your next Tour, because WE MISS YOU, WE LOVE YOU AND WE NEEEED YOOOUUU!!!!!! Without you our World is such a Brutal Planet! ;-) (Yes, really itís true, trust me!!!) Last Year 2007 you was unfortunately not in Germany with your Psycho Drama-Tour, so I went to the UK and saw you in LONDON/ Wembley Arena! I was sooo happy to see you live - Alice, you was so great and your daughter Calico, too! We Germans used to say: The apple donít falling away from the tree! When you know, what I mean! ;-)By the way: I was the woman in the middle of the first row with long, black hair ñ looks like you ;-) ñ and I wear black, sexy clothings (and had a little Camera with me) maybe do you remember me?!? Alice, if you have a little bit of time, Iím very glad, when you write to me. Much lovely Greets and stay tuned, in Love, M______ alias m____ cooper ;-)

***

Hi My name is D______ F________ I am doing a documentary on my father B__ K___ the Balloon Man. Dad made a Balloon of you in the 80's and I would like to interview you for the documentary. Please let me know if you can help. Thank you.

***

Hi Alice, My name is L____. I was doing research on past presidential elections and I found some information that you ran against Richard Nixon in 1972. Is this correct? And if so what was your reason for this? How many votes did you get? any feed back would be great:) Thanks, L____ F_____ Greensburg IN

***

I have not been an Alice Cooper fan all my life...just since 2000 or so. I am 37 years old, I work at the P____ Hotel and Casino as a massage therapist. Alice has some serious medial rotation in his shoulders, I would like to help him. I have noticed that in him for awhile even tho I was not a fan. I lived in Tempe in 2003 and now my 11 year old is addicted to Cooper Eye tatoos and food, so we have to drive from Vegas to PHX everytime she visits...but she has good taste in music. I soon have to quit massage because of an accident in March of 07 that broke my neck and back...and since I live with a brilliant musician and know of their internal struggle with constant noise and such that can be a blessing/curse with creativity I am going to continue to help people by getting into drug abuse and a degree in psych. specializing in the special psychosis that musicians deal with that cause them to try to quiet their mind with drugs and alcohol ultimatly with death...anyway.. .before I have to quit massage I would love to see if Biosync could help with the Medial Rotation that I see in Vincent. I know you probably don't answer people but I don't care about fame, I work with famous peeps all the time...but he is a human being that needs some structural reorganizing. I have worked on Mick Mars, Jenna J., Vince Neil, Vivica A Fox, Tommy Lee...you get the Idea. None of those people need work like I am offering. Thanks. M_____

***

ALICE COOPER U FREAKIN SUCK.. GET A REAL JOB

***

i wish jeffrey morgan would use his own name

WE LOVED YOU SINCE CHILDHOOD ALICE.. SOME OF YOUR BEST MOMENTS WAS WHEN U WHENT INTO WWF..YOU STARTED THAT WHOLE THING /NO ONE KNOWS..

***

whats up Alice, I stayed up last night but it didn't matter because I had OSS today, so right now I'm home alone because my dad and his girlfriend went to pick up my brother from school my brother hardly every gets in trouble, but this time it wasn't my fault, i missed afterschool detention because my dad picked us (my brother and I) up early, so it wasn't my fault that I missed it but they gave me Out Of School Saspention any way my dad was yelling at them, when i got there because he knew it wasn't my fault, so yea it was kind funny that he was yelling at them because when i was in middle school 6th grade threw 8th my mom yelled at them every year. but now i live with my dad because mom moved to North Carolina and even thou it says i live in North Carolina i

Photograph © Denise Firman

don't i live in West Virgina, i have it as North Carolina becasue one day i might live with my mom and i daon't want the entirer world to know where i realy live you get it? I'm going to get my drivers lisence this year too it's gonna be radical, I will be able to get a job which is also pretty rad, i'm gonna work at some place like sheetz until i get out of school then i am going to collage, so i can be better then what my big brother is cuz he didn't go to collage and for awhile he had to live in his own car. so i'm going to go to collage i don't yet know what i want to be but i'm only a freshmen i still have time to think about it. For now Alice i have to go i'll talk to you soon Bye Bye Alice... ^.^

***

i wish ringo starr would use his own name

I know you were a friends of Jim Morrison and John Lennon, I was wondering what were they like? Also I was wondering what drives you to keep being a rock star? Lastly when is your new ablum coming out? I can't wait to get it. Well later days Alice, forever your fan and follower, S__

***

I never got married stud. Must be fuckin' terrific right? I SO love women. I cry everyday they are so good. You Dave Conan and Jay pull me up. I freakin' love you my friend. C____, a local too. He listens at the bike shop. Why woodn't he?

***

i wish chip monk would use his own name.

Hi my name is R___ P_____. I am 18 years old. I live in Waldport OR on the Oregon coast. I was wondering how i could become a roadie for Alice Cooper. I enjoy being on the road. I would like to learn how to set up the equipment and learn how to use it and see how things work behind the scenes. This would be a dream come true for me.

***

I will contact you no further unless specifically directed by you. Peace. Love. I'm out.

***

i wish willie dixon would use his own name.

Hey Alice, I need some advice on a problem which I wish I had a dozen of. A local blues singer, E____ "Blue" L_____, is very interested in one of the 29 blues songs I've written, entitled, "Get Your Blues On". He said that he may want to take it with him when he tours England in mid-March. (So, I don't have a lot of time.) The problem is that I am completely new at this! I know about royalties, basically. But I have only a VERY rough idea what to charge. What is the current standard rate, if there is one? 1/10 of a cent? 1 cent? Do I charge for each performance of the song?... for each recording of it?... for the sale of each CD? And who do I deal with concerning radio plays? Also, I don't know legalese well enough to write up a contract, myself. And I can't afford legal advice, much less legal services. Any suggestions as to how I might obtain free or discounted legal services? Or is there perhaps, a standard form available? Any help you can give this fellow songwriter will really be appreciated, since I am almost completely in the dark on this!! Thank You,"Blues" B__ S_________

***

Hello Mr. Alice Cooper !!! I am O___ M_____, man of 49,russian from St.Petersburg. I was born also on 04.02. I like your music and specially your words of songs. I am a painter. I have a project in my head about costumes and decorations for concerts and shows which can make an image....I mean.... real image.... If you are interested drop me a line..... I ll be waiting.... With my respect, O___ M_____

***

I LIVE IN ROCHESTER, INDIANA. NORTH OF INDY ON 31 NORTH.

Photograph © Dwight McCain

Photograph © George E. Orlay

ANYWAY, WHAT MADE YOU WRITE THE SONG ONLY WOMEN BLEED? THE SONG IS VERY GOOD AND I LIKE IT. I DON'T HEAR IT VERY MUCH WAS IT A SIDE B SONG?I SEEN YOU AT DETROIT STATE FAIR AND YOU PLAYED WELL. I ACTUALY WAS ON THE SIDE STAGE OF YOUR SHOW. WASN'T BOB SEAGER THERE ONCE WITH YOU IN THE RAIN? HA YOUR SHOW ON Q95 IS AWESOME. I SOLD RED BARN ELEPHANT EARS THERE WITH FRIENDS!!!IN TALLAHASSEE FL. I HEARD YOU ON A LATE SHOW FOR A WHILE AND THEN IT JUST DIED. YOU MADE ME FELL LIKE I WAS HOME HEARING YOU ON YOUR SWOW THANKS.B_____.

***

that's some college?

Every time Alice is in Jacksonville my husband, son (he is 18 now)and I go to the concert. They are always fabulous! Additionally, every year for the past 6 years, my son, C____ and I go to Phoenix to visit family. And every year we go to Coopertown to eat and shop. We always have hopes of seeing Alice, but have not yet. The reason for this email is, we are applying for college scholarships this spring. One of them requires a picture of the applicant, C____, with a celebrity. C____ would love to meet Alice and have a picture taken with him for this scholarship. Is there a possibliity of Alice being in Florida or Georgia soon? And if so, could we get a picture of the two of them?

***

Dear Alice to Hi! I am your fan living in Japan. T________ U____ name is and I am. Recently the radio, you listen and come to Japan in March, once in a lifetime you can, please get together with thought. Your music is the first time I met 12 years ago, his brother-in-law has been introduced. The songs under my wheels. Shocking. Late buying a CD or videotape or necessary. 4 CD box set of three pairs of them. My house is right in the middle and Tokyo Narita, Chiba lived in the town. We hope your time even if you do not eat? Japan to introduce delicious restaurant. Aware, not to ask, but do want to see. This email address is alicecooper@______.ne.jp. Catchy. However, this address in Japan's mobile phone from the set not only to receive. Please be patient. Please respond whether once. Sorry illegible writing. Thank you for your patience.

***

canadiasna alice ment for air earlyer was for alice... 4message: Hey again alice (now that i am accuainted with your site.....emails..may flow more freely......) a poem for alice...the coopmistery hey the man in the bay.....has seen a new way....the maganeer of tours ... flowen....throy mysterious BOOZE surcumstaintail life evidence....and coincidence....ps/ andy whorehole Roks Gj G____ the bay....canada

***

Hey alice....im g____.....im sort of a triped out dude as of late......My bipolar.....whatever that is.... has kicked in to overdrive......and alass i feel like a person... After 10 years....i feel Reality under the holiest of gouhst.....by the way my internet skills as well as Guitar Skills are becomeing excellerated by HIM. The new learning prosessise am achieveing under god...... sorry if tis is hard to read....im new at alote....but alot is alreaddy hear....love under god in human ity is good inhmanity is hell...but i feel better...Al.ce, Mr Vinny.....you are a blessing to my ears any time i can catch you show.....which is eazyest three nights a week off a local k rock broad cast..... thank you for recieving this and BEING Alice Coooppper....yopu rock al ot e of worlds....i hve been listening since Trash....and i am just a musisian....still pleaged by my anti sosalist Past. thanks... I will be listinig tonight.....PEACE AND JOY TO ALL WOrlds as colisions as the hatred seeps out of a revolating world.....LUV to a world from an X cracckheaned dude G___ j____ G____...

***

Alice i love you. I went to ur concert at the dodge county fair in wisconsin. it was my first live concert and u made it special. i love u so much im doing a biography on u. and on ur B-day im dressing up like u D__ E___

***

y'all come back now, y'hear!

hey alice,really enjoy your radio show,i listen to it on 96.9,out of louisina.after all these years we still listen to the same music from jr high school(1969)i'm 49 now, but i'm really ageless like you!how long can this go on?saw you in beaumont,tx during the 80's flush the pan?almost saw your welcome to my nightmare tour in houston in the 70's.i live in a hollow 10 miles from the sabine river,if you ever get a chance to come to texas again,give me a call and i'll show you wher we hang out under hwy 63 bridge during the summer!do you have a family?i havn't heard you mention it on air,if you do, bring the kids!e mail me back and i'll give you my number,hope to hear from you! b______ c________

***

My name is H_____ R______ and I live in Sweden. I know this is a longshot but I feel that I at least have to try: I'm trying to get in contact with Mr Alice Cooper because I'm planning to write my third book in Swedish about learning the harmonica. It has been very hard to find harmonica books in the Swedish language. The first book was for beginners where I wanted to give the reader the basics in playing the harmonica and the second had alot of more or less famous melodies that the reader could practise. I'm now thinking of writing a book about bluesharmonica and one of the first reasons to do this is that I wanted to give the reader some 12 bar solos to practise. I found it very difficult to find solos to practise when I learned the harmonica. Then I realised that the book maybe should consist of some more than just the solos. So there I am for the moment. If I write this book about bluesharmonica I want to talk a bit about blues - what is blues etc. Then I came up with this idea of maybe having some famous harmonica- and bluesplayers explaining what blues is to them, because blues is so much more than speciffic notes and chords, and I think that it would be a nice approach to explain the blues!? So the thing that I wanted to ask Mr Alice Cooper was if he maybe would consider to explain

Photograph © George E. Orlay

what blues is to him so that I could have this as one of the apprehensions in the book? It could be just one word, a sentence or more. So I would be very greatful if this message was sent to Mr Alice Cooper. Thank you for taking your time to read this!

***

i was wondering why you or the record company hasn't put out a double dics set of Welcome to My Nightmar and Alice Cooper goes to Hell together because their're pritty much the same story. also i would like to find out how you do the guilliten trick but im sure you get this a lot so im not expecting an answer but if you could that would help my band S_____ The H____ with the stage show I'm trying to get togher

***

I am the clean cities coordinator in Tucson, AZ. My program is charged with reducing dependence on foreign oil through the education and deployment of alternative fuel vehicles like biodiesel, E85, CNG, electric and hydrogen. I am trying to find a speaker for an upcoming meeting, someone who is well known and pro environment. I would love to see if Mr. Cooper would be willing to speak at this meeting. I would help him with a quick education on alt fuels, what I really need is a face that people will know and attend the meeting. Is it possible to book Mr. Cooper to speak?

***

Are you my father or not? My mom and the rest of the family is trying to tell me that I have mental problems. So I would appricate some kind of contact so I can talk to you. Also I tried calling Shep Gordan in Florida and that is a persons home. I also sent a letter to them, I hope they put return to sender on it and not get mad! So again, I didn't change my birth certificate, I didn't make up, I'm not afraid of you, and I do need your help! Not unless you think like my mother!!! Even A_____ was trying to tell me that I have mental problems. "everytime a reality show comes on you think you know them and you want to be them." I don't want to be anyone but myself. That's all I know how to be. Some Christmas. K__

***

I remember listening to you when i was in high school. i dated a guy named k____ cooper that always claimed to be your third cousin. and he did at one time get a signed picture and backstage passes in the mail. Of course we were in jr, high and did not get to go. He passed away after a motorcycle wreck. he was living in Lubbock, Tx. Please get in touch with me.

***

why you unplubg me? as if I don;t know? just a honky white power bozo in control. you know alice cooper would not agree? some typical racist white power honky bozo in control unplugs me. kinda noticed the board mwas a bunch of dumb misfits and started to notice a clan of white honky fools. racist that could not admit it ...typical and predictable. it ain't over honky blood.

***

kee-ripes

alice or should i say vincent, if you ever want a side kick i am the one, my stage name what else kay cooper, alice's younger brother I know most all ur songs up thru poison. and with make-up on i could pass as my hero AlICe himself. also would like u 2 teach me 2 play golf. Please email me back. thanx k____ cooper

***

Photograph © George E. Orlay

Photograph ©
Jeffrey Morgan

Photograph ©
Jeffrey Morgan

Photograph © Jeffrey Morgan

Photograph © George E. Orlay

Well this is a first for me!writing to a rock star. I am a mother of a 20 yr old boy, who turns 21 on the 26th of jan 2008. My son has had a very hard life so far, he has a disability and was not good in school because he was picked on all the time, he now has low self esstem and confidence, he has only two friends, he does not work, all he likes is his music, like yourself. we have bought him guitars, as he loves to play around on them, he picks up some bars by ear, I would love it if you could come to his birthday party,I know this is a big ask, and a bit cheeky, but I would like something nice to happen to him for a change, my mobile number is as follows if you think this is all bull, thanks for reading this.

***

on odd question Body: i know your sober i just had a year and went out im on day two know and i don't wanna live sober but i don't wanna drink either i know it can get better but do u have any suggestions on how to get away from the shame part of it so i can start getting better

***

hi! I read that the song 'Welcome to my nightmare' is based on a nightmare from a boy called Steven. But is the song 'Steven' also based on the nightmare of that boy? And who is that boy precisely? How did Alice have contact with that boy? A____ Van der B_____

***

hi. you probly know my dad his name is J____ H_____. my name is A_____ H_____ and i wanted to tell you that i love Hannah montana and I was wondering if you can help me get the tickets for the next concert in Glendale,AZ this concert is featuring Aly and Aj this cocert is Jan.22,2008 and by the way you might want to know I am 10 years old now. THANK YOU SO SO MUCH please email me back so i know that you got this message ok thanks again bye

***

Dear Alice, I don't need Zyprexa. I need a psycholog who can help me. Do you know somebody? In Psychiatrie they'll give me medical. Do you have any idea? Love M______

***

i love the dead,who was my dad.he leave us alone at monday's night and made us cold!i need a piece of 'spider' help me alice,please!i hope that you feel my pain.

***

hi hottness, i was cruising the web-site wishing i would find you on line. i got what you were saying last night. i believe you are saying i'm alot like p__ and l___. ok. gotcha. i will learn alot. i'll also have you as a friend for life. it means alot to have you in my corner. (but, of course, there many places i'd like to have you. wink) giggle. see you tonight. C____

***

HELLO, YA KNOW I'VE NEVER TRUELY SEEN YOU AS CLOSE AS YOUR PHOTO. I ADOPT MILITARY,FIRE FIGHTERS,(SON WAS BOTH) AND I WRITE SONGS. I KNOW YALL DO YOUR OWN WRITING OF THEMSELVES AS THEY DO RESPOND. I AM ON DISABILITY,YOU CANT SEE IT, OR TELL. HOWEVER I WAS DIAGNOSED THAT I HAVE A YR. I'M PUSHING FOR 5 YRS. L___ G_____ OF PYRGYPH, GAVE ME A

CD,SWEAT SHIRT WITH A HOOD AS HE DID HAVINGME FLOWN TO DENVER. PUT ME IN THE RED LION HOTEL.I WAS THERE IN THE ROOM 4 DAYS AND 3 NIGHTS. I SAW HIM MAYBE 6 HORS IF YOU ADD MINUTES. I HAVEN'T ANY MONEY. DISABILITY DOESN'T PAY MUCH. I WOULD BE HONORED IF YOU'D READ MY LYRICS. IF I HAD THE MONEY, I WOULD BUY YOUR MEMORBILIA. WILL YOU HEP MY DREAMS COME TRUE BEOFRE IT IS LATE... THAT DREAM IS TO TOUR WITH A BAND, BECOME FRIENNDS WITH EM AND HAVE A JACKET OR SOMETHING WITH YOUR NAME ON IT. MY FAMILY LOOKS DOWN ON ME. UNTIL THEY LEARNED I CAN WRITE POEMS AND SONGS. IF I CAN GET IN,;THEY CANT DOWN ME ANYMORE. AND I LIKE TO MAKE OTHERS LAUGH. I NEVER GO ANYWHERE HERE. BEEN HERE 2 YRS AND HAVE NO FRIENDS. NOBODY. MR.COOPER, I AM NOT READY TO DIE.. I HAS A 21 YR OLD SON THAT IS SOON TO WED. THEN THEY WILL HAVE CHILDREN.. RESPECTFULLY R______

***

hey, I hear that Alice Cooper lives in Hamilton Ontario. Is that true? And if So I am wondering if he could come do a concert at McMaster university

***

Dear Acey, It's K.C. again breifly. Really I have a problem with where our relationship has gone. Really you'll have to try a little harder to return the respect I show you , just a little.. Love K.C. N______

***

Photograph © George E. Orlay

Iím always thinking Iím being watched I did start talking to my possible hidden microphones I canít say if there is any I wont go there again started off as it be fun I nearly drove myself mental I wonít let myself think of any possible hidden devices and start talking out laud to them again if my neighbors ever heard me theyíd think I had a screw lose or something I was talking about myself and my family I wanted them to know more about me that was the wrong way to go about it plus I was drinking and smoking on my relax time it was the end of my day from work I didnít count on that stuff making some of my shitty memories that I was talking about that it would have effected my emotions so heavily I donít like even thinking of some of the things I decided to talk about straight I donít understand myself some times. The day you were sitting down on one of a few chairs that were placed under a tree next to my building with the big football player sized guy one of your many security people that you have working for you he didnít bother me I understand why he would be there what Iím trying to say is when you smiled as the driver was driving me to the front of my building my hart melted you looked very beautiful Iím looking in amazement telling myself thatís Madonna I think I went numb or something I didnít look over to the driver dropping me off from there repair shop and say thatís Madonna I kept telling myself holy shit what should I say I was going over to say high and instead when I got out I went up to my apartment I wasnít shaking so I know I wasnít nerves I am shy but nothing like when I was a teenager I donít understand why Iím still asking myself why as time goes by. And I think about it and how much time it would take just for you to even be there and I never said high and I truly did want to anyways I am pissed off with myself about that fucked up thing I did not saying high for what ever reason Iím truly sorry. I hope you donít mind I do keep a desktop picture of you as my desktop. Just knowing you through your videos has helped me change as a person so when I look at my desktop image of you I donít know what it is but it helps me to think first before doing something I normally would have done and get know where go know where attitude something along those lines thanks. My old online name use to be P_______7 then K________ the idea for M-Thirteen came from watching your videos I did learn a few things about you over time from watching them hope you like it. Cheers oxoxoxís

***

my friend was due to go to one of alice's concerts on friday night in cardiff wales uk. due to a taxi driver letting him down he was unable to go and was very upset at not going. I found out that this has been the second time he has been let down. he had spent £40.00 on a ticket did not get to go.he is a massive fan of alice cooper, and after listening to an album lent by my friend i also was impressed. is there any thing that could done to cheer him up as luck has not on his side twice. many thanks m_____ e____

***

that is some pitch.

Backstage and Tour Caterer looking to offer My services. 12 Years of backstage and tour catering expeince. Name: J_____ C. K___

***

Dear Alice, Hello! How are you? I just got out a the nicest bubble bath. My friend just arrived and needs to use this computer. I'm trying my hand at art. I'm working harder than ever lately. The Federal Reserve in Windsor Locks, CT is closing In February 2009. Check processing will be dissapating. I'll be vested in November 2008. PCO, Pco.... i email you for many entries into Publishers Clearing House for ten Million dollars. I hope emailing you wins me that money. I'm at work playing blingo search for publishers clearinghouse. I thought maybe you could write a song for me about my past emails. I'm ready for a new life. Take me away! Thanks, Your Friend, C______ K______

***

I have a movie idea called werewolves on wheels which has nothing but rock stars playing the parts . Except for Jack Nicholson who plays a CHP Officer. You and Zakk Wylde drive across the country in a sherman tank killing werewolves. Who are mostly bikers. If you have any interest let me know and I'll start writing my story idea's. Thanks Coop.

***

I would like the chance to meet and talk about my dreams and projects about "from the inside" i know that

Photograph © George E. Orlay

***

Dear Alice Cooper, What's going on now in the world of Rock n' Roll? Thank you. R_____ A. S____

***

Photograph © George E. Orlay

this can make a stage show and musical with my know how and alice's know how and get together and know how with me it can work - please give me this chance i have been waiting for this for more than 20 years - please reply bak

***

Hello! I want to tell my husband how much I love him, during Alice's Moscow show, I want to say it from the stage!How Can I get in touch with Alice to ask him about it? It's very important for me! Moreover, my husband's make up will be like Alice's one during the show! But it will not be possible to find Alice before the show and ask him, I want to make such a surprise, but on the day of the show we will go the club together with my husband! Can you give e-mail or ask Alice instead of me?

***

I was wondering if you could re-write the song "18" to "50" and change it to a woman's song. It would be quite fitting for a group of 50 year old women getting together to celebrate their birthdays. Please let me know. Thanks, M____

***

COOP. im going to try this again? i think i finaly got my email add.down.i had to.to get a responce from sites like,horneymatch.or sizzelen hot married babes that dont want to get caught.im abought 110%sure i had it wrong when i sent you a email sometimes back. i never did see any thing on this contraption from you,which didnt surprize me.because i didnt see anything from anyone.then a night or 2 later I thought ill listen to nights on KCRR c.f waterloo iowa.i thought,since I mentioned our old friend GLEN you may mention somthing.guess what???no nights with you?this kinda makes me think there could be a consperìcy behind all this? you probley know more about GLEN tan i do,since i was in the county jail when he passed away.otherwise mail me.i will get you any info i can.or you can drop me a email hopefully i have the right add.PS what happened to NIGHTS??on kcrr take care ol friend DIEKEN??!! 1997 better late than not at all;dont ya think?!

***

My son would love to see Alice in concert in Birmingham, UK, on 10th November. Please can you tell me whether there will be any very sudden loud bangs (eg gun shots, cannon shots or fireworks) as he has a condition that makes these very painful. He loves loud music though and any loud noises that aren't sudden and would hate to miss the opportunity of seeing Alice perform live.

***

hi hottness, i hope it's been a great day. monday the health dept will be

Photograph © James Pappaconstantine

here to evict me from my home. it would be great to know if you are going to let me borrow enough funds to fix this bs before i wind up being homelss . unfortunately i am not lying or exaggerating in any way. the watermeter was removed and the power is off we have been stealing power and roughing it for over a month. i hate to add to your overloaded schedule but, please help me out. C____

***

i had just pick up your book yesterday i find it very humerus.A doctor at my dad's (former occupation at long vue country club)gave him a copy for your book. To a lower middle classy framily a 24$$ book is kinda alugury. I run a small business with my friend I__. we goto the worst golf course in the world, g___ v__ golf course. I think it would be a challenge for g______ and others.If you would like to buy discount golf balls just email me. Back to the point i was going to make i beilve i can go big in the futur with a band but these days it's hard to find people willing to play and peractace. there so much violence just the other day i got robbon in the day light i can't really fight im kinda skinny im tall though. no one takes me serious i play the trumpet and my singing is farly good I have a lower pitched voice because of my huge adams apple.well i have togo the steelers game is on wer'er facing arazona today and my mom can't if her football poll. your billion dollar kid,C___

***

hi hottness, i'm waiting on pins and needles but youshould know that i'm loosing hope since there has been no word at all from you and you did say yesterday. i spent my mortgage money to get ready to go with you and if you don't show, i;m gonna loose it all. anxious you bet pleasw do something to let me know whats going on as for me, i took the biggest leap of faith i could have. and if you let me down i will fall and loose everything. and, i did it all on your word to me. please hottness don't let me fall. wink c____

***

Does anyone actually read these e-mails? And, does anyone inform Alice of them? I'm not looking for a handout, but I did send what I thought was a rather sad story of my son missing his first concert ever (Alice, of course) due to the flooding in Indiana earlier this month and I'm surprised not to even get a reaction! Alice seems like such a great guy. And believe me, I have been a fan forever - I'm 46 now, and when it comes to the Coop I'm like a little kid. And my son doesn't like rock-n-roll, but he likes Alice! Anyway, if you are reading this, thanks!

***

hi alice, how are you tonight? i'm good. there has been a stranger in the neighborhood off and on for over 2 yrs now we being all of the neighbors and i have called 911 on this guy and today all the cops would say was they are sure it is a private investigater. how do i find out who he is what he wants? any suggestions? also, hottness i would love to get wild with you . also, i haven't been able to contact k___ about the back stage ticket he says he could procure.. i hope i will see you after the show. only wanting you wink c____

***

Let us know if he shows up!!!!!!!!!!!!!!!

hi alice My name is W______ M_____. My qustion need not be read on air. My mom says that you are coming to my house tonight after the show. Please forgive my impertence but people in the past have told my mom that they are coming and didn't show up. So you see my problem. It's like the boy who cried wolf. It's been said too many times and nothing happened. It would actually be nice to be proven wrong. The last time I was to believe this it was chirtmas last year and Dee Snider was to be here christmas day. I wounder if you could picture the crushed look my mother had to find no sign of him all day. She cried on christmas day of all the joyous days of the year. I hope you come.

***

HI ALICE, YOU SAID SEE YOU AFTER THE SHOW ABOUT BORROWING MONEY ONE FRIEND TO ANOTHER. YOU ARE MOST GENEROUS TO ME. IF YOU WOULD LIKE TO TALK ABOUT THIS PLEASE GET BACK TO ME.I AM STILL WONDERING WHAT YOU MEANT BY I'D BE SEEING YOU SOONER THAN I THINK. (CURIOUS). AND YOU'D SEE ME AT MY HOUSE. YOU'RE SO FUNNY. MISSING YOUR KISSING HOTTNESS C____

***

met you in the seveties.stubbie bud days.fantastic shows.I'm at crossroad.I want to stop the beer.I'm a semi retired Ld and Tech.Worked for the UNtochables.I'm 54'I have slight muscular dystrophy.Financily fair. So the question. How did you beat the stubbie? AA didnt work Name: E_____(Rusty)T_____

***

Sorry if I hit the wrong button. My medication makes my hands shake... Thank you for your time, I would love to at least shake your hand if you have time.We are in orch 4 row p seats 101 and 102. thank you, t_____ h______

***

Dear Mr cooper. I am from Bulgaria, livinng in mesa az now. In 1979 it is very wrong to have any western world propaganda in your possetion. I would follow your music and band where ever you were. I found a picture of you in a music magazine with you and your snake! I took it out and put it in my billfold for safe keeping. Unfortunatly I was picked up by the local bulgarian patrol for a rutine check and they found your picture. for this picture they put me in jail for one week.It was worth it. I would love to meet you one day in person if that is possible please let me

know. Thank You for your Time,
P_____

***

Memory Test: 1973, Ft. Worth. A security guard brought you some lyrics with a signed release. You called me at 2:00 am, and said "I like it a lot & I'm gonna see what I can do with it." don't remember? try this: As I sit here in my dark quiet palace, I watch the world's leaders; they're grinning with malice. remember now? What ever happened to 3rd Degree Burns? D____ S______

***

Hey Alice - we can't wait to see you Friday night at our county fair. The last time I saw you was about 30 years ago in Madison, along with my brother and 4 of my sisters. Anyway,if you would like to go golfing, trap-shooting, take tour of our lake on our pontoon boat, let us know. My husband is the president at the gun club, so we can accommodate you. Looking forward to seeing you Friday night. P.S. We stopped at Cooper's Town in Phoenix in May. Cool! E_____ S______

***

Dear Mr. Cooper,im f____ w______, im not a sloppy mess, but you said that you could function the whole time you were loaded on the cocktails, well me too ,im 49 years old married to a wonderfull wife, got a great jobjust tired of being dizzy, ive admired you for years can you give me any words of wise, it would mean alot, thankyou very much

***

Hey Alice, About 25 years ago a friend of mine delivered a couch to you . He said you were real cool. Stay that way. Like your ZRock radio show. Peace JC

***

You don't know me from Adam, but my brother knows you! He has gone to every concert in and around St. Louis since the 70's and talked to you in Carbondale, Il. outside your bus! He also saw you at the launch of your album, in St.L. at Chippewa and Hampton! He has a hard time in his life, with booze and drugs and has finally reached 6 years of sobriety. I moved him to Columbia, Mo. near me and he wants to come see you in July at the Missouri State Fair. He named is second son, Vincent, after you! He loves you and has alot of respect for all the good that you do. If you could give him a special shout out, his name is J____ J____! Better yet, call him, it will make his day, no, year, no life! I probably sound like a nut case, which is borderline truth, but I am serious about this. Holla!

***

another book for you to review. lucky.

Dear Sirs: I'm author of an international book about one of Mr Alice Cooper's

Photograph © James Pappaconstantine

friends (Jim Morrison and his band) and because I really admire Mr Cooper and because the book is full of material related with his friend, I would like to hear from Mr Cooper in order to explain him what the book is about and I really would love to send him one book (my honor) Thanks Best Regards: R__

***

you really need too retire. I have been a fan for a longb time. I have listened to your music and banter for a long time now and I believe it hqas been longtime comming that you retire and let the newer personalaties take over. I used to like want you had too say but it is getting old and it is time for you too move aside. sooo get ovet it and move on and let someone else get into it.... please

***

are you going to review this animal rescue cd?

Alice - May I send you my charity single CD/DVD, "Katrina's K_______"? I wrote, recorded, produced, published, & sell, "Katrina's K_______", to benefit the animals of Katrina? 250,000 Animals were abandoned to Katrina: Only 15,000 were rescued. This must never, ever "happen" again. Thanks. God bless. T______

***

i can talk with alice cooper??

***

i wish Ahmet Ertegun would use his real name.

Dear Alice...I'm only a teenager, but i absolutely love classic rock. I'm working on my Zeppelin collection, and was wondering if you could help me with the title of one. The chorus goes like "a a a a a ah, you don't have to go o o o o oh, and I, I I I I I..." If you could play it and/or give me the title, that would be AMAZING. M______.

***

How can i ask Alice if he remembers A time in 1978. It was the new york hospital,White plains new york.Playing volleyball,a girl of 17 hit the ball and it bopped him on the head??This "girl" would love to correspond with him.Maybe you can help me.I don't have a my space acct. and don't particularly want one . thank you so much.

***

i wish Mr. T would use his real name.

Coop, I hope you remember me. My name is P___ E_____ and I was your body guard in 1977 when you were the Grand Marshall for the Enymion Parade in New Orleans. Please contact me at email or by phone so that we can

Photograph © James Pappaconstantine

talk. Thanks

***

haha, hi, im D____ from Nebraska, i'm a senior, or was in north platte high school, i doubt this will get to alice, but i drew your name and a rock on sign, with the lyrics "schools out for summer, schools been blown to pieces." yeah. so they assumed i wanted to blow up the school... so i got kicked out right before prom, they expelled me.. it was pretty lame. moral of my story.. its not as cool as the 60's-70's were, they take things way to seriously now a day. But i just can't get my head out of the time, i wish i lived in more than anything. I'm not stupid, i'm just kind of, well impulsive is a better word well take it easy man, hope to hear something from you. if not, best to luck of you, and YOU ROCK! 1948-forever. oh yea, and me and the principal were arguing about it, i said it was written in 1975 he said 76, he told me he was alive in it, and he should know, i said i should have been alive in it, and i do know. so i wish I was at least right on that. haha peace man.

***

I wish Bowie would use his real name.

This is a___ again, What it the difference between Glam Rock and Punk Rock? They kind of are the same... I know you were considered to be a Glam rocker so you should know out of anybody. The stupid sites ive been researching on are confusing. I really like Glam Rock, I understand what it is- Makeup the flashy clothes But I just dont get what the differences are.

***

I am interested in recording a few of Alice's songs in a bluegrass type of arrangement. Do you know of any other Alice bluegrass covers?

***

i wish andy griffith would use his real name.

I am a fan who saw Alice on a late night talk show last night and found his story about his new book interesting and inspiring. I am a school teacher, tournament fisherman, and part-time fishing guide. I f Alice is interested and is ever in the Lake of the Ozarks area, have him contact me for a free guided bass fishing trip. It is a great stress reducer. Sincerely, R___ M______

***

i e-mailed you did you get it i never got an answer, well you are the glitter king. thanx bowboy

***

i wanted to know if alice could put more info on his site like isj faverotie song or faveorite type of music becase i'm doing my speech on him and it would be really helpful

***

I've made a translation of "I love the dead" to swedish and I wonder how to get it approved to play live and record.

***

i'm just e-mailing you becouse you just played a great song about stealing cars and i infact just stole a car about a month ago.i however didn't catch the name of the song.i was also wondering if you could play'department of youth' considering the fact that i'm 16.

***

Hello Alice, I just want to say thank you for the music. I was playing your "Greatest Hits" CD while making love to my girlfriend. It was the best experience of my life, and hearing your music in the background made it that much better. We both agreed to thank you for making this experience much better, so as soon as we were done, I hopped on the computer and tried to find a way to contact you. The songs we made love to were "I'm Eighteen, Is It My Body, Desperado, Under My Wheels, Be My Lover, School's out," and we finished at "Hello, Hooray." I seriously can't explain what the whole experience was like, but I mean, a rock n' roll star like you should probably already know that feeling. Man, as soon as you come over to Los Angeles, we are going to go to your concert for sure. No matter what.

Photograph © James Pappaconstantine

Photograph © Jeffrey Morgan

Again, I can't explain how thankful I am, and no words can describe the feeling of your music and sex. PS: It was also my first time. Thanks. And happy belated birthday Alice!

***

hello,alice happy birthday, i love your style and just wnated to let you know back in 88' when i was 7 i got all a's in school and my father told me i could have anything i wanted and i bought an alice cooper tape , my mom was pissed , ya know that was one of the best days in my life , she wanted to take it from mke but couldn't, only women bleed, any ways play me some thing like eric burtin it's my life

***

dear alice a long time ago i purchased the schools out album it came in a wooden desk when opened i found a pair of pink panties and my mom saw those and barked me out sumthin fierce she dint believe me and swore i slept with sum girl nice trick dude and keep rockin and for that yahoo kiss fan you started it all and i think kiss owes you for the whole kabookie idea and by the way you scared the hell outta me as a kid when you did the guilitine thing i wanted to run up an save you but weas held back by my step dad and were on my mind well after the show thanx for all the shock rock you have given life you are truly the shock rock king hats and heads off to you r____

***

a girl i know says she named alice cooper alice cooper . how did the name originally be found. i say it is from a charles dickens novel. could you please help so i can shut this girl up. thanh you

***

Hell-O- Mr. ahhhh..ok..COOPER if you will. People say you are sort of the Britney Spears of rock. I say FORGETAHBOUTIT!!! They ask me"why is it alice and not cindy lou cooper,or catrina?" My reply is "how the bleepin (%#?!%^&@*)would I know.Anyway,like you I'm now a radio monkeyBoy after a life on the edge of R&R fame and fortune.Although yours would be better I know.. THE STORIES WE COULD SHARE!!! and yes I was backstage at Altimont!! OUCH!!!! NO I'm not a HELL ANGEL thankyou.Will we ever talk, or be amigos? I dunno. But if you ever need to be left alone by this cold cruel world...don't count on me! SEE ya..I'd REALY LIKE TO BEYAH!!!! —Rolls R_____ R______

***

I need an artist that can make a picture for a tattoo. I would like a tattoo of my two favorite singers Alice Cooper and Dean Martin, What I need is a split face one half Alice one half Dead. If you can help me figure this out I would really appreciate It.

***

My husband are driving to Phoenix to see Alice in concert! Can you recommend a hotel, moderate pricing?

***

dear alice, i don't know if you know that you have a son born in 0ct 1970, he was put nup for adoption i met him in highschool .he eventually met his birtyhmother in arizona i think at some trailer park anyway she sad you ere his father.no one else belive but dude he got your eloquent ugliness,with respect! nose blue eyes,and a fuckin crazy disposition.i dont know where he is now last time i heard about 3 yrs ago he was locked up in prison in ca.but he could be in texas cuz his adoptive family moved there.his name is m______ j______ k_____ and i am an old friend of his,he doesnt even know i sent this email.but he has had a very fucked up life mentally wise he is very very agry at what i don't know but hE WAS ALWAYS A FIGHTER!.anyways thought you might want to t find him,if you care or not it doesnt matter cuz he doesnt know i sent you this. m______ j______ k_____ 0ct 1970 his birthmother from arizona still living there sincerely, d._______

***

Hay thier Alice Cooper. this is the Tender Hearted Man saying that I will not be going to your show in october at north bay cause I'm no longer a fan or promoting your music to any one else for personal reason's I've spent enought money and you's american never help me out so know I don't whant anything to due with americans. so long

***

Hi,Man,it's too bad that you only have a single shirt for anyone over the size of large. There are many fans who like XL shirts,or even XXL. Is this Alice's way of saying that if you're kinda fat you cant wear his stuff? I hope not. That'd be so sad. Take care, S____

***

Alice,K.C. ,My Freind that you call my trophy wife finally mentioned get him to Pittsburgh, K.C. dirty daimonds. No privacy but you could meet us both. She has dirty diamonds only person I gave it to, but she asks where are you. But E___ loves you too I guess. You thought she was awful, I think but she is 1 inch taller than you. love K.C. Dirty

Diamonds

***

Hey, Alice, please come. I'm sick girl. I have grandma seizuers at night, but they can kill me. If you do come you can bring your wife, daughter and try to bring the band too. Please, Ihope you do come, cause I'm your biggest fan. So is my great uncle, some of my friends,two of uncles are too. Just stay clear of the press. If you come?? The press is bad here in Peru,IN. E-mail me as soon as you can!!!!!

***

hi hillo hello alice cooper or vieancent fearrnneyer this is k___ g_________ really inperson the cood word is abrrackadabbra imwriteing or iv beentrying to e mail you for three dayes now i dont know if your getting this iwould like too wellcom you too my night mare or ask you some percsonley queistionens sorry if im bothering you ithink i have been kid napped from when i was a babby bye someone i dont now who but I got a dead sisster or ithink murrderd sisster inew about elements off the earthe and muscick black and white chipp gas and still flying the polish flag andbull shit and bollienney brains and they think bull dick a dealackacseey paid human psyckickecks and going back in time black or what ever most people are chip gagg or pollish and still are mabby or just dont want too orprobly not that lucky but i aalllwayes new elieamentes off the earth forgod awhite boy and musickeor how i came up with bands but cant prove it or god heleped you looks and everyting looks and every thing or someone picked you out offaline or someonegot ripped off but your the sameone i mite be luckky im stillhear too and some people or they mite off went back in time and changed evreything kid babbyes jobs wifes iallwayes new what mite happen and put it in a song or too orseaverrol soongs i cant say too much or someone mite triey too runn the place they show me there is lie weinkking at me all the time pluse i got god or a angiel or someone like god or some one i callit conecktions bgod i mean but they try too keepup with paid humman psyeckieckes i got your bottom teath too and the deantiestesis isee really triey and tear up most off my teath when i go see them they say i need a clieanning our mead ickead inscurance wont pay for no other work i mean one off the real ones faimliley me was kidnapped as a babby or kid sorrey just checking just try ieng too get a a in the usa eif you now about getting a a in the usa or usa getting a a that's whiey i sined in too amentool klinick but didint tellthem much t illmostly after they still should bee chip gass or pollish but said little stuff went in too move but didnt tellthem much andfor resslessness like i was hipper cant reallax or site for moore then a minnet ortwoo like i was born addected too some they gave me vallume for awhile then my fake parrentes tooked itaway after iquiet getting high I quite getting high a long time be for that they didnt have a exaqucse for nothing they wouldent let me move too my grandmaas eather my brouthers mite not be realatted toothem eather buttthey acked like there monkeys anny ways it seeamed like the houlle nabbor hood was a seat up too except ithought theymite requiet sooner or latter black or black or white go ing backin time or changhing everything babbyes and everything ithought they would nt want anny thing too do with that efficting themtoo or faimmily tree andevery thing pluse i got your eyes and your boottom teth our you now my uncle he from miamie flourida and has ason nammed s___ his vvoice sounds just like yours you canttell your voice apart i geuas I should have called but i dont know allice cooper inc but i dont now please callme person too person k___ g_________ middle name is d______ only talk too me only talk toome ilive with other people pluse ihad back up writteing black people too two of them but got ripped off pluse i wrote satterday night live got ripped off dont go on that show blackpeople mite try too ripp you off or own you go ttoo go now ok see you latter bpleasewrite and callim ok for now polisce dont do nothing about nothing machomb county it mite be them now toooooooo realy they dont vhave no cooopeish I love k___ g_________ for evver callas soon as posiable ok imok plusehow iwrote for kid rock gueuesehow i got it there is only one white writter thankyou dooon goon

***

a coocoo named alice will work for me if it will work for you I will give you 9%off the top of all fights for any foundation you wish all you have to do is say my name out loud coconut kid yes this is acoocoo kid you have my offer and it allways stands just send me a name and a contract of your 9%of my future boxing career i await your blessing love r____ a wana bee

***

Yea... My grandma has this new boyfriend... and hes completely ruining her... he wont let her listen to any of her music that she used to Metalica, Megadeth, you... well anyway... hes younger than my mom and im fine with that but... his son is younger than me and i would like to get rid of him cuz hes annoying... anyway the point of this letter is that you and my Grandma... well she doesnt like being called that so... H____.. and you would be perfect for eachother... im serious... and i would love you forever... imagine... my grandpa... Alice Cooper... holy flaming mother of Wednesday 13 but anyway... yea and i dont really live in Big Bone Lick, KY... though that is a real town here... i live in Lexington... but yea... that has nothing to do with this letter... just... consider it and ... try to save H___ cuz

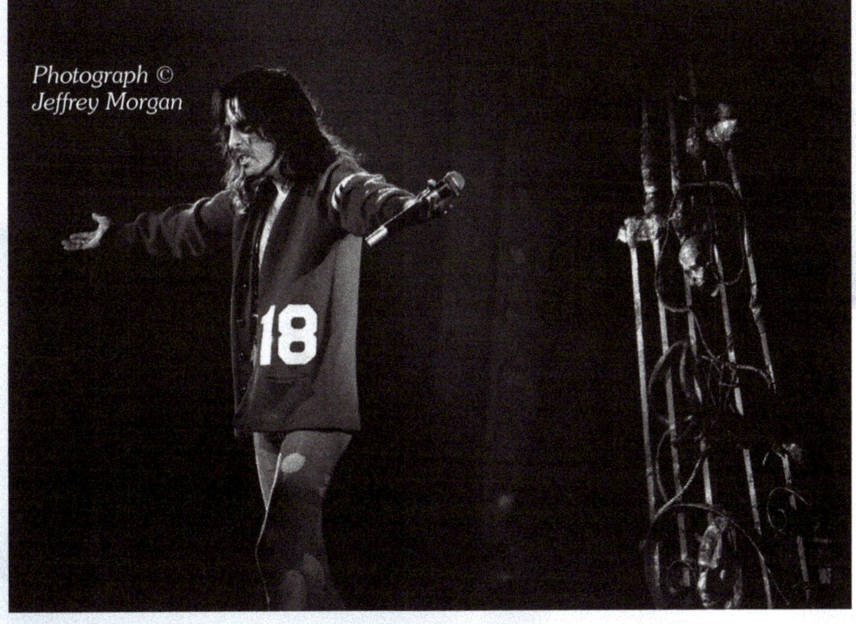

Photograph © Jeffrey Morgan

... shes being turned into some weird country lovin hillbilly... and its scaring me... but yea... my grandma is the shit... I love her even though she tells me to fuck off and calls me a dumbass all the time.. that makes me love her even more and i would like to see her return to her normal state... so please... help me... i beg of you...

***

Alice, I hope you didn't work at Starlight Elecric, once, or twice, this past year, because there was this dude, P___ B______, looked just like you, always picking on me. If that was you, I apologize, that day when you or him, came at me with that big rock, nothing happened, but still. Thanks for the Love it to Death, earlier. I'm stuck at the moment, this is the hardest ever. I would never sell out my family, I will explain everything about our lineage,in an honest biography. I do have the best mom & dad in the world, and that's the way I have to go. You're the first Rock Star I have emailed, Santana, and the stones are next; all the way back to the early 70s, it's like the songs were written for me. My favorite Alice Cooper song is: Nurse Rozetta & Elected. The story they're telling, is only 20% true. I would never, put a video camera in anyone's room, without them knowing. Anyway's, in the middle of a nightmare, that's real ugly, and I have never done an extemporaneous speech, but I will do my best, and get better. Be cool Brother. Respectfully, C___ M_______

***

I was listening to "put the money down" and trying to hear the line - there are bands killing chickens. at first it sounded like there are bands stealing tunes, then, there are bands stealing chickens, and finally I think I convinced myself it was "there are bands killing chickens." Roger says chickens so fast it sounds weird. I'm suprised you picked up that reference to your concert way back in the seventies. Do you think Pete was really refering to you or criticizing you? the song sounds like it's about one of Pete's drunks or something. M___

***

Did alice cooper really sell his soul to satan? or is it just a rumour?

Yes. Yes, he did. The devil came to his house with a contract and... and Alice signed it. With a fire pen. Yes, the devil.

Photograph © Jeffrey Morgan

***

Hey, dude. I saw you show in Ottawa on May 6th, it fuckin' ruled my night, man. You're a divine inspiration to me and my imagination, no doubt. I'm 17 and love your music. I don't think you saw me at your show. But I was the guy jumping up and down like someone lit a fire under my ass, giving the horns solute, screaming/singing along to half you set. just loving your show without a care or doubt to drag me down. I'd definately love to rock with ya again, dude. But my funds are limited (to almost nothing.

***

i just wanted to know if you have any family i texas because im trying to find family that i dont know and that my family hasnt told me about and i just wanted to know if you have family in Tx... and do you know some one with the name I___ K C_____ if you do that is my father so ya just please let me know ok i know no one has probable asked you this but i would like to know so please email me back thanks T______ C_____

***

HI Alice,We share a birthday! As a humane Aquarian, are you planning to protest the seal hunt while in Newfoundland? JP

***

hello, I am brasileiro and a see you in the movie: Monster dog... you is the best...

***

I have been contemplating to build aschool,college and a hospital here in India.Will you please help me.

***

does alice acually cut up a baby in the concerts?

yes. yes, he does.

***

Dear Alice, My husband has PTSD and he is probably your biggest fan. You were always there for him to listen to and give him comfort. If he could ever meet you,it would be fantastic. I know he would love to play a round of golf with you. I know you are very busy and probably will never be in Texas, but if you ever, are please contact me and we will come see you. I appreciate you taking the time to read this, hope to hear from you soon.

***

Hi there, I am a student completing my hsc and I am using "Welcome to my Nightmare" lyrics as a related text. Could you please tell me what it is about and why he wrote it. Thanks, M______

***

dear Alice cooper Ilove your muice Ireally would love too go to your show but idon,t think will get to go Ialways wanted to see you sence i was a little girl but that did,t pan out because my parents could not give us the money to go because we are a family of nineteen kids and we were a very poor family but i do love my mom and dad for all the love they give us now i here you are coming to ottawa canada on may five or six and my dream is to see you but i don,t thing that will happen because i am a single mother that can,t relly aford to by the tickets but i will try to see you but anyways you and me is by fever song good bye for now i hope to see you D____

***

hi my name is t__b____. i am a die hard alice cooper fan . i am 45 years old. i am looking for a different angle in fishing in pro bass tournaments.i am a friend of mike marconi. mike used to play with alice in his back up band billion doller babies tour the band was called battle axe.i am looking for a sponsorship for fishing in pro bass tournaments. such as citgo top 150 and the flw tour. i think it would great to be sponsored by alice cooper.there are alot of different sponsors in todays pro sports.could you please let alice cooper know or where i can send a resume

***

dear mr.cooper!i'm a huge fan of yours!my husband,freinds&myself go to your resturant before your concerts in cleveland when you tour.but I have missed your last 2 concerts on the river.you see, i worked in a locked down psych.unit until a client threw a tempertantrum &bent me over backwards& broke my back&crushed me (she was 383lbs.)i now have metal&cadaver bone in me.i spent a year in a torso cast.as you can tell I didn't get to go to either of your last two shows but,my friends said you were awsome once again.well mr.cooper i was wondering if you could send me a picture i would really appreciate it!you never disappoint us!sincerly a______ v___________ - p_____

***

I am in a bad dental situation and I need $400-500 to get to 1 of 2 particular offices to get a few teeth fixed. If you would help; let me know.

***

Hey Alice you went on tour in Iceland in august. and i was there, and i went backstage with J___ I______ to see you. I was probably the only brownish person there. Just wanted to say great tour loved it. peace.

***

Were they real babies he was chopping up?

yes. yes, they were.

How was it legal for him to do what he did on stage?

the president was a big fan so he got away with it.

Is there any sanity left within his deranged and sick disgusting mind?

no. no, there is not.

I'm sorry but thats the only way to describe him.

you are forgiven.

What else did he do on stage?

had everyone in the audience spit in a

Photograph © Jeffrey Morgan

bucket and then he drank it.

***

my dads your alices biggest fan but hes in prison right now but I was wondering if alice is ever coming to australia again because he was in prison for the last concert it would much appreciated if you could help me thank you

***

I was wondering if Alice ever personally gets to read these e-mails? I have just turned 48 and I have changed the words to his song "Eighteen" to fit my life and others that have gone through the toils of life. I've renamed it "Fortyeight", but since Alice is getting ready to turn 58 maybe he can rename it "Fiftyeight". Ha Ha. Let me know if he's interested. Thank You S___ F_______.

***

sorry, jeffrey....he won't have time for you. and please work on your grammar.

Alice Cooper, I am taking journalism at the University of Lethbridge. We have assignment due at the end of the term to interview someone. And out of 37 students, 2 will be published in the University paper. I am wamting the honor of interviewing you on Oct.24 when you play here in Lethbridge. I was wanting to do a story on how prepare for a HARD ROCKIN SHOW. By following you around for the day. Or if it is too time consuming we can do a Q and A before the concert. Or if it is nice enough we can go golfing the following day and do the interview on the course. Please let me know so I can prepare. Thanks for your time.

***

Dear Alice, My name is J__ T_______ and i am a senior at aitkin high school in minnesota. There are 2 reasons i am writing to you. One is because i am a big fan and love not only your music but the way you present it on stage. The second and main reason i am writing to you is because I have heard that you are not always "Alice". I have heard that 15 minutes before showtime you go somewhere where you are all alone and you can turn yourself into Alice. Well, I myself have battled a sort of depression for over a year now and something happens to me that is somewhat similar to alice. Something comes over me whenever i have alot of emotion inside of me. I turn into a totally different person and sometimes its good but sometimes it is very bad. I have no name for the person that i become nor do i know how to control him. So i was just wondering if there was anything you know about this sort of thing or how i can put all my emotions together and use it when i want to and not when i dont.Thanks for your time.

***

HI THERE MY NAME IS D____ M______ I SENT A REALLY PERSONAL E MAIL TO THE ATTENTION OF ALICE COOPER IT,S JUST THAT I HAVE NOT HAD A REPLY I DONT KNOW IF HE GETS ALOT OF E MAILS LIKE THAT BUT IT WOULD REALLY MEAN A GREAT DEAL IF I GOT A REPLY FROM MR COOPER .I KNOW THE MAN IS VERY BUSSY BUT HE KNOW,S WHAT I,M GOING THROUGH THAT,S WHY I NEED HIS HELP AND HIS SUGESTIONS PLEASE PLEASE CAN YOU SHOW THIS E MAIL TO MR COOPER BECAUSE I NEED HELP SO BADDLY I JUST WANT TO GET THROUGH A DAY WITHOUT HAVING TO TAKE A TABLET SO PLEASE I AWAIT YOUR E MAIL YOUR,S FAITHFULLY D____ M______ XXXXXX

***

Alice, My husband G____

Photograph © Juan Mahoney

C_________ lived upstairs from you in Ann Arbor just before your 1st big concert. He was in row 10 with Nuber when you bit the bat. Still thinks it was a great show. He was a student/musician then. He was a pro musician from the age of 14 and quit touring after his kids were born. He has two songs in the Library of Congress. It hard to restart at 50. Recommendations please?

***

DEAR ALICE WE ARE TWO ITALIAN FANS OF YOURS AND WE WANTED TO TELL YOU THAT FOUR YEARS AGO WE WROTE YOU A LETTER DID IT ARRIVE ? WE ASKED IF YOU MIGHT PRESENT US SOME ALBUMS OF YOURS. WE HOPE YOU'LL COME IN ITALY TO SING. WE LOVE YOUR NIGHTMARES. CIAO BY C_______ AND A_________.

***

hey alice how are you. how is the tour going where are you now. are you taken care of yourself. getting the rest you need to buid the energy you have to have for your preformance on stage for all your crazy for alice fans like me. but i'm in michigan well alice i've got to go i've got to finish putting my furnutre back in place i had just got done painting the inside of my hole house man i'm beat not from painting but from moving all the furnutre around. got to go piece. bye for now. s_____

***

?alicecooper???? I'm a chinese student,like rock music very much,especially yours. "shool's out"and "I never cry" give me a deep impression. Now I learn playing guitar ,and hope someday I could be a rock star like you. I think you don't need to make yourself look terriable,after all,music is the most important thing. I wish you could come to China ,so I could go to your concert. I'll be glad to heard from you. Good Luck

***

Hello, Alice! Are still a gulfing. I look forward to seeing you in more commercials. Keep up the good work. Please send me some recipes of your finest foods from Cooperstown Restaurant. I saw some of the recipes from your website. I might see if I can get more. See ya, and stay sober. C_____ S_________

***

Well thought I would give it a shot , been working on the follow up to Welcome to my night mare Alice ,on and of for the last 15 years if your interested , get in touch ,Thanks K___

***

Dear Alice, I have a personal favor to ask. It's sort of a biggie & I expect that you're too busy to grant it But I'll ask anyway, it would do many things at many levels for me: IF I sent you something I'd done at home on my very meager four track Would you add a vocal track and send it back to me? I'm Not a pro (after my ex lead singer took a dump on my band I lost the taste for it) But was looking good in Milwaukee in the late 80's. I MAY just be a long lost relative of a very good guitar player (well, maybe also a real despised historical figure for that matter too) SO as a long lost bad seed I have a rep (bad) to live up to y'know.... I play the whole thing, drums, bass & lead guitar. Take care – M___

***

Listen alice suprised to here form me bet your drinking coffee yoning sleepily. Dear MR. cooper I,m not to surebut I think we met or it was one hell of a trip. Remmber st.paul mn I have a story for you . I have always been a big fan a would consider it a honor if you would come to my house for dinner sometime. I'm 40 wife four kids . any ways i know you are a bizzy manand will not even get this someone who works for you will throw this awy and laugh.(just anouther loser) thanks for all the menories and there were alot.please call me.

***

Photograph © Linda Weatherburn

Photographs © Jeffrey Morgan

Photograph ©
Jeffrey Morgan

HELLO,PARDON MY GRAMMAR BUT I JUST WANTED TO LET YOU KNOW SOMETHING,I KNOW I'M ONLY 13 BUT I AM PLANNING A 1ST ANNUAL ROCK AWARD SHOW CALLED THE HMR'SMEANING HEAVY METAL ROCK THERE WON'T BE A RED RUG THAT THEY 'LL COME OUT ON , IT WOULD BE BLACK.THEAWARDS WOULD BE SKULLS.

***

Hello alice cooper just thought you are defently a cool singer oh and im 16 years old your one of my favourt old rock star part from one band and thats defleapperd do you like defleapperd cooper well the best songs i like that you song would oh hat to i think its called i might as well be mars i like the words to that song and the song pioson that song i can play on my guitar well i supoes you hear this all the time take it easey cooper oh what you sed to the band meagdeth cooper that was bluddy good advice but even know your one of my favrout singers the best song in the wrould has to be every breath you take soung by the polic well thanks for reading this dude take it easey man

***

ich bin durch zufall auf eine seite im net gestoßen in der irgendwie etwas erwähnt von einer jungen frau mit der du mal was hattest und da sollst du einigen mist gebaut haben. Ich bin total geschockt!!!!!!!! ich liebe deine art und deine show, aber ich bin verwirrt, bitte erzähle du mir was ich glauben soll! es sollen noch weitere infos folgen ich werde weiter im net schaun um zu wissen was es neues über dich gibt. bitte, bitte antwort bald. ich kann es kaum erwarten in liebe deine p__

***

can u send me a copy of classicks! please as it is my birthday and a sighed photo and deatails of your fan club please . from J____ H______ (big fan!!!!!)

***

I'm not a song writer, however some times music comes to me. For the past two weeks one has popped into my mind and it won't go away. I have never E-mailed any one asking them this before, I feel a little strange doing it now! is there any way I can tell you (or your people) my song idea to see if you like it. Let there be no mistke I am not a big fan of your music style (I did like you in waynes world though) I just think that the tempo and tone may fit your image. I don't know if you do political statments in your music. This one that comes to me is based on the sexual indescretions of the catholic priests and how they are destroying what little we have left to belive in. I am not A catholic hater or any thing and I do hope that some how the song can be used for good. Any way i had to ask. Thank You D.S. B___

***

Hi Alice! I have so hard period of my life. I even thinking about killing myself because I'm so confused in my life. The only thing that keeps me alive is Your music, I feel that your life is a best example of a fortitude! I don't want to bother you, I just want to say you: THANK YOU, ALICE!!! YOU HELPING ME SO MUCH! Please keep recording your songs because we need it!!! And please come to Russia again, we are love you so much! I wish you to be happy! You should know that you aregiving the happiness to other people!

***

Yet again I'd like to say congratulations on everything you've achieved. I was fortunate enough to meet you in Grande Prairie (Alberta) two years ago... I was the wacky lady who brought you all the presents :) I was very happy that you came to Grande Prairie (and that I was able to

Photograph © Linda Weatherburn

meet you) and I was VERY pleased to be able to give you tokens of my appreciation. I'd love to know... what DID you think of my poem that I wrote you? It wasn't so much about you as it was for you, it was about inspiration and I meant it as a thank you for giving of yourself all these years. I don't know if I explained it on the bus plus I noticed that you were squinting so you probably had tired eyes and didn't read it very well there. Ok, so, maybe in your life you wouldn't remember a fan from 2 years ago, but I'm hoping that you do. I'd really like to know if my poem touched you as much as your musical personality has touched me for my lifetime. By musical personality I mean I appreciate the fun that you bring to your music and your variety and even your vocal expression. You are a wonderful entertainer and I love the versatility of your voice. Thank you, S____

***

we didn't ask if he wrote the song we know he didn't write it we wanted to know who sang the song the nerve of you poeple i asked who sang the song now i've tried looking on the internet and if it's so easy to find on the internet then why don't you find who wrote it and let me know

***

I was wondering what are all of alice's favorite colors? if you can tell me? and I will e-mail you every day or so, after you e-mailed me back about his favorite colors to find out more about him. that you know of, ok? bye. this is h______ again.

***

Hey, I'd love for Alice to re-do No More Mr. Nice Guy with different lyrics. He should wear an Uncle Sam outfit and portray the United States as being "no more Mr. Nice guy" when it comes to DESTROYING those who caused such tragic havoc in NYC and the Pentagon on 9-11-01. In the song he should include a line; "smoke em' out of their holes". Thanks much, and hope this comes about!! Send a copy to every member of the Armed Forces, and get airplay on every rock station in this nation!! B__

***

well ty for almost ruinin a good

Photograph © Linda Weatherburn

memory but in my mind,there were too many coincidencess that make me beleive i met him.i can not see someone for years and recognize them.i went up to him and asked him if was alice cooper-he laughed and said whos he play for?then he said no i kno who u mean-he told me his name was al-from cooperstown fla-yhe game was sold out but he asked me to go to the next nights game-he was alone and had a good seat behind home plate-so bein a celebrity it would seem logical to come up with an extra ticket-the voice the look was uncanny so i guess it still will be a good memory and i still will always wonder if it was him-he did go to baseball games-i wont bother u anymore-wanna thank u for such a nice website-by the way the person called me the next day n asked me if i was going to the game and my mother said i was only 18 and i didnt kno that was him so she wouldnt let me go-i guess if i would have i would have known-let me kno what u think—

***

Hey Alice, I was just kidding about you being a god and all before. Actually, I really think you SUCK! Yeah, that's right, and there ain't nothing you can do about it because you don't receive these messages anyway, because if you did then you would respond to me since I've bought 5 of your lousy records in the past, so bug off ya mascara running, overly dressed, snake loving jerk.

***

Hello is anyone home? THis friend of my has sent you 20 e-mails and more and you haven't answered them. he's trying to get a backstage pass so he can meet alice when alice comes to berlin or poland, this guy lives on the border of germany, which you know where that's at, right?

***

hey alice i saw u on vh1 alittle while ago on the shocking moments or something like that i did email you before i was the one who talked about doin a alice wedding well i think you miss understood me i meant i might but my girlfreind shot that idea to hell cos she hates you oh by the way i am a huge collector of your memrobilia i got the ash tray the incense burner those are my two newest idems but anyway i g2g oh i will see ur concert in biloxi in august looking forwerd to it catch ya later and you rock ur fan,c____

***

Hi im a up and comming songwriter and i got the idea for a album i have wriiten about 300 sons so far but do not now where to start maybe someone could help me here is a lyric sampIe work and live in a boring shed,so i get heavy daft lyrics pop in my head ive got loads of fresh up lifting lyrics but am unsure where to go or what to do with them if you know of any artist who might be interested in my material please could you let me know i have 18 masterpieces all nicely completed and have shed full of stuff i need to chuck together,but everyone i know says i should try and show some one because it is quite different

***

please give this to Coop. He is so worried about me. I've sent info to him through other people and now I wonder if he ever got it. Please tell him that I live in Apartment #13 (of course), O______ L___, here in Jackson. He knows the rest and he knows my phone number by heart. I know Coop wants to do this himself. But, I feel his feelings. I feel his heart pains and they hurt!!! He's afraid of having a heart attack and I can't stand by and not help him. God has blessed us with good friends who care for a reason. I am sure you have felt his blessing over the years. Please, tell Coop that I love him and I understand the anxiety. God doesn't want us to do this alone. I don't mind if he has someone else call me FOR him. Or he can e-mail me or leave a message on my answering machine. We both need physical feedback to get this going. PLEASE HELP US!!! The e-mail is a Godsend!!! Please give it to Coop!!! You are witnessing a miracle!!! Thank you!!! D___

***

Alice, Here's another album idea... ALBUM IDEA: "THE DEVIL & THE WITCH" (or, alternatively, "THE WITCH") COVER: Some kind of 17th Century scene depicted in colorized woodcut fashion, showing the witch 'Alice Cooper' being burned at the stake (something which can be duplicated on stage via technological illusion). A ouija board somewhere on the cover. The devil in the flames (with Cooper-esque black makeup on) A demonic clown-puppet, skull-like head, somewhere on the cover (also with COoper make-up on) CONCEPT: Showing the origins of Alice Cooper, and the result (in the future) when the rebellious spirit of the witch (Alice) is summoned using a ouija board, we learn via (Steven's?) channelling and communication with her/him/it that Alice was burned after having signed a pact with the devil and tricked somehow. Alice now has unspeakably strong powers—neutral tools that the two sides of Alice fight over in a schizo tug-o-war between good and evil. There is a good side, child-like and full of wonder and hope...and the curiosity which led the witch astray in the first place; and there is the more sinister, malevolent dark side of the character, vicious with greed and sadistic tendencies. MUSIC/LYRICS: Creepy-ballads like "Ballad of Dwight Fry", "See Me In The Mirror", "Dead Babies"... Basically, vintage horror Alice Cooper. Things like "The Awakening" and others off Welcome To My Nightmare. (Keywords to conjure up the idea of mood: The Crow/Raven, The Crone, Nighshade, Old Hickory and Oak, moss and the Autumn night, Harvest Moon, bats, cats, and dead things; spiders and brews, potions and the summoning of spirits...) The basic mood/tone of the album and songs would be very creepy, laced with a bit of history (insofar as it serves the Alice-as-Salem-witch-done-in motif), and can even play as Alice-as-spirit instead of exact gender (i.e., "in the sweet little girl you thought wouldn't bite, in the too tall man that ain't quite right"). More than a concept-theme, and more of an outright story, half the songs could be in the past, the other half in the future (or flipping back and forth). Also, could approach certain songs like: "Bad Moon Rising" "Marie LaVeau" (by Redbone) "Devil Woman" (Donovan) After "Dragontown", most critics/fans

Photograph © Murray Fletcher

outside loyal Alice fans probably wouldn't accept anything so soon without panning it as 'not as hard as...' etc... but if done in a creepy way, that would be quickly forgiven because one thing most people like is the creepy side of Alice—the very horror-oriented side that made him popular. No one else really provides such Halloween-friendly songs these days ;) There's a certain niche there with universal appeal. This album could touch on the 'dark Disney' style, and even set things up for a more metaphysical or new age album after it. Where else is Alice to go, unless more political, or back to his/her witchly mandrake *roots*? But don't promote it as a 'back to basics' kind of thing; instead, just say 'it's downright ghastly' ;) I think 99% of the way albums are received by critics or the press is a recognition of cliche' signals being sent out versus something that doesn't reek of what has come before. It's all perception. It's like Megadeth saying their album RISK was light, and THE WORLD NEEDS A HERO (which followed RISK) was any heavier. It wasn't, really. It was really of similar quality, and good. Not enough "Former Lee Warmer" songs in the Alice catalog, though. The realllllllly creepy, but beautiful ones. (easier to sing in one's older age, I bet, too) ;) – S____

***

Why don't you help me????????

***

Dear Alice Cooper Can you tall my when the date next year of Alice Cooper auble is please because i am a great fan of his and i like his music can you give me his fan mail address please Thank You and some information as well. Your fan A______ S___.

***

What are you trying to prove??? You schedule is insane. I have held you in my heart for too any years and have felt the pain and the passion. I have such a bad feeling I cant explain.PLEASE take a break soon..you don't have to this. If anything happens to you ....I can't even think. You know you're the best let it coast.

***

Photograph © Murray Fletcher

dear alicecooper do you know the sclub7 you do can you tell tham to email me today send me all email to me 24huors all time

***

Greetings to One and A/all I apologize if I am sending this off to the wrong place .. But as a fan of Alice I am unsure where to send anything via email that He or One close to Him might read it My name is R_____ K____ and I live in Toronto Canada .. I have seen Alice a few times over the years .. Yes I am a true fan .. For more years than He or I would dare care to remember I have no doubt. I have read many stories and have a few of My own I have heard of through family of passing meetings with Alice. I also know that Alice recieves a great many requests for visits from fans and for Tv and radio spots .. He is after all ALICE . I know that chances are small He will ever hear of this email .. but as the fan I am I only wish to inquire ... On the 10th of October this year Alice is to be at Massy Hall in Toronto .. So too am I and My wife .. His night here will come about 5 weeks after the birth of My first child .. " Alice R_____ K____ " .. Yes .. again Alice has another baby named after Him ... My small way of saying thank you for all He has shared with Me and so many others .. His music ... His life .. My request is this .. would it be at all possible .. or even likely that Alice would find it a kick to perform a quick mock baptism on My baby girl ? (We have been told it is a girl so I am hopeing) As you who reads this is well aware by now I am either very devoted to Alice and His music .. or just plain insane .. either way I figure if He hears of this perhaps I can bring a twisted smile to His face once, for all the smiles He has given Me. Please if I have sent this to the wrong person(s). Either forward to the correct one, or reply to Me with the correct address for My thanks and request. Thank you. Forever commited, R_____ A. K____

***

How did you quit drinking and continue with the evil show.

***

Hi Dear I saw David Bowie in concert, honey. You work to much I hope you feel okay? I do not want to make you any troubles. Love P______

***

Hello Mr Cooper just to let you know Dragontown"s Great loved it keep up the great work. Can't wait for your next one. I have A very Strange photo you mite like its a vampire skull. Its a very cool shot. You Have to see my work. I work at a photo stuido every one Hate's my work they say i'm sick. But I don't care what they think if they can think. Email me and let me know if you would like to see my work.

***

What happened Friday? Were you waiting for me to approach you? I was waiting for a sign from you or security to let me know that it was OK for me see him. He was so nervous with me there in the house. But it made him so happy!!! I'm real. He needed to see me physically. That's why God told me to go. It helped us both to be that close to each other. The show was fabulous. Coop really looked good. I was watching him for some encouragement so I would know he was ready. I wanted to jump up there and hug him so bad. I didn't want his heart to hurt him. I was ready to stay. I know profoundly that's what God wants me to do. It hurt so bad to leave Coop. Security wouldn't let me go back I love him soooooo much!!! I have complete faith in him. This takes absolute positivity. God absolutely adores him and focusing on that releases the fear. I don't want to wait another year. I was laid off yesterday so I'll be home Friday and Saturday if you guys have time to come to Jackson before Cincinnati. This is a GOD Thing. Our Lord loves us all.

***

Salve, Ho 30 e sono un fan di Alice praticamente da sempre,probabilmente tra i pochissimi fans italiani;posso ritenermi fortunato essendo stato tra I pochi a poter vedere il mio idolo dal vivo,data la sua scarsa frequentazione del mio paese. Incontro notevoli difficoltý nel reperire materiale su lp,potreste darmi dei suggerimenti? grazie. p.s. Per Alice, un saluto dal nostro comune conoscente L____ C____

Photograph © Murray Fletcher

***

Dear very admirated, radical Alice Cooper, we all love you. Your radical performances are super! Specially your performances with dead chickens are cool. I have got long hair too - like you! I love Tarantulas. My name is W_____. Do you like fast-food? I´am, for example, like it. It´s a pitty, that I can´t come to your concert that you will give in munich this year. My mother didn´t allow me this (silly cow). Therefor my sister will go to your show and will take a dead chicken with her to put it into the Freezer to store it for me. I will eat it bloody and with pleasure! Perhaps we can be friends or we can give a performance together. If you have some time, you could, if you want to, write back to me. Yours faithfully W_____

***

Mr. Cooper, I am hoping to make a career as a Pro-wrestler. The reson I am writing is there is a song that somes up the attitude of the character I wish create. And it is one of your's, the song is "hey stupid" and it is the entrance to the song that I am intrested in. However I have no idea how to get permission to use it so I am writing you. If there is any way to accomplish this I would honered to use your song. Please let me know if this is even possible.Thank You, Your humble fan. A____ H______(Lobo)

***

I just wanted to drop a short note to suggest that the new Alice Cooper album be released as an 'Aquarius album', between January 21st and February 21st, which would complete a Grand Trine for the Brutal Planet trilogy: Brutal Planet was released while the Sun was in Gemini (indeed, a *stellium* of Gemini, as is well-known to astrologers—and apparently someone who knew enough to put the symbols of it under Cooper's eye on the album cover...the Sun, Jupiter, etc.) Dragontown was released while the Sun was in Libra, another air sign, trine (120-degrees) to the first album, and compounding its beneficial influence. Both Brutal Planet and Dragontown, by Sun sign, Trine Alice Cooper's Sun in Aquarius. If the third album in the trilogy were to be Aquarius, it would complete a Grand Trine. PLEASE release the third album in the trilogy as an Aquarius album... like, on Alice's birthday or something. Aquarius begins about January 20th, 21st or so...and runs through February 20th. :) –S____ astrologer and Alice fan

***

does it suck not to care about your fans? How bout Dio? Maybe he cares? Later loser hahahahaha

***

Coop, I tried e-mailing you several times over the last few weeks and it would just close out before I could send it. This time I'm praying it works. I Love You!!! I'm so glad you're home. I want to hug you so bad! And kiss you!!! Babe, I feel you so strong and so deep inside of me and I'm going to try hard not to get sappy in this e-mail. When you made 'Eyes' it was so different this time. I love the album and I know that's us in 'Be With You Awhile' and 'This House is Haunted'. I sat on my bed to listen to it the first time as soon as it came out and I cried when I heard you singing those two songs. That's Us! Pure, unconditional, eternal love. God's Blessing for you is growing and there is nothing to hold you back. I'm glad your mom is alright. Did you say you rented a farm? Is that where you and the boys were over the weekend? Sweetheart, please give me a sign. Tell me what to do. If you want me to come there I will. Shaking and nervous (yes, me too!!!) I will come there if I know that's what you want me to do. If you'ld rather come here... come ANY time of day or night. If I'm at work A_____ or A___ should be here. If I'm asleep please wake me up! I'm not sure if I get Saturday or Sunday off or not. They usually don't tell us until the night before. PLease, Coop. You won't have a heart attack, Honey. You're completely protected. All it is is anxiety from fear of fear itself. And God never created it. I understand. I have it too. God convicted me of procrastinating in this and it's just as much my responsibility to come to you as it is for you to go to me. I love you. I feel you heartbeart. I feel your feelings. I feel you white light shining through my eyes. Literally. I just wanna' be with you. Tell me what to do, Babe.

***

Photograph
© Phillip Solomonson
philamonjaro.com

I need help

***

dear alice i was at the rocking the rivers consert it whas the beast sow i have aver seing u sud cum back up to montana agin some time. the sowe u but on is the beas and love the whay u git in to the music it is the beast love to see u agin in consert

***

Al, 2nd Dec, Star by the walk of fame. I'm sitting here and don't know, for what. I miss all the things, and with my jewish co partner, we share this flat, it's not nice anymore. Okay that's all.

***

Coop!!! Congratulations!!!!!!! I felt your heart skip with delight around 2:40pm our time and I knew you were happy. I'm so glad you have your star. I was at work when I realized you have a replica of it. You're wonderful! So Blessed!!! I wish I could've been there; but I know why it would've been awkward. Thanksgiving was nice. And you were here so close. Next Thanksgiving will be perfect... with you. Honey, did you pray about me coming to the house? Please? Before Christmas?? Hang a lot of mistletoe, Babe!!!

***

Photographs © Jeffrey Morgan

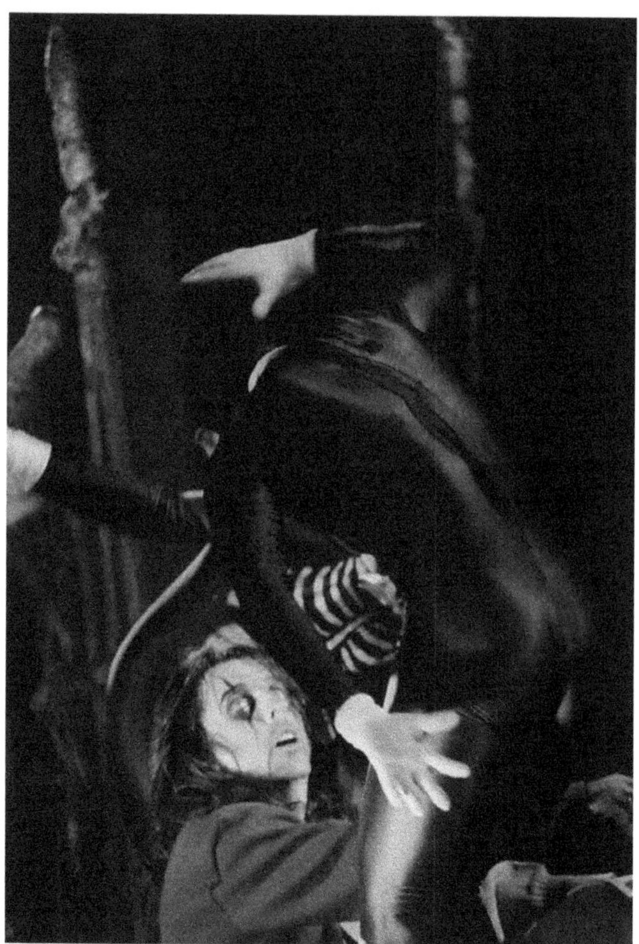

Photograph ©
Jeffrey Morgan

Hi Dear where i cant get a Alice Cooper Autographe? i m a verry big Alice Cooper Fan and my biggest wish is to became an autographe of him, can u help me? lovley greets M____

***

Dear Alice, I have a friend in work who has illegal feelings for u. It would bring us much relieve if u could come to Belfast and do a Gig (but short notice please so we don't have to hear about it). She is your number 1 obsessed fan!! She is blonde, athletic and younger than u!!!!

***

Photograph © Phillip Solomonson philamonjaro.com

Would i be able to get the lyrics to the song Poison? A girl i know wants me to sing her a love song in a few weeks and i want to serenade her with that.

***

Hi this is a question for Alice. I am born on the same day as you and have never met anyone else who shares this day and was wondering what it would take to ask you out on a date on that day. Do you have any plans? Just thought I'd ask. Sarah Brightman plays on day after if you are available then. It's great music not heavy as we both like but it's still great. Let me know if you're interested. Love and laughter, C_______

***

Hey Alice, My name is M_______ and I'm a 22 year old female from Glendale, Arizona. I'm a big fan of your music - you're a talent beoyond words. I am writing this to ask you something, and it's not an easy thing to do. Basically, I've run into some problems and I'm very low on money. My 10 year old car was broken into and trashed. I barely came up with enough money to fix it, when they found other problems with the car that I cannot afford to fix. I lost my job when my car was in the shop for a week. This is hard to ask, and kind of embarrassing, but I'll ask anyway. I've always wanted a new car ever since I was a young kid, I dreamed of being old enough to drive and buy a new car. I'm old enough to drive now, but I just don't have the finances or anyone really to help. I tried to save money, but when my car was broken into, I spent all the money I had saved to fix it. If there was anyway anyone could help, I'd be the happiest person in the entire world. I hope this email doesn't make you mad as that is not my intent. I still love you and will still be your fan whether you can help me or whether I never hear from you in my life. Peace and health, and my God bless you always. M_______

***

perhaps spelling should be the first priority?

Hi Been a fsn for years, worked some dsted in Hawaii in the eighties. I currently work for ProMix as an audi-designer/engineer for TV shums and events.. We are based country-wide and I would like a shot at biddind the tech side of yoyr show, From rehearsal, sound, lighting, crew management, payroll services. Our parent company is well set to cover a large scale theatrical presentation, our touring division is second to none,, and my TV crew gets iall done under-budget. Please give a call Thank tou.

***

hey how u doin just wanted to say whasup i think youre pretty cool im tryin to get into actin got any pointers?

***

Hi,Alice; I don't know if you remember

me. But,we met you 2 Summers ago when you were at Cooperstown,(Yours) and I believe you were doing an interview,and my Brother and I,unwittingly walked behind you. We then chatted,took a couple pix,and you graciously signed some autographs. I was the “fat Ferrari Guy”,who also frequents Charlie Robinsons, We talked about that a little,too. Anyway,we saw you that October,here in Chicago at the House of Blues,while you were on the Dragontown Tour. I added that masterpiece to my coolection,as well as your new work. It's great! As I told you when I met you. “Killer” was the 2nd. Album that I ever bought,back in ‘72 or ‘73.? Led Zep.4 was my first.(sorry) But,after hearing Killer,immediately went out and got “Pretties for You”,and “Easy Action”. Then,”Billion Dollar Babies” and “Schools Out” came out. We were in Rock Heaven! Then,”Muscle of Love” in the Cardboard Box. We had a “Garage Band” back then,(mid 70's) and covered “Under My Wheels”,”I'm 18”,(what respectful Garage Band didn't cover “I'm 18”?) “No more Mr.Nice guy”. “Unfinished sweet” ,and a few more that slipped my decrepit mind.I've always been a huge fan,(and if you recall,thats also meant literally,as I'm 6'2”,and pushin'300#) Too much Charlie Robinsons! (And,BTW,YOUR BBQ is right up there with his,and,as you told me,”A couple more meals like that one,(your BBQ platter) and I won't be able to fit in my 308!”) Anyway,I have a really funny story to tell you,and think back and see if it rings a bell. When I was 25,(1985) I was very thin,had very long hair,that I always dyed Blue/Black. Always wore a Black leather Motorcycle jacket,and Black leather pants. usually,a black T-shirt of some kind. I also share with you a somewhat big Schnozze.I was driving a really Hot Rodded Red 1975 Corvette back then. Twin Turbo hood,and side pipes. I was still in a local band,but only played bars like the (now closed) Thirsty Whale,(Did you ever go there? I swear that I saw you there once) Anyway. I stopped by Charlie Robinson's one afternoon. Pulled up right in front with the Red ‘Vette. went in. And,the older Lady who used to work there when Charlie first started out,(he was still in only 1 or 2 of the storefronts at that time) She was short, a little chubby,older,had Freckles,and Glasses,African American. Anyway,I go up to order,and she's asking me,”Aren't you that Rock and Roll guy?” And,I'm like thinking,”how does she know that I'm in a band”,so I say,”Yeah,thats me!” And,she's all blushing and stuff,and said she'd tell Charlie that I stopped by.

Photograph
© Phillip Solomonson
philamonjaro.com

And,I'm like,”O.O.O.K.?”(how did she know) And,after Charlie put up that picture of you and him,I started thinking,”Oh No! I bet she thought that I was Alice Cooper!” This was back in 1985,so,pretty long time ago. But,do you recall Charlie ever asking you if you stopped in back then? If so,sorry ‘bout that,She musta thought that I was you! No way to get that mixed up now,as,I am fat with short hair. But,I always thought that that was kind of Funny. Hey,all of my Family lives out in Phoenix,and I try to get out there once or twice a year,)wish I could go to Barrett Jackson) If ever possible,would really like a chance to meet you again to chat. Just for a little while,not to bug you or anything. Take care,Alice,and keep on Rockin! Us Fossils(me,anyway) still love to turn it up loud,but,the thing is,is that after all these years,my hearing isn't what it used to be,so,instead of my parents telling me to “turn that damn thing down”,now,it's my KIDS!!! AHHHH! Will I ever get peace!!! RThanks!!! LONG TIME-OVER 30 YEAR FAN...

***

Alice..Dear Alice.. Nightmares to Widows. Scaring all the kiddo's. Charcoal shadow covering evil eyes. You never did die. Only wearing a slimy snake. Making people do a double take. Wearing torn white jumpsuits. And leopard skinned boots. Tearing up a chickens getting you big. Having people pay to walk out of gigs. Making kids wait till summer. To hear the rythm of your drummer. Doing your own thing. Made girls want to cling. Although your growing old. Your still to people, Gold. You have your own twisted palace. Thats why you are the only Alice.

***

Two of Alice's best songs, including "No More Love At Your Convenience" and ... I think it was "Wish You Were Here"... used bongos... when will Alice use bongos in his songs again?

soon. very soon.

***

koo koo

Dear Alice, Well, it's me (again)...M___(aka N_____). Sorry if you or your fan club advisory might have tried the old e-mail which I gave previously but now I have the correct info for my e-mail I hope you have enjoyed the mail that I have sent to you (and website). I feel like some kind of fool seeing that you're making ground for the millenium and the future and here is some kind of "schmuck", sending you stoopid/odd e-mails because he's got ideas....well, I guess alot of people do have good ideas but some are very approachable such as the golf tourny, "Snakes & Ballads", and other crazy ideas (don't worry I'm not crazy BUT, "we're all crazy") ha, ha, ha....... Anyways, just (kind of) hoping that maybe you or Shep or someone with recognition might send an answer back about the ideas which I mailed to your website and with a proper e-mail address too. Keep up the good work and keep shocking the world..before I forget, from before I mentioned to maybe base your radio show out of your Main Restaurant (something like Toronto:Q107 and Hard Rock Cafe). It's simple and "catchy". Maybe very expensive? Broadcast the show up in T.O. Howard Stern had his show with "Q", so can you! I did enjoy your interview on the "Q" too, Alice:Yesterday, Today & Tomorrow. Is it true that maybe someone else will take up on the Alice character? It'll be like American Idol but better judges and better taste in music.... 'till next time.

***

i love it when Goths say "y'all"

Dear oh great and powerful cooper My name is R____, for i am the symbol of all thats dead and dark. I just went and got rob zombies "past, present and future," cd and I read the comment you put on the inside of the last cover page. The comment of there not being to many of us left has ripped my heart open. For I had paronormaly evil tears gushing out my eyes. What I got on here to say was that I believe you are the truest and most expresive artist of the gothic world. Also I swear to all of you that Ill do my damndist to represent you and all the rest of the amazing artist and get people to enjoy y'alls music so much that theyll have no choice but to go get your cds. In probaly 3 months im going to throw the biggest party in the world that displays you. I personaly couldnt give two shits and a fuck about being incarserated for expression y'all. It would be all worth (how do you spell die with an ing?)and the pain Ill get after all of its over with. I hope you see me on the news. My real name is j____ o_____ and if you feel that reporting me would be the right thing to do Id so humbly request that you email me telling me not to do it. For if the king of darkness request not to do this Ill stop it all at once for the respect that I have for you. Its a respect so deep that it can easily be mistaking for love. But in all actuality its my love for the darkness that you helped ,and created, represent. I only hope this touches your heart somehow and that the spirits that gard us lays a burden on your heart for me. Please let me here from you somehow if the spirits lay it on you realy desire to talk to me. MAY DARKNESS AND INTELLIGENCE DRAW US ALL TOGETHER IN MIND, BODY, AND SOUL "FOREVER MORE." R____

***

Photograph
© Phillip Solomonson
philamonjaro.com

i want to know , in wich album is the song baby ah the superstar os oh oh

***

Coop, it's been awhile and I'm sorry. My computer's messed up and I'm using a library computer so I'm gonna' keep this one short. There's not enough privacy here and I don't trust the internet. God Loves You!!! And cherishes you. You're well protected from a heart attack. But I understand the fear. My job has changed. I'll explain later. I want you to know that I'm usually gone between 7:45am and 3:45pm weekdays now. Call me anytime. Beat on my door ANYTIME. Wake me up!!! You're why I'm on this earth!!!!!!! Honey, Happy Birthday!!! 'Wish I was with you now!!! 'Gotta' go... I do love you. Please don't be afraid... This is your blessing, Babe!!!

***

Just wanted to know where Alice Cooper stands politically? Is he Conservative? Liberal? Non-Political? Thanks.

he likes going to the movies and eating popcorn.

***

Hello Alice cooper i'm contacting you because its time to change the world my dad knows how to make perpetual energy a generator that needs no gas or oil but we play in a rock band together and he has been waiting for our band to be signed to build the advanced version we have a great rock band but now days in bakersfield its really hard to get noticed his name is k__ w___ like the sterio thats also the name of our band my name is j______ having free energy will save america no more smog and cars that never break down and prepare for better space travel

***

um. how about the same place you just sent this email to?

Why is their no fan mail for Alice cooper on his official website....My uncle is turning 50.. he's been a very big fan of alice cooper since the beginning. He owns all the vinyls released cds, dvds, vhs, everything!. he would like to send a message but we dont know hwo to locate him or anyone affiliated!

***

he's graduating and he's this stupid???????

Dear Mr. Cooper, My name is R___ M_____ and I am currently a senior at Cranford High School in Cranford NJ. As graduation draws near, many of our students were hoping that you would be able to perform "School's Out for Summer" at our high school graduation party. In fact, our Dean of Students, G___ S_________, thought that your presence would be a great idea. I'm not sure if you remember but Mr. S_________ was once in charge of your concert security, sometime in the late 70's. He has told us a few stories and has only fueled our interest in having you perform. I know that this request is a bit out there but it would a memory never forgotten if you were to perform for us. Thanks again and we hope to hear from you soon. Sincerely, R___ M_____

***

i have song and i don't know the name of it the one how give me this song say that song to alice cooper and i want to know the name of this song and the album tittle ..... if the song not to alice cooper can you help me to know the name of this song please

***

Coop, I'm off the whole weekend!!! Woohoo!!! And... A_____ had a very clear ultrasound Wednesday. It's definitely a boy. Healthy and active baby boy. Her due date is still April 12. With helping mom for the next few months does that mean you won't be touring til May or June? Oh! & when I said that I was glad that your mom is alright I meant that I'm glad she is and that she has you to make sure she is well taken care of. Did you say she her ankles swell so much she can barely walk? I pray for her. She loves you very, very much. I know you love her tremendously. I'm gonna' take a nap. Honey, come anytime. Wake me up. Beat on my door. Throw rocks at my window! I'll come there if you let me know someway. Even if it's a little note on the door with only the time of day written on. I'll keep it secret & maybe ask my brother J_____ to come with me to pray and keep me calm so I won't chicken out. Aside from A______ and A___, he's the only other person I've told. He believes me and he trusts God and knows that miracles happen all the time. He won't tell anyone except maybe K____, his wife. I trust her as much as I trust him. Honey, I won't do anything to jeopardise your privacy in any way. I love you. Words cannot describe how deeply I feel you. I trust you with my soul. AND my sanity! I trust you completely, Babe. I thank God all the time for creating us this way. Our kids will witness our interaction with each other and know that this is through Christ. There is no way we can fake this. Thank you, Lord!!! I'm sleepy. I wish I could kiss you goodnight.

***

Hi Webbies, I looked over a paragraph in your bio introduction that mentioned Alice running for US presidency against Nixon. As hard as I've tried, I can't find any data on this anywhere. was it simply a joke, or is it true? Love your site, by the way :) N____

***

Mr Cooper , I have been a Fan for A long time . I remember my father nutting up on me when I brought the Muscle of Love Album Home. I have seen your Live Shows ..But loved that Night in Cape Cod when I saw you with Joan Jett on the Special Forces tour . Awesome Show . I am getting ready to shoot my Feature Film Dust to Dust in early 2005. I have a part as a Ghostly Card Dealer that you are perfect for . I will meet your payrate and take care of anything else to get you in this Film .I have a couple of Horror Icons already Casted. I know your Time is VERY limited, But please consider this as it would make My life Complete (no pun intended). I know the odds are against this ,But it doesn't hurt to ask .GOD

BLESS ... A fan 4 life

***

My name's A______ C_____ and I've emailed the site a few times tryin to get hold of Alice. If he's interested, my fiance and I have an invitation to my wedding for Alice and his wonderful wife. I'll email the invitation soon. Thanx.

***

Forgive me for asking, but I have to. I met a man named L_______ A_____. He claims he was Alice Cooper from 73-79 and then Vincent took over. I don't know much about Alice and just wanted to check. Is he legit or a storyteller? Sorry to ask

***

I'm dreaming, that a young man kissed me. It was only a dream, but it was good. That my mind tells me what I miss. I hope you can do something for me. In July I had taken a lot of pills and I really want to die. If you don't do anything Alice I would never dance more in my shit live

***

Hi Alice! How are you. My name Is M_____ G_____ from Germany.I sit alone here and think on you. Every day and all the night. I wish I can be with you. My love Alice I cry for you then I love you so. My heart so pain . One life without love is one life without sense. I'm sorry for my English. In love seewiesenstr Bietigheim-Bissingen That's near from Stuttgart I wish you give me answer Please help me please please help me

***

I NEED TO BUY SOME MEN'S COLOGNE (for me, when I'm Alice...I don't want to smell lik a woman) Would you happen to know if Alice wears any cologne or after shave, and if so, what brand? If not, can you recommend something?

***

Hi Alice. What did happen you? Why don't you answer more to ours e mails. Just because we are here from Brazil we are not seriously mischievous. We continued adoring you and awaiting your coming here to Brazil Don't become blunt!!!

***

This anxiety is the only thing holding us back. Please, don't go to Columbus. Please come here to my apartment tonight, anytime you want - or I'll will take a drive at the crack of dawn.. meet me in the parking lot where you know I've looked your way and prayed. You'll see my car. You'll know I'm there. If your're too nervous send someone, anyone! I love you. We can't let this slip away. I feel like I'm dying inside each day we don't do this. And I must have gone to the wrong place again. If my car is not at my apartment duriing the day it's because A_____ (she lives in apt.#6 and you'll welcome there anytime, too, if you'ld feel more comfortable talking to her first) or I might have to run a quick errand and be right back. I did not want to tell you this but I have to - Since God had me quit my job I've run out of savings so we've got to do this before I'm evicted, literally. And that may be within the week. God tells me that this is the reason. I trust God. Please, Honey, get me before that happens. It's just anxiety. God won't let anything bad happen to you. You're completely protected. Babe, I beg you... ask someone to help you do this. It doesn't matter how we do it as long as we do God's will. Send someone over here for you or have them meet me out there. I have anxiety too. I know it hurts sometimes and then it goes away. Your chest hurts you much more in Phoenix than it ever did here. This isn't supposed to be easy. Have someone call me, come here, meet me there in the parking lot. I don't care. Anyway at all to do this is the right way. I love you, Babe. Don't leave me. Please talk to God about this.

***

i wold like to write a book about ALICE which pictures i can use and if want to sell it how i can conect you in a future sincerely m______

***

Well this is a dreaqm come true actually e-maing you.

***

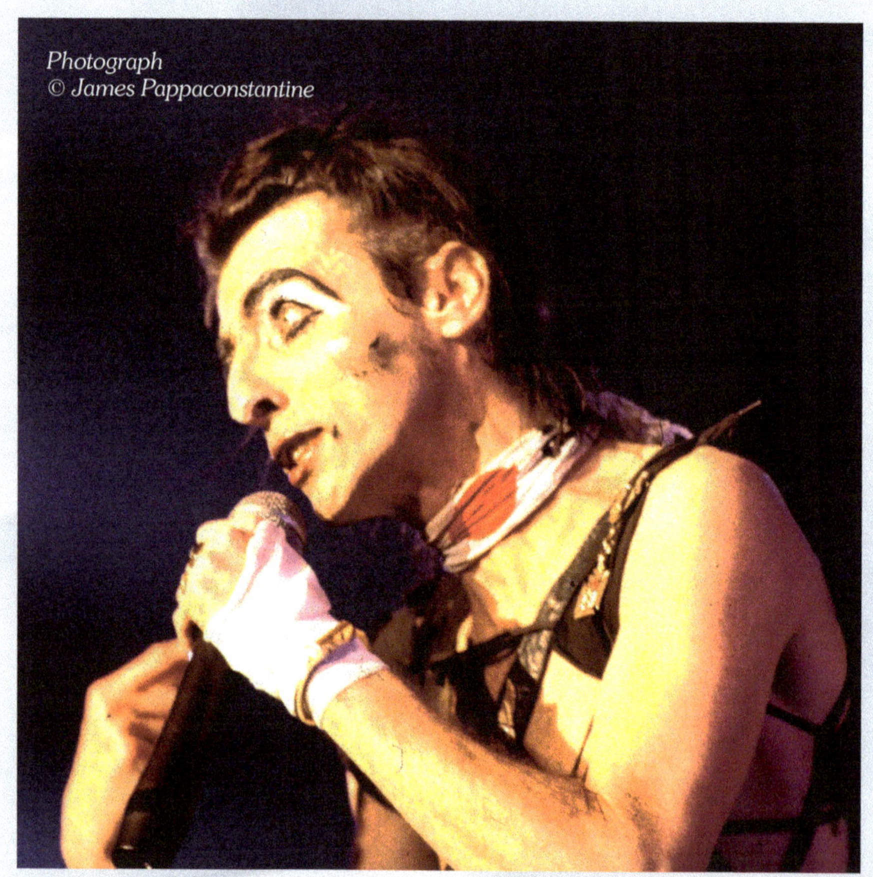

Photograph
© James Pappaconstantine

SECTION THREE

THE CHICKEN COOP

THE CHICKEN COOP

I know, I know. But if you think some of *those* messages were sad, that's nothing compared to this *next* awful offering. Because this truly is an even sadder story. But it's a story that must be told, if only as a cautionary tale to warn what can happen when fandom turns feral.

The following unhinged account is taken from the confidential case files of the School For The Hopelessly Insane. This is what patient "9 26445-2" wrote, in his own words, with all primitive punctuation left intact, given that red crayon on wax paper is difficult to decipher. As you read it, please keep in mind that this delusional detainee actually believes that he is currently enrolled in a rehabilitative "Twelve-track program with six tracks per side!" and is in the process of successfully recovering from his obsessive addiction. He still has a long way to go.

***

Hi everybody, I'm Mac and I'm a Cooperholic.

I was first introduced to "the glorious, wretched excess" of Alice Cooper by a friend in my first year at Wallsend High School in 1972. From that moment on, school was most definitely out for me. Over the following twelve months I acquired the complete Cooper catalogue to that point, from 1969's 'Pretties For You' (released in Australia with 'Easy Action' as the budget-priced double LP set 'School Days - The Early Recordings') through to 'Muscle Of Love.'

I had found 'my thing.' The Coopers' miscreant anti-hero stance resonated deeply with me. Rumors circulated in the press that the group was bringing their "Billion Dollar Babies' extravaganza to Australia in early 1974, but sadly nothing eventuated. Then, suddenly, Alice Cooper the group, disintegrated.

What the...?

When Alice finally toured Down Under with his 'Welcome To My Nightmare' solo spectacular in March 1977 I was there, having organized a bus trip through school. I was there again the next time Alice visited with April 1990's 'Trash' tour. Having threatened to behead their drive time DJ, I miraculously won a local radio station competition to meet Alice backstage in Sydney. I gave him some cheesy Australiana souvenirs including a decapitated Koala key chain, a collector spoon with a swinging dunny door (dunny' being an Australian slang term for a roughly hewn make-shift, outside toilet) and a Ned Kelly tea towel for his mum. Alice laughed, "I don't have any of this stuff, it's total trash!"

I also had the great pleasure of meeting Assistant To The Master, Brian 'Renfield' Nelson, with whom I kept in touch, initially via 'snail mail' and eventually as part of the World Wide Web and the Sick Things Mailing List.

While I was visiting the USA, courtesy of Sony Records' 'Hey Stoopid' competition in February 1992, Ren showed me around all the significant Cooper haunts in L.A. and Hollywood. It was beyond cool cruising down Sunset Boulevard on our way to the legendary Rainbow Bar and Grill in his beat-up muscle car with the 'Live At The Forum '73' desk tape blaring.

He bought me pizza and schooled me on the evils of alcohol and illicit drug use and implored me to understand the differences between 'fans' and 'collectors.' My assertion that it seemed to come down to budget was seen to be too simplistic. Brian could be intense.

In 1995, Brian contacted me and other Cooperphiles to seek assistance with naming a career retrospective Alice Cooper boxed set. I fired off myriad ideas including the suggestion to house the collection in a mental asylum jail cell. I was elated to receive "the good news - we're going with your 'Life & Crimes' title and concept" but disappointed that "the box set is currently on hold indefinitely," though it was finally released with suitable fanfare in 1999.

In early 2005, Brian reached out again with news that Warner Archives and Rhino Records were looking at a complete, deluxe reissue of the Warner Bros. Cooper catalogue with bonus material (demos, out-takes, live recordings) to accompany each disc. Did I have any ideas? I suggested that the discs be housed in a large can and the collection be titled 'Alice Cooper's Chicken Soup.'

The chicken reference was an obvious nod to the infamous poultry incident at the 1969 Rock And Roll Revival concert in Toronto. The can idea harkens back to Frank Zappa's desire for the band to change their name to Alice Cookies and release their debut album as multiple single, cookie-sized discs, encased in separate, small cans. I also felt it appropriate to reference Andy Warhol's iconic pop culture imagery as the original Coopers (especially Alice and Dennis) were acknowledged fans.

Graphic artist Rick Caballo and I collaborated on a prototype soup can and associated merchandise (t-shirts, stickers) and had them ready to show Ren and Alice the next time they were in town on tour in July 2005. Alice laughed when he saw the can and did a great, campy Warhol impersonation: "Oh Mac, I just love it! It's gorgeous! And so perfectly trashy!"

Brian, always the pragmatist, enquired about the logistics of getting the discs in and out of the can. We discussed a central spindle and the possibility of the can being hinged and opening like a book. As well as the inclusion of a t-shirt and

ALICE

Cooper's

CHICKEN

SOUP

800g NET

★★★ NUTRITIONAL INFORMATION ★★★

Box Set Produced by:	Brian Nelson
Executive Producers:	David McLees, Greg Geller
Associate Producers:	Shep Gordon, Toby Mamis
Compilation Assistance:	Dave Kapp, Gary Stewart
Project Coordination:	Jo Motta, Gary Peterson
Licensing:	Michael Nieves, David McIntosh
Sound Produced by:	Bill Inglot
Digital Mastering:	Andrew Garver, Bill Inglot
Art Direction:	Rick Caballo, Steve "Mac" McLennan
Design:	Poo Tickets & Smelly Rainbows Inc.
Technical Advisor:	Trevor Dare

100% fully remastered

INGREDIENTS: PRETTIES FOR YOU, EASY ACTION, LOVE IT TO DEATH, KILLER, SCHOOLS OUT, BILLION DOLLAR BABIES, MUSCLE OF LOVE, WELCOME TO MY NIGHTMARE, GOES TO HELL, LACE & WHISKEY, THE ALICE COOPER SHOW, FROM THE INSIDE, FLUSH THE FASHION, SPECIAL FORCES, DADA.
PLUS PREVIOUSLY UNRELEASED DEMOS & OUT-TAKES

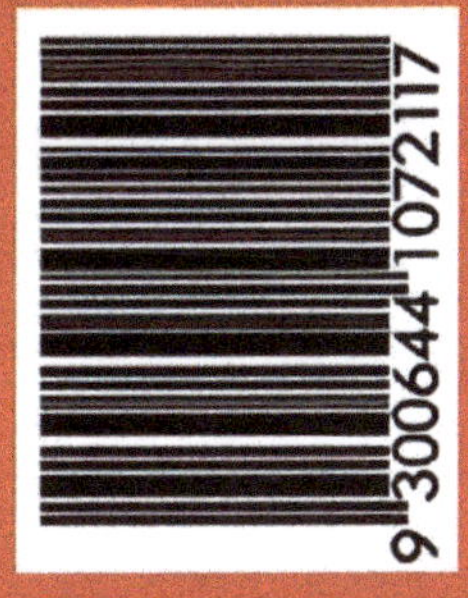

The Producers wish to thank ALICE COOPER

Management: ALIVE ENTERPRISES
Shep Gordon & Toby Mamis

All selections ℗ Warner Bros. Records Inc. except:
"Welcome To My Nightmare" ℗ Atlantic Records.
Produced under license from Atlantic Records Corp.

This compilation ℗ 2006 Warner Bros. Records Inc.
& Rhino Entertainment Company.

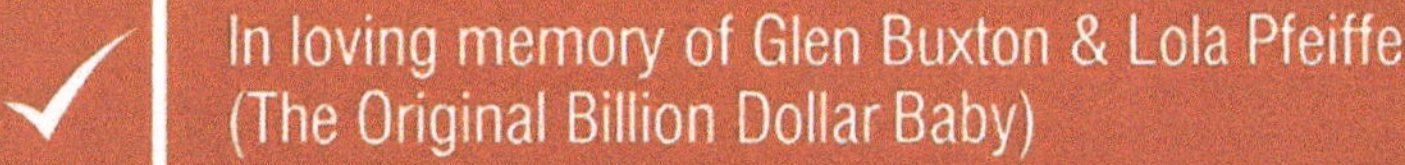
In loving memory of Glen Buxton & Lola Pfeiffer
(The Original Billion Dollar Baby)

Alice Cooper Web info:
www.alicecooper.com
Official Alice Cooper Merchandise:
www.fanfire.com

"Alice welcomes your questions and comments"

Featured contributors:

Alice Cooper, Michael Bruce, Glen Buxton, Dennis Dunaway, Neal $mith, Bob Ezrin, Jack Richardson, Jack Douglas, Mick Mashbir, Bob Dolin, Rockin' Reggie Vincent, Dick Wagner, Steve Hunter, Prakash John, Tony Levin, Jim Gordon, Allan Schwartzberg, Pentti Glan, Rick Derringer, Donovan Leitch, Dave Libert, Jim Mason, Stu Day, Dennis Ferrante, Liza Minnelli, The Pointer Sisters, Ronnie Spector, Sarah Dash, Nona Hendryx, , Paul Prestopino, Jozef Chirowski, Johnny Badanjek, John Tropea, Al MacMillan, Jim Maelen, Bob Babbitt, Jefferson Kewley, Davey Johnstone, Robbie King, Fred Mandel, Steve Lukather, Jim Keltner, Dennis Conway, Rick Schlosser, Sheryl Cooper, Mark Volman, Howard Kaylan, Kasim Sulton, Lisa Dalbello, Karen Hendryx, Rick Kolinka, Graham Shaw, Duane Hitchings, Mike Pinera, Erik Scott, Jan Uvena, Crai Krampf, Danny Johnson, Ian Underwood, John LoPresti, Roy Thomas Baker, David Foster.

sticker in each can, I also suggested chicken feathers and a chicken wish-bone key chain would make for quirky little additions. The conversation was animated, free flowing and very positive so I was deeply disappointed when some months later Brian informed me that "although everyone loved the concept" the can had been deemed "unmanageable" and prohibitively expensive to produce.

When 'The Studio Albums 1969 - 1983' fifteen disc box set was finally released in 2015 it was, in my opinion, an underwhelming missed opportunity. I couldn't help but feel that Renfield would have been as disappointed as I was by the nondescript clamshell box and the card sleeves approximating the original iconic artwork. Anyway, enough of my yakkin'.

I miss Brian. He was truly one of the good guys. I am grateful for his generosity and the authentic connections he fostered with Alice Cooper fans worldwide. He knew what it meant to be a Cooperholic because he was one. Brian really enjoyed sharing his passion and knowledge with like-minded freaks, myself included.

The happy snap of me with The Coop and Soup was taken by Renfield at Newcastle's Civic Theatre on 21 July 2005. I just love it!

Luv, frogs and ZAZZ !!! mac

***

I know, I know. The all too obvious ravings of a madman, right? Am I right? You with me? Still, there is the unsettling matter of the 'can wrap' artwork which is included in the patient's file. Professional to a fault, there's no way that "9 26445-2" could have possibly created it using the 486 DX2-50 dumb terminal that all patients are allowed access to once a week.

Even more disturbing is the photograph of the patient who calls himself 'Mac' with his objet de fixation, Alice Cooper, who is seen actually holding the aforesaid prototype soup can. It was initially assumed that the image was somehow expertly altered to support the patient's fanciful narrative. However, a third party investigation showed, after an intensive three dimensional lighting and shadow analysis, that the image was indeed genuine and untouched.

***

As such, the matter remains open to personal interpretation while the patient remains closed to public interaction.

ALICE COOPER SCHOOL FOR THE HOPELESSLY INSANE
FOUNDED 1978 A.C.
CERTIFICATE OF INSANITY
ISSUED IN APPRECIATION OF THE PROLONGED STRANGE, ERRATIC AND OTHERWISE TWISTED BEHAVIOR OF:
PATIENT MAC
I'M CRAZY, YOU'RE CRAZY,
WE'RE ALL CRAZY –
ALICE COOPER, KEEPER
VOID IN CERTAIN TIME ZONES
NON-TRANSFERABLE

SECTION

FOUR

THE EXEGESIS EXHIBITS

Photograph © Greg York

THE EXEGESIS EXHIBITS

Ladies and gentlemen! Boys and girls! Children of all ages! Welcome! Don't be shy! Step right up! Jeffrey Morgan is the name and writing is the game, which is why I'm grievously humbled to be the official authorized biographer of *the* most spectacular death-defying entertainer of all time, rock 'n' roll's foremost legendary statesman of outrage, that malignantly macabre culprit, the one and only Alice Cooper!

Do I have to tell you that there are few trends in modern music that Alice Cooper didn't anticipate; fewer still that weren't incorporated by this innovative showman into one of the most bizarre and entertaining rock attractions of all time? May it never be! Do I have to tell you that the audacious, precedent-shattering, inspirational, taboo-defiling hoodlum flamboyance of Alice Cooper did more than forever alter the face of rock 'n' roll as we now know it? Perish the thought! Do I have to tell you how he virtually invented rock as theater, created new fashion trends, sparked a new sexual revolution, established higher standards for teenage decadence, and found time on top of all this to write and record a library of classic rock 'n' roll albums? Say it ain't so!

***

But friends, if I may speak personally for a moment, you can believe me when I *do* have to tell you how that amazing colossal biography (the unreasonably exhaustive and titanically titled "Alcohol And Razor Blades, Poison And Needles, The Glorious Wretched Excess Of Alice Cooper, All American") took me seven long arduous years to write before it was finally published by none other than Sam and Jack, the Warner Bros. themselves, in the best-selling, high-fidelity, *fin de siècle* sonic sarcophagus *The Life And Crimes Of Alice Cooper*. Impressive, I know!

Ask anyone who bought it and they'll testify on a stack of first-borns that when *you* buy it, just like them, you'll also receive, free of charge, four bonus long-playing records that are oozing with hours of malevolent music, all masterly played over the past half-century by the cadaverous Coop and his various cool cat combos. Limit one per customer!

However, that's not all because I subsequently had the ominous honor of writing the liner notes to two (count 'em) two *additional* Alice Cooper albums: the no-nonsense nerve-racking companion compilation *Mascara And Monsters: The Best Of Alice Cooper*, which was discharged in 2001; and the 2002 reanimated exhumation of his incredible inaugural solo soliloquy *Welcome To My Nightmare*. A veritable trifecta of terror!

Prior to that, I had the grave good fortune to write about Alice during the '70s and '80s in CREEM: America's Only Rock 'n' Roll Magazine, where I was predestined to become CREEM's longest serving rock critic with a prodigious record-setting rock writing tenure of twenty unsurpassed years (you could look it up). And friends, I'm here to assure you that it was those self-same prosaic pieces of prose which caught the attention of Alice's very own late lamented personal assistant and which are single-handedly responsible for my being here today. Please doff your hat for the dear departed!

Finally, as if all *that* wasn't unnerving enough, way back in 1974, at the tender age of twenty, I was compelled to appear on stage at that venerable venue Massey Hall, dressed as the aforesaid Alice Cooper, resplendent in top hat and tails, singing "Hello Hooray" to a solo piano accompaniment. And because seeing *is* believing, you can view an historic photograph of that prescient performance on page 43 of my profusely illustrated, full color, coffee table autobiography *Rock Critic Confidential*, along with Alice's riotous reaction when he saw said photo for the first time forty years later. Turn to the last page of this book for more information. I'll wait here while you do!

***

Welcome back. Did I mention that Alice himself wrote the afterword to it? He most certainly did, but don't take my word for it. Buy your own copy of *Rock Critic Confidential* and see for yourself what Alice has to say on page 134 and then decide for yourself if these words he speaks are true. Available at no extra charge!

So it would be a bona fide unabashed fact to say that I've been an Alice Cooper zealot for quite some time. Still am, as a matter of fact. He's my number one rock 'n' roll hero. Always was, always will be. In fact, I'd be willing to wager a crisp uncirculated billion dollar bill that he's *your* rock hero as well; that *you* know far more about Alice Cooper than I ever will; and that *you're* Alice's biggest fan. So shoot the works and, if your number comes up, you can cash in your chips by passing through the egress on your way out. You bet your life!

***

But before you *do* pass away, if I may, I'd like to draw your attention to the errant item on your left. Yes, that's the one. It's the first of many such atrocity exhibits here on display and it's the oldest, if not the oddest. Strange little thing, isn't it? Uh huh. Well, come closer and I'll tell you all about the first time I encountered this abnormal offering. I can still remember how it happened to enter my life as if it were only yesterday…

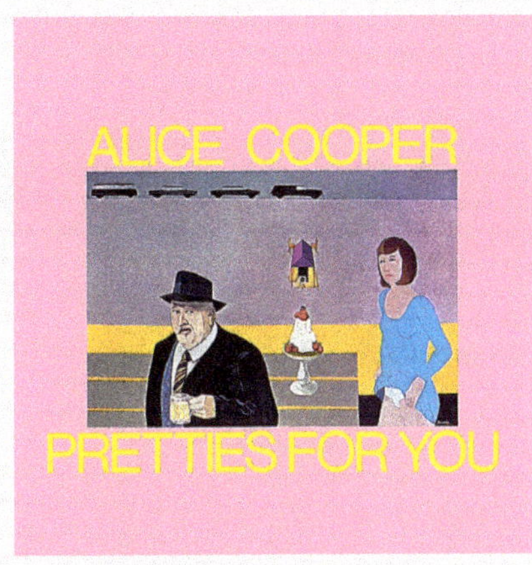

Exhibit #1

PRETTIES FOR YOU

Acquired: 1969

It all started when I bought *Pretties For You* the same day it was released. Cutting my last class at high school, I trucked on down to Sam The Record Man where *Pretties* was listed for a special, one-day-only, same-day-release sale price of a mere ninety-nine cents, marked large in red grease pencil on the factory wrapped cellophane. Of course, after they slit the shrink-wrap and played the first side (assuming they even *got* that far), most first-time buyers felt that they'd overpaid to the tune of at least ninety cents, if not more.

Not that any of them would be able to *do* anything about it because, thanks to the dozens of refund requests demanded by irate teenie boppers who had previously purchased *Their Satanic Majesties Request* in 1967 (all of whom were blissfully oblivious of the drug-addled anarchy that awaited them within), the beleaguered retailer was forced to impose a standing 'No Refund Or Exchange' policy to ensure, from that point on, that anyone who didn't like what they'd heard, having bought it, was stuck with it.

However, unlike most of the others who inquisitively put their hard-earned dollar down that sweltering day in June 1969, I had no remorseful need for any such post-purchase reimbursement. I was stuck with my copy of *Pretties For You* because I was one of the few who actually *liked* what I'd heard—but I was in a distinct minority. The majority viewpoint mirrored that of the anonymous author who reviewed *Schönheiten für Sie* later than year in the October issue of West Germany's underground rock newspaper *Heil Rockenplatz* and wrote (translated from the original German):

"Anybody who buys the new record by Alice Cooper called *Pretties For You* expecting it to have anything to do with *The Wizard Of Oz* is going to be very disappointed. I know I was, because it certainly does not. For one thing, the scene where the Wicked Witch calls Dorothy "my pretty" is not mentioned in any song. Also, there is nothing on the record that refers to the "Fly, my pretties, fly" scene also featuring the Wicked Witch. This is just misleading. In fact, the only connection between *Pretties For You* and *The Wizard Of Oz* can be found on the back cover photo of the Alice Cooper band members. They look more ugly than the Witch and her flying monkeys do.

"But perhaps I should not have been surprised because the lewd cover painting by Edouard Beardsley depicts the kind of unhealthy debauched imagery that one would expect to find from someone who is a distant relative of the equally decadent Aubrey Beardsley. Why anyone would think that such a cover would sell a record is beyond me. "As for the songs, they are all beyond me as well. To say that there is not anything on the record that comes close musically and lyrically to "Somewhere Over The Rainbow" would be a gross understatement. In fact, the Alice Cooper music is as gross to hear as the Alice Cooper musicians are as gross to look at.

"In conclusion, the new Alice Cooper record *Pretties For You* is neither pretty nor for you. It certainly is not for me."

Several months later, this anonymous review was reprinted in the Spring 1970 issue of *Pop Music Scene*, which was a mimeographed ten page (five sheets, double-sided) newsletter mailed out to several hundred subscribers who paid publisher Rhonda Nabolt a dollar for four yearly issues. But because she wasn't fluent in any other languages, Nabolt had to ask a high school friend, who was taking first year German, to translate the review into English. The result was less than accurate and turned what was originally a negative appraisal into a rave review.

Even worse, the mistranslation said that *Pretties For You* actually *was* a *Wizard Of Oz* tribute album, and that the group had recorded the record live while watching a rented print of the film, projected in the studio.

When I asked Alice about this decades later, he laughed. "We could barely afford to rent studio time, let alone a print of *Wizard Of Oz*. Besides, we were more into *West Side Story* back then. But I guess that's where Pink Floyd later got the idea to do *Dark Side Of The Moon* as a tribute album. They could certainly afford to rent a copy of *Wizard* by then. Come to think of it, by that point in the early '70s, so could we!"

There were other unforeseen consequences as well. Dave "Homily" Frankson, a disc jockey at alternative Detroit radio station WABX-FM, was suspended for two weeks after he played *Pretties For You* repeatedly for three hours during "Homily's Happenings," his overnight shift. After the torrent of complaints that followed by dusk-to-dawn denizens (many of them cruising cab drivers and short order cooks in all night diners), the station manager issued an edict that the record not be aired, even going so far as to personally razor blade it himself on both sides to ensure that it could never be played again.

Perhaps most disturbing of all was the report that a number of all-male "Cooper Clubs" were springing up in colleges around the Midwestern United States, with an initiation rite that required prospective male members to wear wigs and dresses to emulate the group's futura-fashion look on the back cover. In retaliation for being blackballed from the proceedings, all-female "Cooper Cubs" were formed by the liberated distaff side to combat what they deemed to be rampant gender discrimination. The Cubs' initiation rite had potential women candidates pose with their dresses hiked up, just like the woman on the front cover painting of *Pretties For You*.

However, a scandal erupted at several colleges when it was discovered that some of the "women" making the female Cooper Cub initiates pose (and often be photographed) in such a revealing manner (with some not wearing the requisite white underwear) were in fact actually male Cooper Club members, dressed in their wigs and dresses. As a result, all college clubs with the name "Cooper" in them were summarily disbanded and prohibited from being formed. Perhaps inevitably, covert Kooper Klubs and Kooper Kubs were rumored to be formed off-campus (reportedly in the back rooms of pool halls and bingo parlors), although there is no hard evidence to support this ever occurring.

Speaking of which, before we move on to the next exhibit, may I take a moment to reveal, here and now, for the very first time ever, the real reason why Alice Cooper performed the song "Goin' Out Of My Head" on *The Gong Show* in 1977? For although many theories have been posited over the ensuing years, I can tell you with absolute authority that it was sung to settle a long-standing lawsuit wherein the publisher of that pop tune claimed that the first track on *Pretties For You* (the instrumental "Titanic Overture") was a direct melodic steal of their very own "Goin' Out Of My Head."

Although this preposterous accusation was made without a single shred of evidentiary proof presented whatsoever to support such a flimsy supposition, the group nevertheless made a very munificent offer to pay damages in the form of any back royalties owed. When this offer was deemed to be insufficient punishment and unlikely to serve as a deterrent to other duplicitous rock stars, the publisher then petitioned for an even harsher sentence. After deliberating behind closed doors for close to five minutes, the jury came back with a unanimous verdict that scapegoat Alice receive the death penalty and be decapitated by *Gong Show* host Chuck Barris, live on national television, while singing the litigated ditty in front of a studio audience.

Despite strenuous scurrilous objections that the execution was instead performed on tape and in syndication with canned applause, the court was nevertheless satisfied that justice had indeed been served. When an appeal was filed by the music publisher on the grounds that, once beheaded, Alice didn't *stay* deceased, the court ruled that it had no jurisdiction over the undead and the case was summarily dismissed.

Even so, there was one *additional* legal requirement that Alice had to fulfill, which he also publicly did in 1977. But we'll talk about that later. For now, let's proceed to the next piece.

Exhibit #2

EASY ACTION

Acquired: 1970

Next we would have had the opportunity to inspect the devious misdirectional come-hither con of *Easy Action*, wherein what appeared to be five topless babes with long hair on the front cover turned out to be five ornery male freaks on the back—a duplicity that didn't stop at the outer packaging and continued unabated within, where additional far more surreptitious layers of deception could be found.

However, as you can see, this exhibit has been temporarily removed for repairs, the unfortunate result of it being vandalized last month by a maniacal woman who believed that the final song "Lay Down And Die, Goodbye" was telling her to act out her repressed power fantasies. I believe it was the line "You know what you can do" that set her off. The last I heard, she was undergoing an experimental form of transorbital rehabilitation that severs the main… It's where the… I won't dwell upon it. Let's continue to the next display.

RA0520 F4 15 11 JARTST ERA0520
PRESENTED BY
CASINO RAMA
19YRS-GOVT PHOTO ID REQ
ALICE COOPER
WWW.ALICECOOPER.COM
FRI MAY 20,11 9PM/DRS8PM

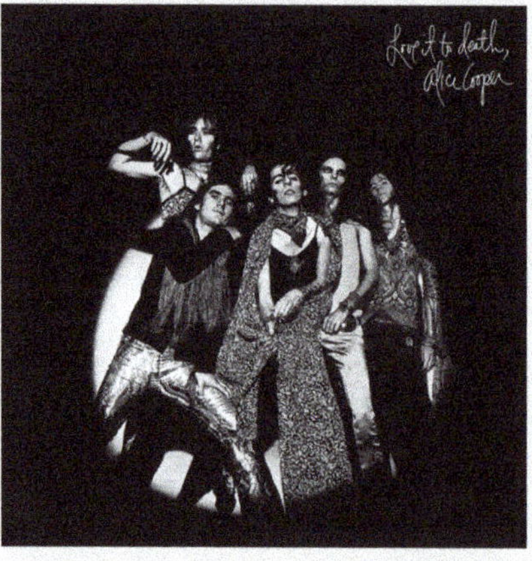

Exhibit #3

LOVE IT TO DEATH

Acquired: 1971

Ah, yes. *This* is where it all begins in earnest. Let those who have eyes see! *This* is where the Alice Cooper manifesto of malfeasance was writ large to be an unrelenting, rampant commitment to the wholesale slaughter of every civilized tenet known to society. Let those who have ears hear! *This* is where a designed-to-shock dynasty of decadence was created by pushing the limits of both rock 'n' roll and theatricality. Let those who are afraid fear! *This* is where the Alice Cooper Group decided to play for keeps and relentlessly pursue a higher level of satirical sonic brutality that would ultimately take outrage to its inevitable and heretofore unimaginable extreme.

That's because *Love It To Death* is the foundation for an astonishing and unparalleled ascent that, within two years, would culminate in the crowning of Alice Cooper as the undisputed number one heavyweight champion rock 'n' roll act in the world.

The very first song, "Caught In A Dream," perfectly encapsulates many of the themes that audiences have henceforth come to expect from Alice Cooper. Let me count the ways: The punk attitude: "I'm caught in a dream, so what?" The greed: "I need everything the world owes me. I tell it to myself and I agree." The confusion: "Thought that I was living but you can't really tell. What I thought was Heaven turned out to be Hell." The insanity: "When you see me with a smile on my face, then you'll know I'm a mental case." I could go on, so I will.

A plethora of other now-familiar Cooper topics also rear their severed heads here *en masse* for the very first time. School's in, so pay strict attention as educator Alice instructs you to open your *Love It To Death* textbook that you might learn all about the three Rs: Religion, as found in the chapters "Hallowed Be My Name" and "Second Coming." Resurrection, as found in the chapters "Black Juju" and "Sun Arise." Relationships, as found in the chapters "Is It My Body" and "Long Way To Go." But be prepared to stay late because the life lessons never end when Coopernican class is in session.

You'll also learn that teenage years are never the easiest of times, which is why "I'm Eighteen" was such a revelation. Never before had anyone ever talked to teens on their own level about the awkward pain and loneliness of growing up and mutating into something altogether…*different*. But Alice did. And this time when Alice spoke, the youth of the world listened. And what they heard was that Alice *understood*. And the *reason* he understood was because he was just as messed up as *they* were! He was one of *them*. It was that bonding between artist and audience that helped "I'm Eighteen" climb to #21 on the pop singles chart.

And whereas The Who's mildly rebellious "My Generation" might have been an appropriate enough pop proclamation for the '60s, the '70s needed a much stronger rock anthem and they found it in the overt recalcitrance of "I'm Eighteen." But if "I'm Eighteen" was the tender morsel that first drew people into the Alice Cooper web, it was "Ballad Of Dwight Fry" that paralyzed them into staying longer than they had planned.

As every horror fan knows, the song is named after character actor Dwight Frye who, in 1931, appeared as a raving lunatic in both Universal Pictures' *Dracula* and *Frankenstein*. A six-and-a-half-minute harrowing descent into one man's madness, "Dwight Fry" is a torment made all the more chilling by Alice's superb vocal stylizations and adept skill at concocting various personas. The voice that was only hinted at on *Easy Action*'s "Return Of The Spiders" is now in full fetid bloom. But enough of that. Over here is something I'm sure you'll *really* like.

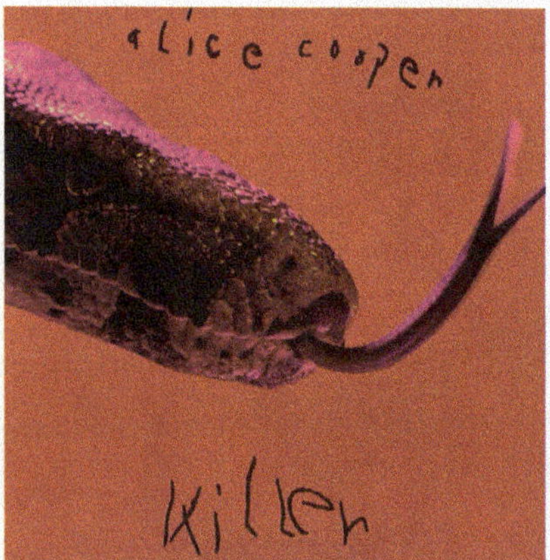

Exhibit #4

KILLER

Acquired: 1971

I'm afraid this one *still* upsets people to this very day. However, it's worth remembering that, for all the bloodletting prevalent, at the center of this uneasy action is a morality play, acted out on record and on stage, in which Alice was always executed at the end of each show. At first, during the *Love It To Death* tour, he was strapped into Old Sparky and electrocuted. Then, as his transgressions escalated from bad to worse, so did the punishments: on the *Killer* tour he was hung nightly from the gallows; and by the time of the *Billion Dollar Babies* tour, he was being strapped into a life-size working guillotine and beheaded.

Of course, Alice *had* to die as a way of absolving the audience from the sin of vicariously reveling in his crimes. No one, however, ever said that, having been killed, he had to *stay* deceased. Just ask the publisher of "Goin' Out Of My Head," who never understood that resurrection is an important element of the Cooper *oeuvre*. Accordingly, Alice always rose from the dead just in time for the encore.

As you can see here, from lady killers on "Be My Lover" to baby killers on "Dead Babies," the Cooper's fourth album is an extremely conceptual one. A veritable soundtrack for the calculated outrage and disruptive, corruptive congestions of their stage show, *Killer* focuses on the alienated outcasts of the world, either through premeditation for gain as on "Desperado" or as a result of society's neglect as on "Killer." From the bludgeoning metasonics of "Under My Wheels" and "You Drive Me Nervous" to the extended disciplined meanderings of "Halo Of Flies," *Killer* had something for everyone.

Look closely and you'll see that Alice's wardrobe was evolving from thrift shop trash 'n' drag rags to attire more befitting a hard-working master agitator. Torn tights, thigh-high boots, and leather bondage vests were now the new issue. The most important change, however, was in the evolution of Alice's eye makeup from mincing to menacing. The fem-demented spider-eye design was gone. In its place were now two dark, malevolent orbs of death, which—along with a newly carved on clown frown—would instantly become known as Alice's trademark visage. Accordingly, his new persona was as chief instigator of a new brand of dementia: Evil as a commodity.

Nobody ever before *looked* like him, *sounded* like him, or *acted* like him. And nobody could shred the speaker of an AM transistor radio like Alice Cooper. He was a first-class hit disturber—and his greatest class disruption exploded onto the airwaves in the summer of 1972 with all the subtle impact of ten fingernails shrieking across a classroom chalkboard. This way, please.

5880240 **The Exegesis Exhibits** 5880240

Exhibit #5

SCHOOL'S OUT

Acquired: 1972

A teen paean to indelicate delinquency and academic insurrection, *School's Out* is a reprobate record that contains more hoods than a used car lot. From the lawless brass-knuckled back alley brawls of "Gutter Cat vs. The Jets" and "Street Fight" to the wistful nostalgic mobocracy of "Alma Mater" and "Grande Finale," there's something here for every rascal and miscreant—and that includes the real cool ersatz jazz make-out piece "Blue Turk" as well as the greatest apocalyptic song ever recorded, "My Stars."

And then there's the title track itself, the number one single that *Entertainment Weekly* deemed to be one of the Top 10 Greatest Summer Songs ever, right behind The Lovin' Spoonful's "Summer In The City" and The Beach Boys' "California Girls." Not bad company for a song that contains some of the rawest, snarkiest, punkiest, and wittiest rock lyrics ever written.

Which isn't to say there weren't repercussions. Within five weeks after *School's Out* was released, the crime rate for juvenile delinquency in the United Sates rose by four hundred percent—a statistic not seen since the '50s and one that was comparable to those documented in other countries shortly after the album went on sale.

Writing in the International Edition of the prestigious psychological journal *Grafisches Gedächtnis*, Dr. Lubna von Domina summed up the prevailing professional opinion when she proclaimed that: "A comprehensive study of the combined residual effect of listening to these songs, all of which extoll the virtues of leering sexuality and blood-drenched violence, has prompted me to conclude that immediate global legislation, based on the public health ideal, is not only needed but necessary to prohibit the circulation, display, and sale of Alice Cooper recordings to all teenagers, especially those under the age of fifteen, without medical supervision."

Thus, the flames having been fanned by such incendiary rhetoric, the outrage continued to spread unabated. After numerous lawsuits across America failed to ban *School's Out* on the grounds of indecency, one particularly frustrated lower court appellant judge was heard to mutter: "If only that pesky First Amendment didn't apply to the free speech of rock 'n' roll, we'd finally be able to clean up this country once and for all."

And speaking of infamous flames, because every copy of *School's Out* contained a pair of women's panties with twelve inches stuffed inside it, the album left itself exposed to be spread wide open for even more attacks. Determined not to be stymied in their anti-Cooper crusade, a united coalition of interstate citizen committees pressed on to prohibit the album from being sold on the grounds that the pink panties which were wrapped around every vinyl disc were a menace to public health and safety due to their being made out of highly flammable material. In this they were slightly more successful than their earlier less cannier counterparts and had *School's Out* taken off the market—albeit only temporarily until fire-proof panties were hurriedly manufactured and shipped across state lines.

As for those panties, a survey in *Classroom Curriculum* magazine later confirmed that it was the first time many a young male fan had ever managed to literally get his hands on a pair. Please use the sanitizer before going any further.

Exhibit #6

BILLION DOLLAR BABIES

Acquired: 1973

Now this one you can take to the bank. Screaming it out loud and clear with a typically defiant and brazen shamelessness, *Billion Dollar Babies* is the number one album that crowned the Alice Cooper Group as the biggest and most magnificent rock 'n' roll band in the world. And although Alice was pumping up the economy by blowing his wad all over the place, money wasn't the only thing on his mind this time around.

As the victim who was left "Raped And Freezin'," reverse sexual harassment was still yet another taboo subject that he tackled with unabashed bravado. On the uneasily hilarious ballad "Mary Ann," he also proved that he could still genderbend with the best of them. On the precognitive "Generation Landslide," he stuck his finger deep into the pulse of the prepunk zeitgeist. On that NecroExplorative double dosage of disgust, "Sick Things" and "I Love The Dead," he delved into pulseless nocturnal defiling. And then he had the temerity to top it all off with "Unfinished Sweet," a song about that scariest of all experiences: a trip to the dentist. Needless to say, but I'll say it anyway, Alice also set yet another lasting trend when he teamed up with Donovan to record "Billion Dollar Babies," the world's first duet between two rock 'n' roll superstars.

Last but unleashed, we have the hit single about rampant Americanism that blitzed straight to number one in England. What better sacred cow for Alice to slash to ribbons in the middle of Main Street USA than that much-vaunted symbol of democratic pomposity, the American electoral system? Following their fearful leader, his fans responded in droves by casting their votes for "Elected."

Knowing that it takes money to make money, Alice seized his campaign donations and formed a PAC (Party Alice Cooper) to fund the new and improved Cooper hellbox of unearthly on stage delights which now contained a guillotine, swords, whips, mannequins, hatchets, baby dolls, blood, fist fights, leopard skin platform boots, balloons, giant teeth and dental drills, free posters, free money, smoke machines, bubble machines, snakes and ladders... Just about everything, in fact, except for the proverbial kitchen sink—and even that would come later.

Meanwhile, just as before, everybody was a critic. Writing in the book *Billion Dollar Baby*, an erstwhile *Esquire* columnist perceptively perceived that: "The reason Alice Cooper is currently the biggest of all rock 'n' roll bands stems from the Cooper stage show. A combination of leering sexuality and blood-drenched simulated violence that has prompted in-print reactions labeling the group as sick, perverted, obscene, and 'Nazi-like.' "

Seconding that demotion was Leo Abse, the British member of Parliament for Torfaen Pontypool, who requested that the government ban the group from performing in England, claiming that Alice was "peddling the culture of the concentration camp." Said Abse: "Pop is one thing, anthems of necrophilia are quite another."

Upon hearing this aspersion and unwilling to roll over and stay dead, Alice flew to London that July in an attempt to speak before the UK parliamentary committee investigating the Second World War's influence on rock music. When members of the Parliament Home Guard prevented him from entering the august chamber, Alice called an impromptu music press conference outside the Palace Of Westminster.

"The power of our show is just the whole idea of bringing back Cabaret," he said to the NME and Melody Maker. "We are really doing a '70s stage thing on decadence. The cabaret was a period in German history when they were interested in decadence. That's exactly what we're doing. Only we're doing it with rock music instead of old beer-drinking music. And that's not too far away either; we do beer-drinking music, too. The whole idea behind the *Billion Dollar Babies* album was exploiting the idea that people do have sick perversions."

Such sentiments foreshadowed the moment when, a mere two years later, the coolly satiric "Cold Ethyl" so totally offended advice-slinger Ann Landers with its theme of NecroSexuality that she devoted one of her syndicated newspaper columns to it, railing against its vulgarity. Good thing Ann didn't listen carefully to Alice's massive hit single "Only Women Bleed," which was his most deceptive song yet—not just because it was a ballad, but also because of its neo-feminist subtext.

However, there were opposing viewpoints which offset the offended. Writing in their landmark textbook treatise *Criminology: Explaining Crime And Its Context*, erudite authors Stephen E. Brown; Finn-Aage Esbensen; and Gilbert Geis astutely assessed that: "Crime and deviance continually test societal constraints, thus forcing an ongoing evaluation of group norms. This confronting of the legal limits introduced the possibility for social change. Think, for example, of the changes in society brought about by such 'criminals' and 'deviants' as Socrates, Jesus, Mahatma Gandhi, Martin Luther King, and Alice Cooper."

Well, two out of five ain't bad. Follow me.

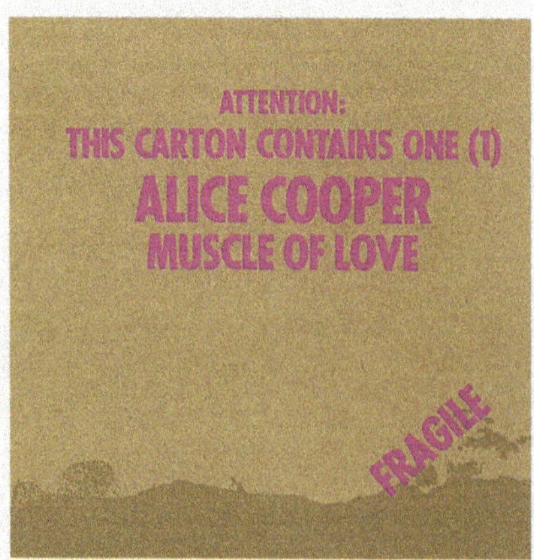

ATTENTION:
THIS CARTON CONTAINS ONE (1)
ALICE COOPER
MUSCLE OF LOVE
FRAGILE

Exhibit #7
MUSCLE OF LOVE
Acquired: 1973

This, I'm afraid, is a classic case of more definitely being less. Recently unsealed files from the Warner Bros. audio archive show that *Muscle Of Love* was initially intended to be the first Alice Cooper extended play record. In an inter-office memo dated 20 May 1973, department head Morry Ostrofsky wrote to his staff:

"I've been listening to these new Alice Cooper band songs and I think we would be better off cutting our production costs and putting some of them out as an EP instead. For those of you who don't know, an EP stands for Extended Play which is basically a single with two songs on each side, not one. We haven't put out an EP for a while and it might be a really good promo for us while the Cooper band is still hot.

"Of the songs I've heard, these are the ones that Irv and I feel have the best potential to chart: "Big Apple Dreaming" and "Never Been Sold Before" on the A side and "Working Up A Sweat" and "Muscle of Love" on the B. The only other song I heard that's any good is "Teenage Lament" which might make a reg single if we can find a good B.

"The songs seem to be about sex in the big city, but we'll play that aspect down so the retailers won't squawk like they did the last time. Shirl in accounting says that even the title Extended Play has a 'big sex' feel to it so I don't know. I've cc'd Marv in the art department to see if he can come up with something that won't offend anyone. Marv, if you do think of anything, give me or Irv a call. But don't waste too much time on it because I hear the band is on the way out anyway so it won't matter what we do."

Had it come to fruition, an Alice Cooper EP would have been an occurrence which would have heralded the resurgence of a format not seen in years, instead of being a missed opportunity.

As for department head Morry Ostrofsky, advanced Cooperologists will know him as the man who once wrote a belligerent three page Alice Cooper biography which famously concluded by saying: "If you can stomach any more of this kind of crap… contact Warner Bros. Records."

And while it would be ironic in the extreme to report that, shortly thereafter, Mr. Ostrofsky choked to death on a chicken bone, the truth is far less sanguinary and far more straightforward in that he died suddenly from acute chronic depression after being told that the Alice Cooper Group was to be inducted into the Rock Hall.

Mr. Ostrofsky was surrounded by family members who report his last words as being… Well, they're far too vulgar and disparaging to be printed here. Let's move on.

Exhibit #8

ALICE COOPER'S GREATEST HITS

Acquired: 1974

Everybody says that 1939 is Hollywood's greatest year, but that's a buncha hooey. As far as Alice Cooper is concerned, *1931* is Hollywood's greatest year because that's the year that gave the world Béla Lugosi and Dwight Frye in *Dracula*, Boris Karloff and Dwight Frye in *Frankenstein*, Edward G. Robinson in *Little Caesar*, James Cagney in *The Public Enemy*, and the Marx Brothers in *Monkey Business*. Take *those* actors and *those* films and blend them with an unwholesome dose of Busby Berkley on a bender and you'll know why the cover to this exhibit fittingly portrays music's most monstrous public enemies as gangsters billed as the "hit men of rock." But there's more to the story than this, much more. For not only does this album write a fitting epitaph to the end of an old era wherein one group is all messed up with nowhere to go, it also heralds the dawn of a new era whereby a rekindled covenant will forever cement Alice Cooper's lasting commitment.

Love 'em or leave 'em, y'just *gotta* feel sorry for the kids of today who are constantly turning over every slimy stone in sight, earnestly searching for a new rock 'n' roll antihero who's *truly* worthy of their worship—and not just another second-string hollow shell of a shill fronting for a trendy mass-marketed franchise that's actually nothing more than a flimflam scam of a sham.

Managing to suss out such flash-in-the-pan swindlers is a tough enough job at the best of times, but when you're slogging waist deep through a musical miasma clogged with fakes, it's an even tougher task. Now as any carny barker will gladly tell you for a price, gibbering sideshow freaks are a ripe dime a dozen nowadays. But without the big hits to back up their brag, they're all nothin' but a buncha would-be contenders who'll barely be remembered as third-rate pretenders—if at all. Many music mavens can shock for a short while, but only a select few are predestined to possess the virile visionary vitality needed to successfully rock out for the long haul on a consistently creative basis.

Now, when it comes to spinning homespun recipes for rebellion, you can easily find scores of them online, but let's face facts. In today's disposable fast paced prepackaged world where every second counts, more often than not you've gotta splice together your own slice of anarchistic action—and what budding anarcho-syndicalist is gonna take the serious amount of time necessary to laboriously follow downloaded instructions these days? If only someone would make it *easy* for 'em to rebel…

…which is exactly what Alice Cooper's been doing his entire life: dumping all his rotten eggs into one basket case after another and providing the listless, restless youth of the world—you know, the ones who are running things now—with a ready-made resource for raucous revolution by issuing a series of primo primers for perversion, each one lethally loaded with enough corrosive custom-designed terrorist tunes to send severe seismic shock waves all across the strictly staid culturally repressed landscapes of this fallen world.

And like all great deleterious weapons with an extremely long half life, Alice's albums still reek with the classic contaminate stench of seditious success. An insurrection collection enviably undimmed by the passage of time, the hit parade slug-fest serenade of Alice Cooper remains—now, more than ever—nothing less than the perfect personification of pure pop incarnate.

This immortal immoralist continues to fulfill his magnificent manifest destiny of doom by influentially infecting generation after generation of jaded juvenility. Just as a leper can't change his spots, Alice can't escape his inevitable fate as rock's ultimate underworld leader. With a rap sheet twice as long as your arm and a rebellious reputation that's three times as strong, he's on everybody's blacklist and in everybody's black book.

Shunned by society, Alice Cooper is the original outlawed outcast who restlessly roams at the edge of your community, ostracized and alone. Unstable, unstoppable, and unpredictable, he's the malformed nocturnal monster who's capable of anything. Audaciously atrocious and deviously inventive with a wild animal's innate cunning, he's the savage unbridled brute let loose in your home who relentlessly does what he wants *when* he wants…and *not* because his actions are part of some demographically-designed, fan-demeaning, callously-contrived con job but because—just like *any* out of control creature let loose in a civilized world—its his natural intrinsic nature to *do* so.

I tell you, it's enough to drive you crazy.

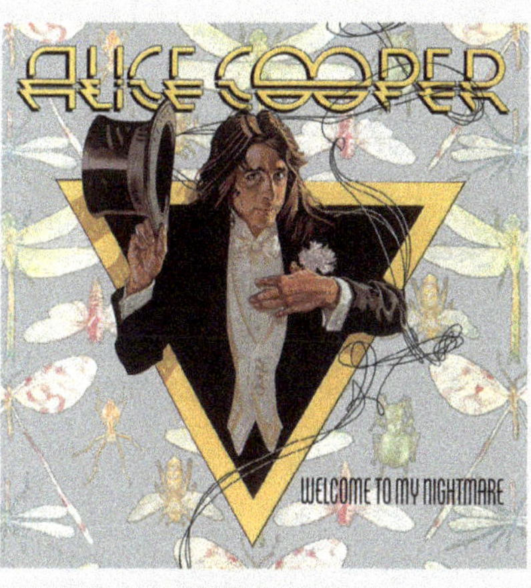

Exhibit #9

WELCOME TO MY NIGHTMARE

Acquired: 1975

And *speaking* of crazy, the next time you find yourself so depressed that you're ready to toss a rope over a wooden crossbeam and do the herky-jerk, here's a little something you can do instead that's guaranteed to yank you out from under that dark cloud and make any hopeless situation seem positive by comparison: just close your eyes and pretend that you have to spend the rest of your life committed to an isolation ward in a mental institution with no chance for parole, ever.

That's right, imagine yourself being thrown into a padded cell the size of a broom closet; hearing the iron door being dead bolted behind you as you lay sprawled in the corner; and feeling the constant hollow churning in your guts that tells you you've been drop-kicked out of the world. Permanently.

Now that's a long time for anyone to be incarcerated, but for a world-class professional master agitator like Alice Cooper, it's only a light slap on the wrist. Because no matter which side of the death penalty debate you happen to support, the unanimous prevailing public sentiment when it comes to Alice Cooper is that giving him a mandatory death sentence is more than enough reason for the State to automatically lodge an immediate series of appeals, all of them based on the grounds that the judgement is too light.

That's why Lady Justice is blindfolded: she knows that every time Alice Cooper meets death, Alice Cooper *cheats* death; and she's so sick and tired of seeing him literally get away with murder that she just can't take it anymore.

You know how everyone in prison constantly claims to be innocent? Not Alice. Always man enough to brazenly admit his transgressions, he's the first one at a crime scene to not only cheerfully admit that he did it, but that he's *glad* he did it and wishes he could do

Photograph ©
Jeffrey Morgan

Photograph ©
Jeffrey Morgan

Photograph ©
Linda Weatherburn

Photograph ©
Linda Weatherburn

Photograph ©
Linda Weatherburn

Photograph ©
Phillip Solomonson
Philamonjaro.com

Photograph © Linda Weatherburn

it *again*. Yet no matter how many of these true grue confessions prosecutors get, there never seems to be enough evidence to garner a guilty conviction that sticks.

Witnesses, judges, juries, it doesn't matter who they are: when Alice turns on his legendary snake-charming charisma, he has them *all* eating out of the palm of his leather-gloved hand. And on those rare occasions when it *does* appear as if the hangman is finally going to knot the noose around his scrawny neck, Alice simply frames a patsy to serve in his stead.

And *that's* why a certain kid named Steven is celebrating yet another anniversary confined in solitary. Oh sure, the Governor commuted his death sentence years ago, but that's small consolation at this point because, just like all the others cooling their heels in stir, Steven also says he's innocent.

Says he really *didn't* do what they said he did.

Says that the *real* culpable culprit responsible for all the blood 'n' guts is this Alice Cooper character.

Alice, meanwhile, disavows any knowledge of the kid's existence.

So whaddya *do* when a kid professes his innocence while America's Most Wanted continues to flaunt it? You do what any great society like America would do under the circumstances: you dust off all the available testimony and give the kid a second hearing. And *upon* second hearing, *Welcome To My Nightmare* steadfastly withstands the true test of time as one of Alice Cooper's most daringly innovative and richly radical preeminent audio excursions.

Everyone likes to joke about what killed vaudeville, but only Alice would dare put his shovel where their mouths are and irreverently disinter the hoary old genre from its moldering grave. Having *other* uses for its dead decaying body, he not only resurrected and reanimated vaudeville, he cleverly reinvented it for a whole new generation of rock 'n' roll adherents who could never be weaned off electricity.

A plundering culture-vulture infamous for always taking his creative cues from movies and television with brazen unabashed audacity, Alice saw that the time was ripe for him to use those classically corrupting influences and invent a revolutionary new form of rock theatre: an extravagant multi-media event the likes of which the world had never seen before.

His sinister scheme was to jolt rock 'n' roll out of its stale stagnant state of complacency by rejuvenating it with a dynamic new stage show, infused with dramatic excitement and spectacular special effects. It would be the kind of sick Coopernican creation that only a certifiably diseased mind like Alice's could conceive: a cadaverous crypt cabaret of truly monstrous proportions. Once assembled, he then unleashed the beast upon an appreciative world-wide rock audience that was severely starved for a new form of musical entertainment.

But *Welcome To My Nightmare* was more than just the hyper-hybrid result of Alice's masterful Moreau-like mutant mating of Rock with Broadway. Not only the veritable blueprint-cum-soundtrack for his record-breaking world tour of the same name, it single-handedly set the highest benchmarked standards for every rock 'n' roll show that's ever followed in its wake, an influence that's spanned two centuries.

The *Welcome To My Nightmare* world tour was a wildly successful series of spectacular shows which did more than just enhance Alice's already heady reputation. By astonishing his audiences, captivating the critics, and exceeding all expectations on a nightly basis, these performances forever solidified Alice Cooper's legendary status in the hearts and minds of the public by confirming what the world had known for years, yet never dared to publicly admit: that Alice Cooper was nothing less than rock 'n' roll's supreme theatrical showman.

Many of those who were lucky enough to have had their senses shattered by Alice live in concert during his ground-breaking *Welcome To My Nightmare* tour still suffer from the traumatizing scars he so expertly inflicted upon them. These fortunate victims number in the high hundreds of thousands, but even those impressive numbers pale in comparison next to the millions upon millions who have been aurally inoculated by Alice over the decades, via the deviant sonic seductions of his original *Welcome To My Nightmare* album.

Just one listen is all it takes to understand why Alice aficionados the world over have deservedly deemed his first solo album to be a universally acclaimed masterpiece. From the ominous opening strains of the title track to the final syncopated mind-break fade out of "Escape," *Welcome To My Nightmare* is a delirium-soaked, non-stop roller coaster ride that takes you way out to where the buses don't run and then dumps you, abandoned and alone, deep inside the delusional mind of a cold-blooded killer.

But lest you let obvious Laff In The Dark spook show serenades like "Cold Ethyl" and "Department Of Youth" lull you into a false sense of security, be forewarned that every dream has a slivered lining and Alice is only softening you up for a sobering sucker punch once your guard is down and your back is turned.

It's about having fun, but it's no joke.

Getting you to tap your toes in time to a tune like "Some Folks" is just part of the ploy to get you hooked. Although on the surface it appears to be nothing more than an innocent sounding good times song, this apparently innocuous jaunty little jingle carries within it an insidious seed. Soon its rhythms involuntarily infect your body and, before you know it, you're merrily singing along with Alice. Then it suddenly dawns on you that the lyrics you've been cheerfully crooning deal explicitly with cannibalism and necrophilia.

And that's only the fourth track. But you let your guard down anyway. You thought that after the dual degradation of tracks two and three it couldn't possibly get any worse. Then you heard the mellow music and you thought you could breathe easy again. You should've known better than that but, then again, how *could* you? Because that's the pure evil genius of Alice: before you even know yourself what your next move is going to be, he's already made three moves to *counter* it.

He knew that after Vincent Price weakened you with the repulsive snack attack combo of "Devil's Food" and "The Black Widow," you'd be ripe for the picking. But little did you suspect that after the base humiliation dealt you by "Some Folks," Alice would take advantage of your freshly shredded defenses by landing an even harder body shot called "Only Women Bleed" that leaves you reeling on rubber legs for a standing eight count.

Then, just when you're at your most vulnerable, the melodies distort and the façade melts away as Alice triumphantly wields his masterstroke: *Welcome To My Nightmare*'s climactic trilogy of terror. Delving deeper to expand upon his *Love It To Death* and *Killer* straitjacket persona, "Years Ago," "Steven," and "The Awakening" claustrophobically harvest the unholy sanity schism which has been percolating to a fever pitch right from the very beginning.

Unfortunately, despite whatever false assurances the final track might have you believe, escape is not an option; it's only a cruel illusion meant to raise your hopes one last time before your spirit is finally broken for good.

And as you look up, dimly aware that the wallpaper surrounding you is patterned with an assortment of large spiders and bugs, you can't help but notice that these selfsame insects are beginning to somehow inexplicably extract themselves from the smooth lavender surface and slowly skitter down towards you…

Welcome to your nightmare.

Welcome home.

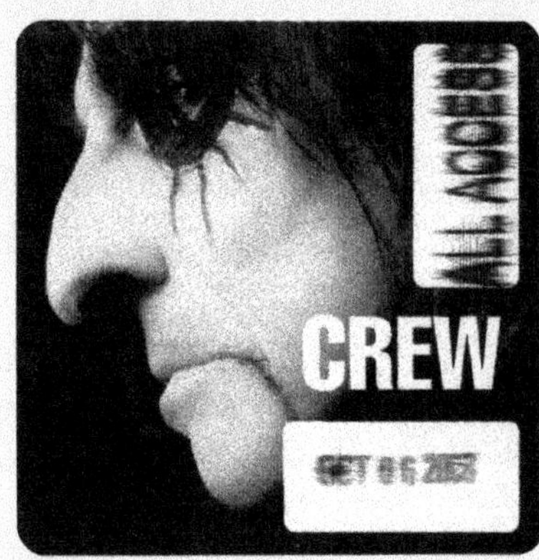

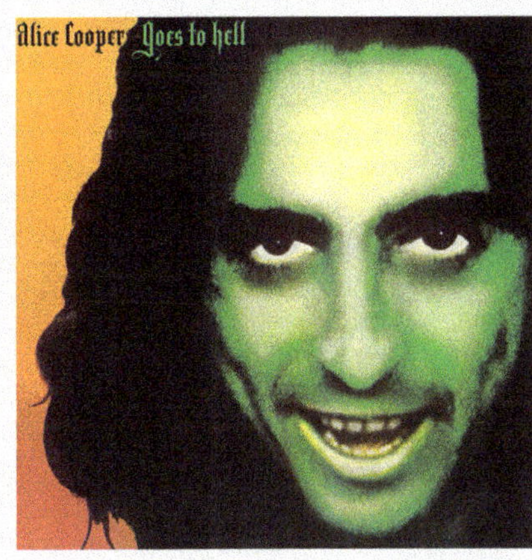

Exhibit #10

ALICE COOPER GOES TO HELL

Acquired: 1976

It's an age-old adage that whatever comes up, must go down. And so, after laboriously scaling the lofty heights of success with *Welcome To My Nightmare*, it was an inevitable axiom that there was only one direction left for Alice to go—and only one final terminus. Ostensibly an "Alice's Inferno" purgatory saga, in actuality this album expertly delineates the Eleven Circles Of Musical Hell, as follows:

First Circle: "Go To Hell" (Rockschmaltz)
Second Circle: "You Gotta Dance" (Discoschmaltz)
Third Circle: "I'm The Coolest" (Funkschmaltz)
Fourth Circle: "Didn't We Meet" (Cheesyschmaltz)
Fifth Circle: "I Never Cry" (Balladschmaltz)
Sixth Circle: "Give The Kid A Break" (Cornballschmaltz)
Seventh Circle: "Guilty" (Aschargedschmaltz)
Eighth Circle: "Wake Me Gently" (Snoozakschmaltz)
Ninth Circle: "Wish You Were Here" (Ploddingschmaltz)
Tenth Circle: "I'm Always Chasing Rainbows" (Vaudevilleschmaltz)
Eleventh Circle: "Going Home" (Overproducedschmaltz)

Let's keep moving.

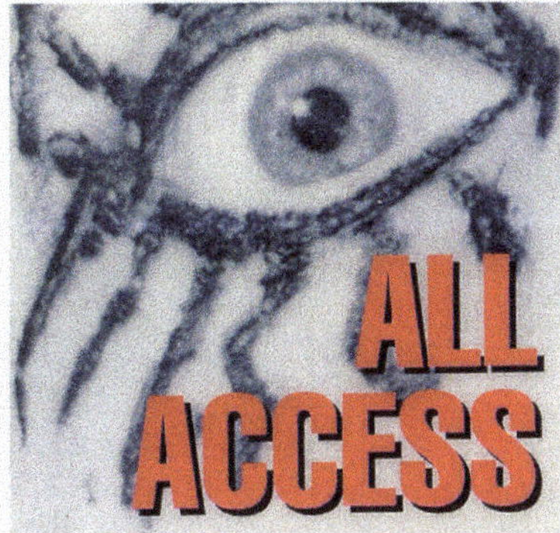

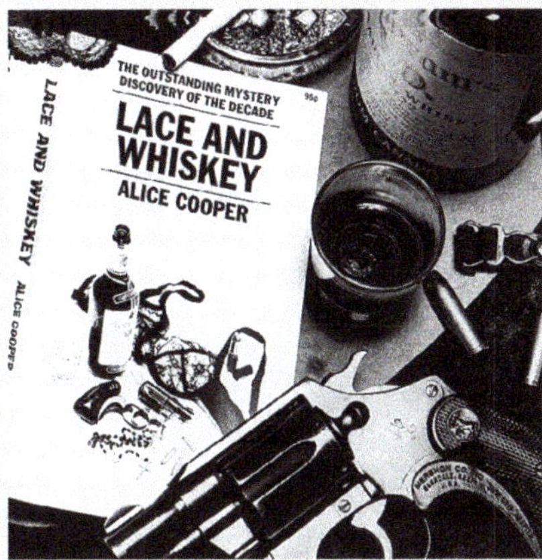

Exhibit #11

LACE AND WHISKEY

Acquired: 1977

Now here we have a *real* rarity. The following uncredited review was originally published in the Nov-Dec 1977 issue of the short-lived counterculture magazine *Men's Adult Detective & Music Bimonthly*. Although the end of the review suggests that it was to be in two parts, no second installment ever appeared because the magazine ceased publication with this final issue.

*** *** ***

I soon found out that she was no stranger to Scotch and that she loved to dance. We split the booze can just before three, and when we arrived back at my digs I was more than ready to call it a night, but it soon became evident that she had other designs and was still raring to go.

My hand was slipping inside her elastic when two men slid out of the bedroom closet. The pair didn't say anything, but I heard a click. One of them had a switch; the blade looked as long as a saber. I drop-kicked him in the crotch and watched with satisfaction as the navy tweed covering his groin turned wet and red. By that time, the other one was halfway to the door. He never made it. Lunging, I grabbed him by the collar and redirected his head into the nearest wall. Plaster and shattered cartilage massed into a pulpy smear as his bloodied face painted crazy new patterns on the already hip wallpaper. Not wanting either one of them to soak the plush white carpet, I opened the door and the slobs staggered out into the hallway, leaving a trail of puke all the way to the elevator.

Adjusting my tie, I looked over at Eileen who was lying nude on the bed, looking infinitely desirable. Crossing the floor, I started to remove my jacket when my wingtip struck something that one of the thugs must have dropped. Bending over to pick it up, I saw that it was a record album. Unable to make out the lettering on the front cover, I flicked on the end table light.

It was an Alice Cooper album. A new one.

The cover photograph intrigued me with its combination of booze, broads, and bullets. That's a winning trifecta to bet on every time. Clearly, here was a man with a thirst for more than just justice. Turning, I entered the living room and snapped on the hi-fi. Slipping Jackie Gleason's *Music For Lovers* back into its jacket, I used the discarded switchblade to slit the shrink-wrap on the Coop disc.

As I placed it on the turntable, Eileen came bounding out of the bedroom, still naked. She splayed herself suggestively on the love seat. I considered showing her the album cover, but decided that she'd already had enough excitement for one night. Besides, what Eileen wanted from me was something far more urgent; already her undulations were beginning to soak a large stain into the upholstery. Women.

I pushed the automatic start and waited. Instant on and out, the JBLs started spitting guitar and drums. Eileen began to writhe urgently in time to the steady throb punching out of the twin speakers, and who could blame her? Not me. Already I could tell that this gumshoe gavotte might be a contender. The voice sounded strong with an even dose of snarl and snark, evidence that he might be writing straight-ahead rock songs again, instead of the reeking stale-dated baby food that stunk up the aptly-named *Goes To Hell*. Yeah, I was impressed all right.

Then I looked at the track listing and froze. Ten song titles. Sure, maybe to the untrained eye they looked like song titles. But not to me. I saw the secret map code in those song titles just as easily as I could look over and see Eileen rhythmically flex her smooth inner hamhocks.

Ignoring the obvious invitation, I sat down on the couch in front of the coffee table and brushed aside last month's skin magazines. Tearing open the album jacket, I smoothed it flat on the table, face down. Then, uncapping my silver and gold Cross fountain pen, I began to make the necessary connections on the blank cardboard, marking them down as each song played. It didn't take long before I had it all figured out. Ten tracks, ten parts of town you wouldn't go without a pistol.

"It's Hot Tonight" referred to the dog-barking tenements in Sinister Heights. That's where a local loser named the Jazz Geek would prowl for open roof doors. Then the peeping pudknocker would literally hang out on tar beach and scope the naked pieces of fluff who romped around in the buff because they didn't have an air conditioner stuck in the bedroom window.

"Lace And Whiskey" was an obvious nod in the direction of Shamus Flats, where all the retired flatfoots drowned their sorrows with a self-inflicted shot, either from a bottle or a service revolver. The lucky ones who had a frail to squeeze got to make another kind of shot. Ohhh yasss…

"Road Rats" was easy to peg as a loose collection of bunko boys who loitered in and around Thieves' Highway by the truck stop. They'd pilfer anything for a price and sometimes did finger jobs for free, just to keep their chops up. I remember that the Cosmetic Kid had a thing for beauty supplies and specialized in casing the makeup cases at upscale department stores. The kid was vain, so he would have been pleased to know that he looked great in the open casket, even after an armed security guard put an end to Cosmetic's career by drilling a couple of hot slugs into his dome. The mortician used part of the Kid's own stash to touch up his perforated mug.

"Damned If You Do" was the slogan printed in chalk on the locker room ceiling at The Precinct. And although nobody knows who actually climbed up to put it there, the general consensus is that it was scrawled by "Vicious" Aloysius "Gonzo" Gonzaga who, in addition to having two nicknames, was actually monikered after Saint Aloysius de Gonzaga, an Italian aristocrat who grew up amid the violence and brutality of Renaissance Italy and witnessed the murder of two of his brothers. Unlike his namesake, however, Vicious Gonzo was anything but a saint and spent his entire career at war not only with gangland writ large but with his own inner demons. When VG disappeared one night after an especially arduous night shift in the Danger Zone, bets were made as to whether he was a victim of the mob or of himself. No one has collected to this day.

"You And Me" could only mean a one way trip to the steep precipice at the end of Losers' Lane, where lovers either jumped or were pushed to their eternal reward while under the influence of love or some other equally noxious substance. And because Mother Nature had the good sense to place the local tar pits right underneath the overhang, the town was saved the added expense of having to spend thousands of tax dollars to scrape up and remove the splattered remains since the falling bodies all sank down into the black pitch, never to be seen again.

Hearing a click, I got up and turned the disc over. As expected, the flip was a good flow that was ripe with additional information. I continued to make notes.

"King Of The Silver Screen" referred to the run-down second run movie theatre near Knockover Square that specialized in gangster melodramas. That's where certain unimaginative mugs would sit and plan their next job. More often than not, they'd pattern the heist after whatever poverty row double feature was playing at the time. When the joint was temporarily closed for renovations, the crime rate went down for a week.

"Ubangi Stomp" couldn't have been more obvious. It meant walking the beat-up beat down on Hate Street, where every resident was a passo-aggro who either put the boots to someone or had the boots put to them, often at the same time. These back alley brawls provided a good side living for the local cops on the take who would make book on who would survive and what would be left of them.

"(No More) Love At Your Convenience" was a not too subtle nod in the direction of Vixenville, where peroxide bottle blondes cashed checks with their mouths that their weak-kneed customers readily wrote with their... Well, you know.

"I Never Wrote Those Songs" was such a confused confession that it could only result in a one-way ticket to the Psych Ward, where such delusional babbling was the only currency that all the pixelated residents had in common. In fact, the song was so sincere in its insanity that, for a split-second, it occurred to me that Coop might actually be a candidate for confinement in the rubber romper room. Then I immediately came to my senses and dismissed the thought as being the one thing that would never happen.

"My God" could only mean Blind Alley, the one place where blind faith ruled the religious roost. Of all ten locations, this was the one location I was most familiar with, having grown up in the projects. Father O'Brien was a former light heavyweight who was known as "Battling" O'Brien before he hung up his gloves for a higher calling. Not only was he my boxing coach in the ring at Sammy Luftspring's gym, he was a good friend behind the pulpit who showed me the importance of using my brains as well as my fists.

The flip side ended and the tone arm reset with a solid click.

I looked over at the love seat. Empty.

I looked over at the front door. Open.

She'd be back. I went over to the hi-fi and shut if off. Picking up the disc, I noticed one final clue as I was putting the record back into its inner sleeve: the matrix number etched into the vinyl at the runout groove: BSK-3027.

Looking at the rotary dial on my telephone, I transposed the first three letters and came up with 275-3027. I immediately recognized it as a local number that could only mean one thing because it belonged to none other than...

TO BE CONTINUED NEXT MONTH

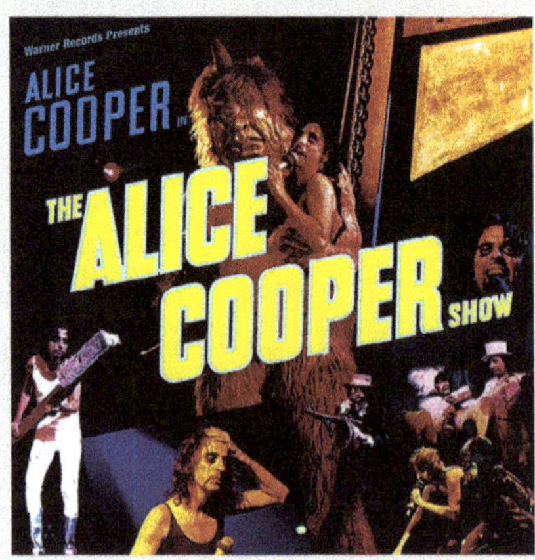

Exhibit #12

THE ALICE COOPER SHOW

Acquired: 1977

And now if I may return to my earlier exhibit dissertation on the "Goin' Out Of My Head" lawsuit, you will recall that there was one *additional* legal requirement that Alice had to fulfill, which he also publicly did in 1977. It has to do with this album and I'm wondering if you can tell me what it is. Go on, take your time. No, it has nothing to do with that particular song. In fact, it has nothing to do with *any* of the songs, so what does that leave?

That's right, the album cover. So I ask if

Photograph © George E. Orlay

you would now take a good look at the album cover and see if you can discern for yourself what additional legal requirement Alice fulfilled. I'll give you a hint, it's not on the front cover. Oh, I see you only have a digital copy. No vinyl? That's too bad because, if you *did* have a vinyl copy, you'd see a photo of Alice in the bottom right hand corner, fedora-adorned with his hands down at his sides and his index fingers extended in a perfect impersonation of Chuck Barris hosting *The Gong Show. That's* the additional price he had to pay.

But if you don't believe me, just ask Renfield. One night while Brian and I were having dinner, I asked him: "Am I the only person in the world who noticed that Alice is impersonating Chuck Barris on the back cover of *The Alice Cooper Show*?"

Whereupon the Assistant To The Master immediately looked up at me and promptly replied: "Yes."

Exhibit #13

FROM THE INSIDE

Acquired: 1978

And *speaking* of back covers, almost everyone who saw the reverse of *Pretties For You* knew beyond a shadow of a doubt that Alice Cooper was balmy, barmy, bats, batty, bonkers, brainsick, bughouse, certifiable, crackbrained, cracked, crackers, crackpot, crazed, crazy, cuckoo, daffy, daft, demented, deranged, gaga, haywire, kooky, loco, looney tunes, lunatic, mad, maniacal, mental, meshuggah, moonstruck, non compos mentis, nuts, nutty, psycho, psychotic, scatterbrained, screwy, unbalanced, unhinged, unsound, wacko, wacky, dotty, loopy, touched in the head, aberrant, delirious, delusional, off his rocker, disordered, disturbed, neurotic, obsessive-compulsive, paranoid, schizoid, schizophrenic, sociopathic, eccentric, odd, oddball, pixilated, strange, irrational, unreasonable, amuck, ballistic, bananas, berserk, frantic, frenzied, hysteric, raving, fixated, monomaniac, monomaniacal, obsessed, and flat-out wigged-out.

Still, it wasn't until "Ballad Of Dwight Fry" that such errant assumptions were actually made manifest—which is why it came as no surprise to anyone when *From The Inside* was released. However, having seen *Arsenic And Old Lace* more times than he could remember, Alice knew that it wouldn't be easy for anyone to commit him into an insane asylum without proper cause and proper paperwork. That's why the improper authorities requested that eminent psychiatrist Dr. Fredric Wertham give Alice a written exam to medically establish just how krazy the kat actually was. The Nuremberg-born author of such scholarly tomes as *Seduction Of The Innocent* (1954); An Exploration Of Human Violence (1968); and *How Rock Music Leads To Mass Murder And Cannibalism* (1976) readily agreed.

Now, for the very first time, in the interest of full translucent disclosure, we dare to present the actual questions that Dr. Wertham used in his examination of Alice. These are the exact self-same queries which ultimately led to the rock legend's inevitable state-sponsored incarceration. Given how heavily the deck was stacked against him, it remains a mystery to this very day and is anyone's guess as to how Alice flew the coop.

*** *** ***

SECTION ONE:

For each statement, say whether it applies to you or not.

When in the dark do you often see shapes and forms even though there is nothing there? Are your thoughts sometimes so strong that you can almost hear them? Have you ever thought that you had special, almost magical powers? Have you sometimes sensed an evil presence around you, even though you could not see it? Do you think that you could learn to read other's minds if you wanted to? When you look in the mirror does your face sometimes seem quite different from usual? Do ideas and insights sometimes come to you so fast that you cannot express them all? Can some people make you aware of them just by thinking about you? Does a passing thought ever seem so real it frightens you? Do you feel that your accidents are caused by mysterious forces? Do you ever have a sense of vague danger or sudden dread for reasons that you do not understand? Does your sense of smell sometimes become unusually strong? Are you easily confused if too much happens at the same time? Do you frequently have difficulty in starting to do things? Are you a person whose mood goes up and down easily? Do you dread going into a room by yourself where other people have already gathered and are talking? Do you find it difficult to keep interested in the same thing for a long time? Do you often have difficulties in controlling your thoughts? Are you easily distracted from work by daydreams? Do you ever feel that your speech is difficult to understand because the words are all mixed up and don't make sense? Are you easily distracted when you read or talk to someone? Is it hard for you to make decisions? When in a crowded room, do you often have difficulty in following a conversation? Are there very few things that you have ever enjoyed doing? Are you much too independent to get involved with other people? Do you love having your back massaged? Do you find the bright lights of a city exciting to look at? Do you feel very close to your friends? Has dancing or the idea of it always seemed dull to you? Do you like mixing with people? Is trying new foods something you have always enjoyed? Have you often felt uncomfortable when your friends touch you? Do you prefer watching television to going out with people? Do you consider yourself to be pretty much an average sort of person? Would you like other people to be afraid of you? Do you often feel the impulse to spend money which you know you can't afford? Are you usually in an average kind of mood, not too high and not too low? Do you at times have an urge to do something harmful or shocking? Do you stop to think things over before doing anything? Do you often overindulge in alcohol or food? Do you ever have the urge to break or smash things? Have you ever felt the urge to injure yourself? Do you often feel like doing the opposite of what other people suggest even though you know they are right?

SECTION TWO:

Do you see yourself as being...

Extroverted and enthusiastic or critical and quarrelsome? Dependable and self-disciplined or anxious and easily upset? Open to new experiences and complex or reserved and quiet? Sympathetic and warm or disorganized or careless? Calm and emotionally stable or conventional and uncreative?

SECTION THREE:

Are you the kind of person who...

Worries a lot? Gets nervous easily? Remains calm in tense situations? Is talkative? Is outgoing and sociable? Is reserved? Is original and comes up with new ideas? Values artistic and aesthetic experiences? Has an active imagination? Is sometimes rude to others? Has a forgiving nature? Is considerate and kind to almost everyone? Does a thorough job? Tends to be lazy? Does things efficiently?

SECTION FOUR:

Which of the following statements do you agree with?

I often make a fuss about unimportant things. I often talk to strangers. I often feel unhappy. I am often irritated. I often feel inhibited in social interactions. I take a gloomy view of things. I find it hard to start a conversation. I am often in a bad mood. I am a closed kind of person. I would rather keep other people at a distance. I often find myself worrying about something. I am often down in the dumps. When socializing, I don't find the right things to talk about.

SECTION FIVE:

How often in the past month did you feel...

Happy. Interested in life. Satisfied with life. That you had something important to contribute to society. That you belonged to a community like a social group or your neighborhood. That our society is a good place or is becoming a better place for all people. That people are basically good. That the way our society works makes sense to you. That you liked most parts of your personality. That you are good at managing the responsibilities of your daily life. That you had warm and trusting relationships with others. That you had experiences that challenged you to grow and become a better person. Confident to think or express your own ideas and opinions. That your life has a sense of direction or meaning to it.

SECTION SIX:

How often in the past year did you...

Take calls or spent time with a sponsee? Guide an alcoholic or addict through the twelve-step program? Hold a service position in a twelve-step program? Say something positive to an alcoholic or addict? Listen to an alcoholic or addict? Say hello to a newcomer? Reach out to an alcoholic or addict having a hard time? Share a personal story with an alcoholic or addict? Read program literature to an alcoholic or addict? Encourage an alcoholic or addict to go to a meeting? Donate money to Alcoholics Anonymous or Narcotics Anonymous? Put away chairs after a meeting? Record an actual rock 'n' roll album that doesn't include any pansy power ballads?

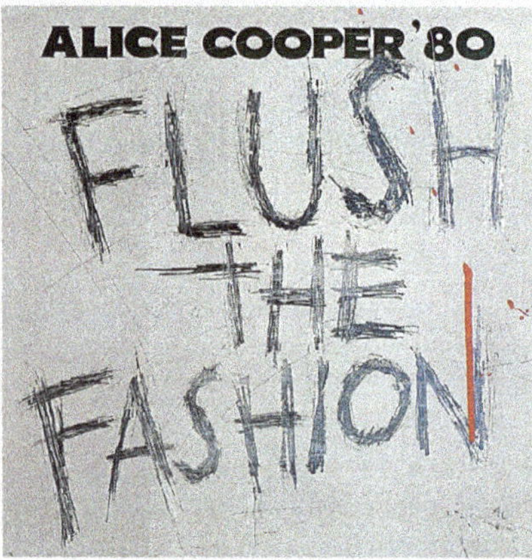

Exhibit #14

FLUSH THE FASHION

Acquired: 1980

More than just a side order to go, these famous last words accurately describe Alice Cooper's futurist fashion plate.

SIDE ONE: THEN

A real man knows when it's time to admit his mistakes, and I'll be the first one to publicly confess that the skinny little weasel sure as shootin' had *me* fooled. Hell, I thought he was *washed up*. You know: Finished. Kaput. Had the bun. He probably had *you* fooled, too. I mean, how long did *you* stick around after the glorious wretched excess of 1973's *Billion Dollar Babies* belched up the last gasp remains of the original Alice Cooper Group via the flaccid *Muscle Of Love?* Could *you* bear to watch one of rock's great originals slide into a nickel and dime decline?

I couldn't.

So now it's seven years later and, as late as two weeks ago, there was no way you'd get me to listen to an Alice Cooper album at this late stage of the game—let alone go out and actually *buy* one.

After all, we know what the statute of limitations is on a body missing in action, right? Wrongo, boyo. Raise that curtain, hello hooray, old snake eyes is back with a two-sided disc-dose that's more fun than freebasing with a polyester shirt on. After years of scamming us with a tightrope walk between rock 'n' roll and bleeding-women bull, Alice has finally dug down, come up, and put his money where his meat is.

Still, seven years *is* a long time to be playing footsie with the die-hard rock fans of the world but, I kid you not, on *Flush The Fashion*, Alice shows the stuff that got him elected CREEM's 1973 Punk Of The Year in that year's annual readers' poll (and when I say *punk*, I mean *smartass* and, make no mistake, they just don't come any punkier than Alice).

So why, do you ask, is this new long player gonna stick to the roof of your skull like a wet gob of Dubble Bubble?

1. The title. *Flush The Fashion* is a *great* rock 'n' roll title—especially in this day and age of terminal vagueness.

2. The cover. Etched in fury with a rusty nail by old Salvadork A.C. himself, it's a brilliant work hailing from the "who-gives-a-shit" school of design.

3. The songs. "Clones" you all know about by now. It out-*Replicas* Gary Numan by adding a sense of humor tempered with a streak of masculinity. Then there's "Leather Boots" that sounds like epileptic warriors on speed-balls and isn't what you think it's about. 'Nuff said. No? Well…

4. The lyrics. "Pain" contains some of Alice's best lines since "Second Coming" and, as for "Model Citizen," can *you* find fault with a guy gutsy enough to sing a line like "I'm a friend of Sammy Davis (casually)"? *I* can't and I don't even *know* old glass eye.

5. The vocals. Maybe those nights in the detox tanks really *did* do the trick, 'cause Alice sounds like Public Animal #9 again. When he snarls "I'm the burnin' sensation when the convict fries," he sounds just exactly like you'd *want* him to sound.

6. The back-up vocals. Flo & Eddie, for that classic T. Rex sound. No Liza or Labelle in 1980.

7. The production. Jackhammers. You can thank Roy Thomas Baker for this one.

8. The credits. It's about time *somebody* gave credit to Basil Fawlty for inspiration on a rock 'n' roll album.

9. The concept. The concept this time around is that there *is* no concept this time around, other than Alice declaring war on the new decade.

10. The score. Alice: 1, New Decade: 0.

11. The moral. It's 1980. Do you know where *your* heroes are?

SIDE TWO: NOW

Hey, just because I was only twenty-six when I wrote that doesn't mean I didn't know what I was talking about. After all, when Lester Bangs personally invites you to write for America's Only at the tender age of twenty, you're expected to make some smart calls along the way—and having the prescient foresight to refrain from knocking this album was certainly one of them because history in her infinite wisdom has shown that, as Alice Cooper records go, *Flush The Fashion* has steadfastly stood the test of time.

Truth be told, I liked it enough back in 1980 to assign it to myself for review, and I still like it enough to heartily recommend it now, some four decades after the fact.

Y'see, *Flush The Fashion* is one of those rare Alice Cooper albums that exists purely as a light bit of entertainment; a mere diversion as you slog your way from point A to point B. I said it then and I'll say it again: the concept this time around is that there *is* no concept this time around, other than Alice declaring war on the new decade.

And given how Alice has so adeptly taken to the bully pulpit in recent years to wage war on the new *century*, it's kinda refreshing to have a cool, calm oasis, devoid of chaos, to drink from in these troubling times. Yessir, this is one agenda bender with no axe to grind and absolutely no message to import. None whatsoever.

Aw, nuts. Who am *I* trying to kid with that load of malarkey? That passive party line may have fooled the rubes in the idyllic eighties, but that was long before any of us knew what new terrors were destined to come savagely roaring down the pike. Back then, nobody had the faintest clue what the future would hold; we were all blissfully unaware of what was yet to transpire.

All of us, that is, with the notable exception of NostraAlice who, having parted the veils of tomorrow, then imparted his visionary wisdom to us in a cautionary *début de siècle* album that was released a full twenty years before the chickens would come home to rule the royal roost in the year 2000. But time flies when you're on the run which is why, an additional two decades later, it's now the perfect occasion to crack this musical time capsule open and reexamine it with fresh eyes, aided by the added benefit of hindsight.

And under closer scrutiny, I gotta admit in retrospect that *Flush The Fashion* exhibits all the hallmarks of being one of the greatest subliminally precognitive concept albums ever recorded.

So what, do you ask, accounts for this sudden radical reversal of opinion?

1. Uncivil liberties. Having lived his entire life basking in the accusatory glare of authority's spotlight, Alice knew from experience that a clever updating of the Music Machine hit "Talk Talk" would provide the perfect opening metaphor for

a future society—*ours*—where nobody ever assumes responsibility for their actions anymore and everyone's fifteen minutes of blame someone else are on constant display, perpetually rerun twenty-four hours a day. Put down that smartphone and pay attention to me.

2. "Clones (We're All)." Follow the science. *Et tu, Coop?*

3. The longest track. The anguished four minute epic performance piece "Pain" acutely foreshadows Alice's duplicitous personifications on *The Last Temptation*.

4. The shortest track. The harrowing ninety-second grim urban dispatch "Leather Boots" treads menacingly down the same dark districts later delineated in depth by Alice on *Brutal Planet* and *Dragontown*.

5. The Food And Drug Administration. For decades they've been studying the merits of Alice's medical prognostications *vis-à-vis* his addiction predilection on "Aspirin Damage."

6. The pro-nuke 'n' no-nuke factions. Unbeknownst to each other, both sides have avidly embraced Alice as one of their own as a result of his thermo atomic attitude on "Nuclear Infected."

7. The social activists. The 'Sammy Factor' notwithstanding, they *still* can't agree whether Alice is a boon or a bane to society due to his candid confessions on "Model Citizen."

8. The parents of the world. They continue to take comfort from Alice's pro-parental words of wisdom on "Grim Facts."

9. Their disenfranchised whelps. They continue to take comfort from Alice's anti-parental words of wisdom on "Dance Yourself To Death."

10. Dennis Rodman. You might remember that the tattooed beat rebounder made headlines around the world by literally taking the advice of self-promotional guru Alice who, on the aptly named "Headlines," counseled: "I called a conference with the press, announced my marriage plans in a wedding dress."

11. The concept. The concept this time around is that there *is* a concept: Alice paving the way for a future declaration of war against the Four Horsemen of the new century.

12. The score. Alice: 2, New Century: don't ask.

13. The moral. It's not 1980 anymore. Do you *really* know where your heroes are? Well, you'd *better* 'cause one of them is out there on a solitary watch, and he's sounding a cultural clarion call to arms like never before. And *that's* why *Flush The Fashion* is one of Alice's greatest concept albums ever: it's an early warning shot across the bow for all of us to stay ever vigilant about what's going on around us. And *this* time around, there's no room for defectors.

Oh, I'll admit that I strayed from the fold for a while; who *hasn't* from time to time? Just so long as you know that I wasn't retreating: I was just advancing in another direction. But this is the album that pulled me back into the ranks with a vengeance…and look where *that* got me. "Glorious wretched excess," indeed.

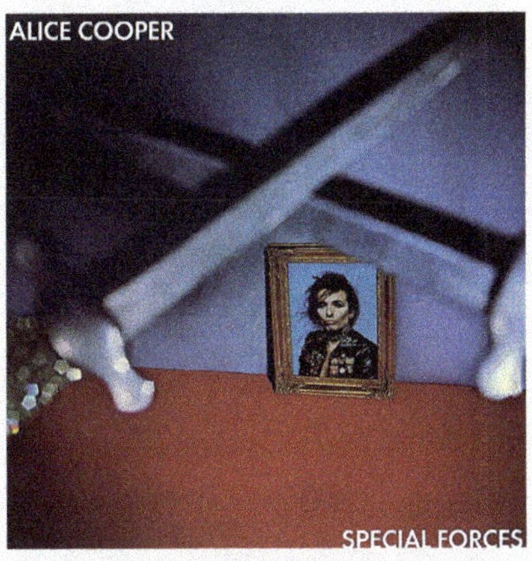

Exhibit #15

SPECIAL FORCES

Acquired: 1981

Wherein the futurist new wave look of *Flush The Fashion* gives way to the traditional old wave look of *Special Forces*. However, as always, there is far more to this story than meets the eye. It all began when Alice saw the following two advertisements while flipping through a 1980 issue of *Soldier Of Fortune* magazine:

> COMBAT MUSIC – We're looking for 100% all-American rock music that graphically portrays the life of the professional. The pain, the fear, the loves, the hates, the joy, and the toil. We want to hear music that will nourish your heart and mind for years. Send demo tape with SASE to PHMA, P.O. Box 15344, TN 38556

> DRESS THE PART – We have the gear that makes the man look military. For a lot less than the price of a crate of ammo we can provide. Ask about our standard AG-44 dress uniform, tailored like suit/sport coat. Leather trench is our specialty. Give size with alternate. Box 391B, Sandusky, OH 44870

Putting the two ads together, Alice took his new image a serious step further with the unveiling of his next twisted sartorial statement that bridged the gap between shock rock and shock troops: military drag. The theme of *Special Forces* had the Degenerate General adopting a Field Marshall Cooper persona, replete with lipstick, leather, and false eyelashes.

As always, there were a number of naysayers who didn't fully understand the concept. And although Warner Bros. bought several full color back cover ads in both *Soldier Of Fortune* and *Guns & Ammo* to promote the album, that financial contribution didn't placate the many grizzled veterans who were offended by the idea of Alice Cooper being one of them—and *Soldier Of Fortune*'s FLAK letters page showed it.

> A DISGRACE…
>
> Sirs:
>
> I am a gunner in the U.S. Navy and a strong supporter of your magazine, up until now. My stomach churned at the sight of "Alice Cooper" dressed in a military uniform. No, make that tarnishing a military uniform. This is a disgrace!
>
> GMG3 Bob Henderson
> FPO, New York, New York

> HAIRCUT NEEDED…
>
> Sirs:
>
> Are you really that desperate at SOF that you have to start running ads for bad albums instead of body armor? This is not what I buy SOF for. Enclosed is my two cents to give that thing a haircut, preferably with a straight razor.
>
> Jack Ackuna
> Captain, USAR
> San Antonio, Texas

> FOR SHAME…
>
> Sirs:
>
> I'm writing to tell you how irked I am to see a rock musician on the back cover of your magazine. It's anti-American filth such as this that my brothers and I fought hard against and it's what's wrong with this country today. By running such an ad, you remind me of the immoral drug dealers we used to come across, whose motto was, "Hey pal, if your money's good, your money's good." For shame.
>
> Dixon Siegel
> Post Falls, Idaho
>
> *These letters are representative of the hundreds of mail and phone responses SOF has received concerning this issue. We've also received a few replies like the one below. — the Eds.*

> KEPT US GOING…
>
> Sirs:
>
> As a Vietnam veteran (I was squadron dental surgeon for 1/7 Air Cav in the Delta, 1969-1970), I can't tell you how pleased I was to see an ad for Alice Cooper's new "Special Forces" album. When we weren't listening to incoming, we were listening to a lot of heavy music to get us through the tour. Alice wasn't around back then, but his albums like "Killer" would've kept us going just as much as Hendrix and the Stones did.
>
> Sincerely,
> T.G.V.
> Jasper, Missouri

But that was nothing compared to how the International Association Of Chiefs Of Police reacted when the truly transgressive video to "Prettiest Cop On The Block" was released and went into heavy rotation on every local music show around the country.

Writing in their magazine *Police Chief*, the IACP requested that off-duty officers working for police forces around the country should withdraw their services and not provide close security at any Alice Cooper concert. An editorial in the July 1981 issue bluntly titled "This Crap With A Crop Is No Cop" posits the police position in no uncertain terms:

"Not since this eminent organization was first formed by Sgt. Augustus "Weeb" Weeble back in May 1893 have we ever encountered such an affront to our front line officers. For the majority of you who aren't familiar with such smut unless it comes to your attention either in a bulletin or across your blotter, all members should know that Alice Cooper, a well-known deviant known to every interstate department, has besmirched the entire corps in a new film during which, looking like Joan Crawford and wearing a poor imitation of a police uniform, he extols what he deems to be the virtues of male police officers dressing like women while being on duty.

"It has come to our attention that Mr. Cooper (for those who are unaware, Cooper is a man who goes under an assumed alias using a woman's name) will be performing this song in American arenas across the country for the remainder of the year. As such, it is therefore the strong recommendation of this organization that all off-duty officers refrain from working these shows. We realize that many of you depend on this added income to support your families, but officers who are able to show just cause for compensation can apply for equivalent reimbursement through the IACP Fund."

The fact that Alice never performed "Prettiest Cop On The Block" live did little to assuage their ire. Follow me to the next exhibit.

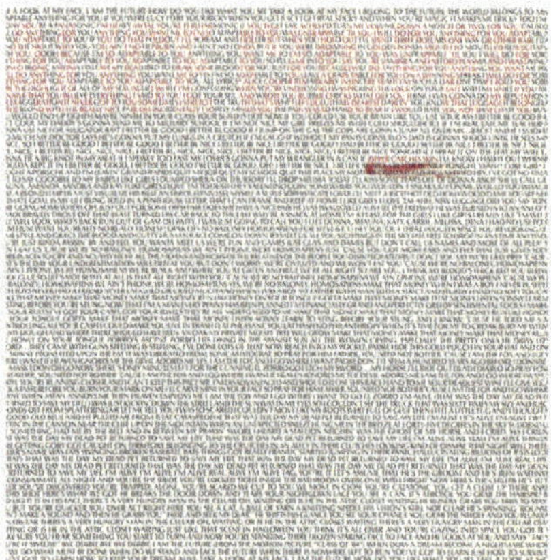

Exhibit #16

ZIPPER CATCHES SKIN

Acquired: 1982

This is an album that might best be described as featuring songs which displayed a lyrical stream of consciousness style, wherein Alice explored a myriad of topics ranging from throat-slashings to alien life forms to fanciful dark fantasies of Zorro.
I could go on, but this time we have bigger flesh to fry.

Exhibit #17

DADA

Acquired: 1983

Well, you've come this far so you might as well take another few steps and get all the way in. That's it. Now step into the light over there so's I can get a good look at you. We don't get many visitors out here these days. Specially at night. Used to, but that was before the incident. Traffic's kinda dried up since then. This is the last stop, you know. Ain't nothin' out there after this so it's a good thing you dropped by when you did. A fella can get lost in these parts real easy if he's not careful. Go on, pull up a chair and sit a spell. Take a load off. That's it. So where you from? What is that, a big city? Thought so. We don't have much use for big cities out this way. Y'see, out here we like to keep things small and manageable. Private. Why, I reckon I haven't been more'n twenty miles from this house since the day I was born. I was born here, you know. Long time ago. Of course back then there were a lot more people walkin' around but, well, you know how it is. People get tired of a place, they up 'n' leave. Wake up one mornin' and there's one less person in town. Just up and gone overnight. Soon there'll be no one left but us. Didn't I say? My boy, Sonny. Yeah, he's outside preparin' dinner right now. You damn right you can smell it. Sonny's got a whoppin' messa meat on the barbecue out back. Says the smell can bring a dead man back to life. Now I ain't seen that yet, but I know for a fact there are plenty of folk who'd die for it. I can see the smell's got you. You're lookin' right hungry so why don't you just shuck that jacket and stick around for some vittles? Ain't no bother at all. Like I said, company's slim pickins these days so we'd love to have you for dinner. You just sit yourself right down over there at the head of the table and I'll bring you a plate of Sonny's finest, soon as it's ready. That's it. I serve everyone who drops by. Why, here comes Sonny now. This is the last stop, you know.

If, as Alice says, "Dead Babies" is his most misunderstood song, then *DaDa* is his most misunderstood album.

Like any demanding problem child, it's extremely difficult to handle; almost impossible to ignore; and requires a serious investment of time and effort before you can even begin to understand what kind of language it's speaking. But then again, the severe strain of dealing with a sick family member is never an easy task even at the best of times, and *DaDa* is no exception to the rule.

So don't be lulled into a serene state of complacency when it occasionally opts to adopt a somewhat sedate manner, because lowering your guard for even a split second will result in you being lured teetering to the slavering maw's brink and then suddenly sucked in without even the slightest hint of warning.

But if you think I'm being overly melodramatic and would like to know the *real* gospel truth behind *DaDa*, go ask Alice: I think he'll know.

On second thought, don't waste your time because these days even Alice can't recall what was going on back then. And we're not talking about a mere memory lapse of just a song or two over the past forty years, we're talking full-fledged forgetfulness: Alice doesn't remember writing or recording any part of *DaDa* whatsoever.

Which is only fitting, given that Alice's albums are riddled with classic crime *noir* scenarios—not the least of which is the constantly recurring theme wherein a hapless protagonist mysteriously blacks out for an extended period of time, only to regain consciousness with gore-streaked hands, lying next to a dead body.

Still, never before in the history of rock 'n' roll (and most likely never again) has a premeditated total aesthetic blackout of such extreme magnitude ever occurred. The end result is Method recording in its purest form, taken to its ultimate inevitable extreme. And it's precisely this unfathomable edge that not only gives *DaDa* its strength, but its bone-chilling authenticity as well.

Of course, given what we now know about how successful and influential Alice's career has continued to be since then, it's tempting to look back at *DaDa* and see it not as the arcane masterpiece that many fans have fervently taken to their hearts but, rather, as just one of Alice's more unfamiliar albums.

Indeed, even diehard Alice fans at the time considered *DaDa* to be little more than his latest release. Only much later did they realize that this dark harbinger heralded the dawning of a unique artistic period in the career of their horror hero.

In the fall of 1983, however, none knew the awful truth: that *DaDa* would be the last Alice Cooper album for exactly three years. An album whose last song was ominously titled "Pass The Gun Around." An album that ended with the abrupt roar of a handgun, followed by the faint rhythmic *plip plip plip* of falling blood drops.

And while it's true that *Killer* also ended with a death, that sonic demise was the State-sponsored public execution of a convicted felon. Besides, *Killer* was the soundtrack to what, literally, was Alice's new death-defying stage show, thus maintaining a steadfast covenant with his audience that Alice would adhere to year after year. For no matter what fresh horrors he served up on record, fans could always count on Alice showing up in their town after every new release, dishing out the kind of innovative, show-stopping, hard-rock entertainment that only he could deliver. Even the intimate inmate padded cell confessions of *From The Inside* were followed up by Alice's raucous Madhouse Rock tour.

But not anymore. After *DaDa*, there was no tour. After the final echoing gunshot, there was no duking it out on stage with giant spiders or oversized liquor bottles. After the final *plip plip plip* there was absolutely nothing but a prolonged deafening silence for three long years. And if only for that reason alone, *DaDa* remains Alice's most unsettling and harrowingly apprehensive record.

But as is the case with most Alice Cooper albums, there's always far more to the story than just what the exposed surface reveals. And underneath *DaDa* in particular there swirls a churning miasma of malaise unlike any other; a pale pall of queasy uncertainty that lingers even to this day.

DaDa stands in stark contrast to all his other records because, unlike the humorous vaudevillain shock theatrics of *Billion Dollar Babies* or *Welcome To My Nightmare*, it's the one Alice Cooper album that doesn't deign to wrap its punches in punch lines. Which is precisely why listening to *DaDa* is such a claustrophobically suffocating experience: because this time you can't shake the inescapable sinking feeling that Alice isn't fooling around anymore; this time you intuitively know that it's as serious as serious gets.

This time he's saved the beast for last.

And lest you're of the opinion that the patriotic paean "I Love America" single-handedly belies what I've just said, then the joke's on you because this highly acclaimed song is the aural equivalent of driving through the desert on an empty tank and coming across a shimmering service station sign that says LAST GAS FOR NEXT FIFTY MILES only to find that your imminent salvation is slowly dissolving before your very eyes into nothing but a cruelly mocking mirage.

So make no mistake; when Alice ad-libs "Ain't going to catch me at no May Day rally, buddy" during the song's final fadeout, what he's *really* saying is: Last Humor For Next Three Years.

*** *** ***

Accepting and deciphering such apparent dichotomic contradictions is key to comprehending the uncanny enigma that is *DaDa*; a morbid mosaic inherently doomed by its very nature to be a thick thumbed-through catalogue of conflicting dualities, tethered by a thin skein of brittle psychosis.

Your descent into this depthless depravity begins with the cover painting which is nothing less than a clever construct that subtly alters the middle detail of Salvador Dali's famous illusionary painting of 1940, *Slave Market With The Disappearing Bust Of Voltaire*.

Much has been written about Alice's periodic dalliances with Dali over the years—and rightly so, as their notorious summits of surrealism continue to be the well-publicized stuff of envious legend. Ironically, however, it's this once-removed bold cross-breeding of iconic imagery which remains their most enduring legacy.

It's important to note that *DaDa*'s cover painting deviates from Dali's original masterpiece of perceptual rivalry in one critical paranoia way: its sole alteration is specifically in the area of Voltaire's eyes (nun); an intentional "de-facing" that symbolically suggests a form of extreme body modification which is entirely in keeping with the album's sinister subtext of congenital cannibalism (none). Seen in this context, an alternative meaning hidden in the painting's title becomes apparent by deconstructing the words "Slave" (to be in thrall), "Market" (a source of food), and "Disappearing Bust" (as remains gradually diminish upon consumption).

Even the name 'Voltaire' itself denotes a series of dual connotations in that Voltaire was the alter-ego of renowned author/philosopher François-Marie Arouet (a binary gendered name); he lived on an estate at Ferney (note the similarity to Alice's maiden name); and, of course, *Voltaire* is reminiscent of *volte-face*: literally an about-face.

It's no surprise then that, thus altered, Dali's perceptual reversal of an ambiguous image should become the very visual embodiment of *DaDa*'s Coopernican torment.

But if you find Alice's eerie sallow-faces on the front cover disturbing, you'd best brace yourself because that's nothing compared to the heightened cringe factor incestuously induced by the back cover's creepy locket-linked father and son portraits.

Despite years of speculation and intensive research, historians have yet to discover the true identity of the wan old geezer seen gazing over at his young malleable prey with knowing predatory leer. However, more than one astute critic has commented on his striking resemblance to Germany's infamous Dr. Caligari, whose real life exploits were the subject of a famous expressionist documentary.

Writing in an undated copy of the German underground music pamphlet *Euro Rockwerk*, noted enviromusicologist J. Mark Berkowitz cogently summarized this similarity in an article entitled 'Muse Mabuse Musik' when he wrote: "The Caligari resemblance on the back cover is an especially significant one given Caligari's much vaunted hypnotic willpower. *DaDa*'s wizened domineering father figure could very well in fact *be* Caligari, albeit much older in a post-incarceration incarnation. It is worth remembering, though, that despite initially appearing to have the upper hand both socially and psychologically, the criminal Caligari is ultimately seen to be clinically insane and at the very mercy of those whom he had sought to control."

By applying this role reversal template to *DaDa*'s delusional framework, it's easy to see the ever shifting power dynamic that comes into play as a result of the intense psychic struggle which is continually waged between father and son throughout the album. Is Alice forced to do the bidding of the father? Or is the father surreptitiously under the control of Alice? Indeed, one can even ask with some justification whether the Alice character actually exists at all or if, as many have surmised, he's but a chimeral phantasm of the father's imagination.

That such crucial questions should lack clearly defined rational answers only serves to further enrich *DaDa*'s already withered psychotic tapestry; and after Alice, no one was more capably adept at sculpting such dissipated environments than one of his oldest studio stalwarts, producer Bob Ezrin.

Formerly Ezrin had collaborated with Alice on such precedent-setting concept albums as *Love It To Death, Killer, School's Out, Billion Dollar Babies*, and *Welcome To My Nightmare*. But whereas those albums owed their successful stench of decrepit decadence in large part to a rabid mutation of the carnal and the charnel (ably augmented by a heaping helping of popular culture), *DaDa* would prove to be an entirely different stinking kettle of fish. For instead of drawing from Alice's traditional triad of societal influences (television - movies - theatre), *DaDa*'s raw source material would, by necessity, have to come from the secluded insular confines of a truly diseased mind.

Not since he helmed the sparse Weimar weeper *Berlin* exactly ten years earlier would Ezrin be called upon to fabricate what would turn out to be an even starker canvas of depleted dissonance. What he came up with was a cinematic soundscape unlike any other: a lush bubbling electro-acoustic cauldron in which Alice could cadaverously cavort.

And who better to provide the driving rhythm for such an introspective album than guitarist Dick Wagner, who had previously worked with Ezrin on both

Berlin and *Welcome To My Nightmare*. One listen to his majestic swirling solo on "Pass The Gun Around" will tell you all you need to know about how seriously he took his responsibility this time around. Aided and abetted by the other members of their grue crew, Ezrin and Wagner did an admirable job of transferring Alice's terrible torments onto tape—but now the rest is up to you.

So listen, learn, and try to discern which songs are based on reality and which ones are but fractured fragmented figments. Keep in mind, though, that all of them are dopplegängers, from the excruciating 'emotional plurality' of "No Man's Land" to the weary world-inversion of "Dyslexia." As such, decoding *DaDa* won't be an easy task by any means but, as with all great works of art, what you get *out* of it depends entirely on what you *bring* to it.

Y'see, Alice brought everything he had to bring up until that point, with such debilitatin' results that it took years before he fully recovered. So I reckon it's the least you can do to meet him halfway. And don't you worry none about shortchangin' Alice any by only goin' so far, because I guarantee that DaDa's mesmerizin' pull will do the rest. How do you think you got here in the first place? Weren't no accident, I'll tell you that. You knew where you were gonna end up, didn't you? Yeah, I can see it in your eyes. That's it. Well, gotta go now. Bye bye.

Exhibit #18

CONSTRICTOR

Acquired: 1986

Although you and I may have discerned the complex machinations behind *DaDa*, Alice found himself releasing such misunderstood albums into a rapidly changing marketplace where hard rock itself was floundering as a viable commodity. Everyone was feeling the same detrimental effects as rock 'n' roll underwent yet another transformation. Alice wisely used these turbulent times to lay back and assess the situation during his above-noted extended hiatus. The result would be the following two exhibits, both of which heralded Alice's long-awaited return to the roar of heavy metal.

And just like its title warned, on *Constrictor* Alice tightened his grip around the scrawny chicken neck of what was passing for rock music at that time and single-handedly squeezed new life into it. But there would always be those poor deluded souls whose only reason for living was to squeeze the life out of Alice. Which is why the man who invented controversy and turned it into an art form once again found himself in the craven crosshairs of countless numbers of grassroots organizations who, all around the world, had mobilized anew with the sole fanatical mission of trying to ban Alice from appearing in their town.

Indeed, the German state of Bavaria actually *did* manage to censor Alice's doll chopping performance of "Dead Babies" by threatening both him and his audience with imprisonment should Alice proceed with his act as planned. And although Alice didn't mind being sent to the big house, he wasn't about to subject his fans to the same unjust sentence.

"What have they done to deserve such a fate?" Alice asked the media during a scrum outside of Bavaria's historic Landsberg Prison. "But if any screw thinks he can keep *me* locked up, he's got another thing coming." Then, gesturing behind him, he sneered with a look of utter contempt. "The slammer ain't been built that can hold The Coop!" he snarled to a vigorous round of applause.

But some weren't clapping. As if on cue, Alice's old nemesis returned to rear her comely head, nearly a full decade and a half after she unsuccessfully tried to have the master tapes of *School's Out* destroyed, along with all existing copies. Once again, Dr. Lubna von Domina took to the pages of *Grafisches Gedächtnis* to vent her frustration with all things Alice:

"Oh, humanity! I ask you! How long must we have to put up with this vile blot? How long when we should be heralding

Photograph © James Pappaconstantine

instead people like my good friend Lorna! My good friend Lorna was a very accomplished woman! She took matters into her own hands and showed people that women can do anything they set their mind too! A woman with lots of courage and respect! My good friend Lorna is the kind of person we should be heralding! Instead, while Lorna lays forgotten, the world remembers, nay, champions, the likes of a man (no longer will I deign to mention his name) made infamous because his music was different from all of the others who just wanted to sing! He put more gore into his concerts! And many people went to see him because he sang scare songs about the Frankenstein and the Freddie Jason with the creepy Kiki Mama chant. Oh, humanity!"

Fortunately, shortly after this irrational piece of pandering saw print, Lubna von Domina suffered a complete nervous breakdown and was institutionalized for an indefinite period of time. Should you ever be in the region and have the opportunity to visit the *Grafisches Gedächtnis* building, you will see a small brass plaque affixed outside the main entrance, dedicating the edifice in her name. She deserves a lot less.

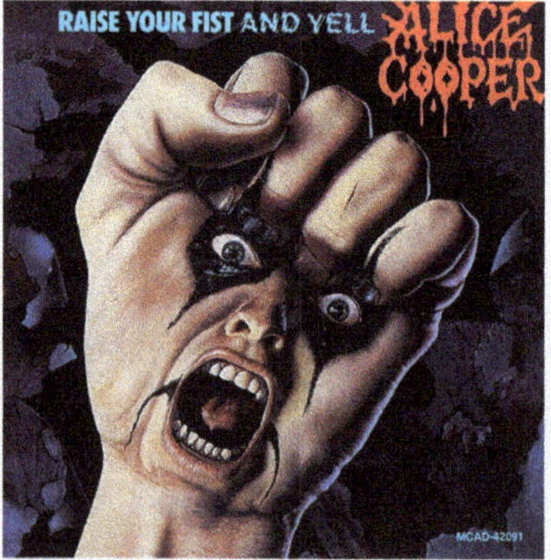

Exhibit #19

RAISE YOUR FIST AND YELL

Acquired: 1987

Meanwhile, back home in the land of the free, the rock-hating record-rating Parents Music Resource Center immediately installed Alice at the top of their Most Wanted list after reading a review in *Meat Beat* magazine that called *Raise Your Fist And Yell* "a grisly ensanguinated butcher block aural offal offering." As always, Alice wore the blue-rinse brigade's disgust as a badge of honor and publicly proclaimed as much during a media availability held after the world movie premiere of John Carpenter's *Prince Of Darkness*—a film made all the more memorable by containing a classic cinematic Coop cameo featuring a bi-psycho built for two.

Needless to say, it did not sit well with the PMRC when Alice referred to them as

"Prudish Mothers Repressing Coop" and they doubled down on their indignation by buying a full page ad in the *New York World-Telegram* headlined A WARNING TO ALL FAMILIES! "Alice Cooper's out forever!" it read in part. "PARENTS! Forget all the other bands we told you about because ALICE COOPER is the one you have to worry about the most!"

This muckraking scandalmongering text was accompanied by an equally exploitive paparazzi photograph of guitarist Kane Roberts liberally lathered in baby oil and lounging on a beach, wearing only a skimpy loincloth. However, this sensationalistic stunt backfired when hundreds of suburban housewives rushed to their local newsstand to buy up every copy of the *World-Telegram* containing the ad with the guitarist's photo. The rest of the newspaper went straight into the…

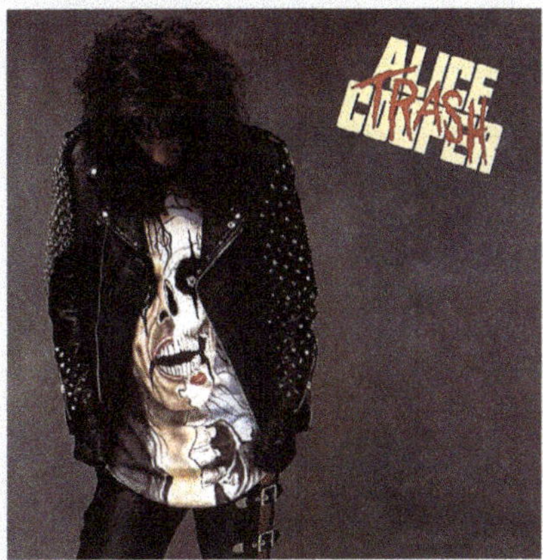

Exhibit #20

TRASH

Acquired: 1989

With this exhibit, we now enter into a new era of rock 'n' roll renaissance in the career of Alice Cooper. To quote what one rock rag wag wrote upon its release: "Having strongly re-established himself as one of the premier live rock 'n' roll acts in the business, Alice (who by now had worked the blood 'n' guts of the MCA *Constrictor* and *Raise Your Fist And Yell* years out of his system) signed with Epic Records and trained his creative sights on the making of what would become one of his biggest successes ever. Once again, he turned his attention to a familiar subject that had served him well since the days of "Yeah, Yeah, Yeah" and "Is It My Body." There was no denying that the old dynamics of sex and romance had, over the years, severely mutated into something scarier than even Alice could have ever envisioned. It was a source of inspiration just waiting to be used.

"Enlisting esteemed hit maker Desmond Child to co-write and produce his new album, Alice once again headed into the studio, accompanied by Aerosmith and Bon Jovi, both of whom were recruited to sit in on a few tracks. The result was *Trash*, which spawned the megahit 'Poison' and became the biggest-selling album of Alice's career. *Alice Cooper Trashes The World* was the new tour's theme, and the title was more than a fair description."

A tad on the patronizing side, perhaps, but I'll let this contributor continue as we move on to the next exhibit, if only to see if his words become less monotonous.

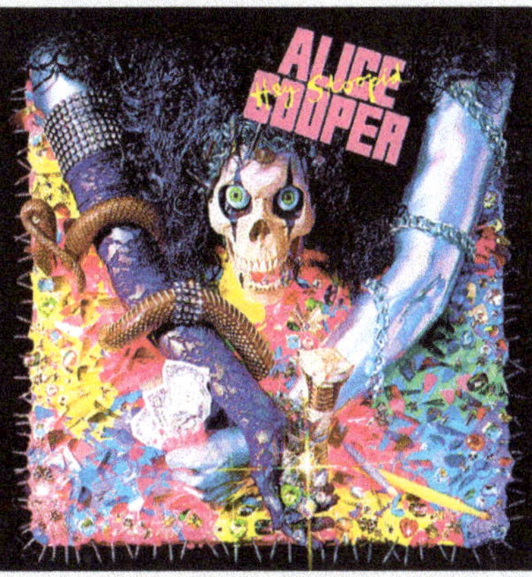

Exhibit #21

HEY STOOPID

Acquired: 1991

"Upon its completion, Alice went to work on the follow-up, *Hey Stoopid*. Included in the sessions this time around were special guests Ozzy Osbourne, Joe Satriani, Steve Vai, and Mötley Crüe. Also making an appearance was Guns N' Roses guitarist Slash, thus continuing an association that dates back to the first time Alice and the Gunners toured together in 1988—tandem teamwork that includes two collaborations: a hot-wired version of 'Under My Wheels' and *Use Your Illusion I*'s 'The Garden.'

"Their respect for Alice, however, is by no means an isolated incident; countless others in the music business have also showed their appreciation by covering Alice Cooper material. A double-album tribute entitled *Welcome To Our Nightmare* features the talents of numerous alternative bands, while *Humanary Stew* is a tribute album that includes, among others, Roger Daltrey and Megadeth."

Still awake after enduring that perfunctory piffle? Good. Shall we continue?

Photograph © James Pappaconstantine

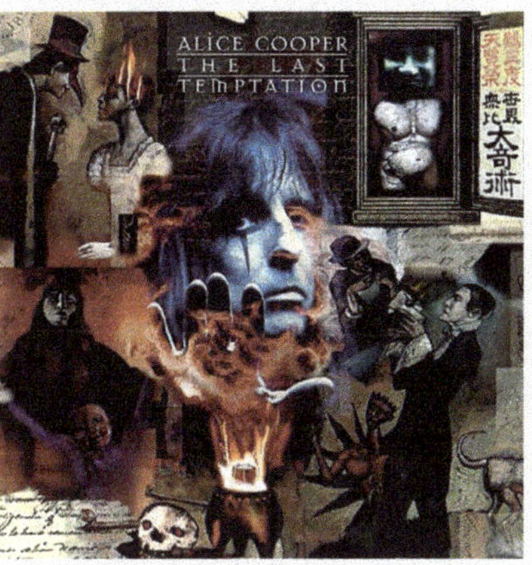

Exhibit #22

THE LAST TEMPTATION

Acquired: 1994

And now, if I may lower myself to such a dire depth of desperation, you see before you an actual record company press release, prepared exclusively for this exhibit. And while we usually abstain from acknowledging such lower forms of expression, in this specific instance you will note that it differs from all other promotional items in that it is bound with an actual glossy cover. Opening it, one finds several sheets of matte black paper, upon which are printed white letters. Those letters form a series of words which, in turn, comprise a number of paragraphs, all of which could, at best, be charitably described as being written in a breathless over-the-top fashion—one hesitates to use the word *style*.

And although Epic Records wisely decided not to attribute the author by name, one need not look far to see the tell-tale signs of what could loosely be called a literary technique. The very fact that the anonymous comma-eschewing author actually interviewed Alice Cooper and then had the temerity to bury his learned words under a puerile weight of rampant alliteration and exhausting run-on sentences tells you all you need to know.

Then again, what *else* do you expect from someone who obviously has no compunction about tossing around ten dollar words while using a shameless surfeit of hackneyed recycled phrases extracted from past pieces? Truly I say to you that it would be foolhardy in the extreme to hazard a guess as to the authorship of this singular self-serving promotional document, which is why the reader is strongly advised not to draw his or her own personal conclusion as to who is responsible for writing it.

*** *** ***

Sigmund Freud believed that our dreams provide us with vital clues to the nature of our psychological problems. But Freud is dead.

So, given that today's new standard of currency on the shock markets of the world is nothing less than one long screaming nightmare, is it any wonder that we're in dire need of a new messenger with the communicative power to lead us from the depths of doubt and dark despair? And having come to that conclusion, there's no one better qualified for the job than the man who wrote the book on nightmares: rock 'n' roll's master agitator of the mind, the legendary Alice Cooper.

On his new Epic album, *The Last Temptation*, Alice isn't fooling around. One look at the cover—a powerfully disturbing graphic created by artist Dave McKean—is enough to make clear his present intent. "*The Last Temptation* is the first album I've done in a long time that's a true concept album," says Alice. "It has such a definite story line that I really didn't think I could do it justice by only putting it out on record."

Which is why *The Last Temptation* comes packaged with the first issue of a trilogy of Marvel Comics based on the album. Both arose from a concept jointly conceived by Alice Cooper and comic book writer and novelist Neil Gaiman (whose very Cooperesque character, "Sandman," is his best-known creation). Unlike *Tales From The Inside*, Marvel's previous Alice Cooper comic book (based on his 1978 album *From The Inside*), this atmospheric new series—written by Gaiman and illustrated by Michael Zulli—complements and expands upon *The Last Temptation* in a depth of detail unavailable anywhere else.

As Alice explains: "*The Last Temptation* takes place in an average Middle American town where one particular group of young boys, who think they've done and seen everything, stumble across this old vaudeville theater that they've never noticed before in an old part of town." Emerging from the shadows within to greet them is a mysterious figure called The Showman (based on the classic Alice Cooper character) who runs the theater along with his beguiling female assistant, the temptress Mercy.

None of the kids accept the invitation to enter for a free show, except for one brave boy named Steve—who will be instantly recognizable to fans as the selfsame schizoid protagonist of Alice Cooper's groundbreaking concept album, *Welcome To My Nightmare*. Once inside, it is indeed showtime, and Steven's temptation at the hands of The Showman begins in earnest. But will he succumb? "It's all based on the question of whether or not Steven gives in to modern-day temptation," says Alice.

Creating the proper sonic atmosphere for The Showman and his theatrical environment was so essential to the success of *The Last Temptation* that Alice never considered working with just one producer. He teamed with three different aural experts to sculpt the richly powerful sound he desired.

Andy Wallace was recruited for the grand opening and closing numbers "Sideshow" and "Cleansed By Fire," as well as Alice's collaborations with Soundgarden's Chris Cornell on "Unholy War" and "Stolen Prayer." Don Fleming, on the other hand, was responsible for the street-tough sound of "Lost In America," "Nothing's Free," and "Bad Place Alone" while the team of Duane Baron and John Purdell took the helm for the more melodic explorations of "You're My Temptation," "Lullaby," and "It's Me."

Aside from the two Chris Cornell background vocal performances, *The Last Temptation*—in contrast to Alice's previous Epic albums, *Trash* and *Hey Stoopid*—features no guest musicians. Backed solely by his current touring band, this time the music is pure, unadulterated Alice Cooper.

The incidents, adventures, and achievements which comprise his career proclaim Alice Cooper a true original in a world where originality is disdained and complacency is the norm. His precedent-shattering audacity did more than alter the face of rock 'n' roll. Alice Cooper virtually invented rock and theater; influenced the entire field of fashion; brilliantly satirized America's obsession with sex, death, and money; and wrote and recorded a library shelf of classic albums like *Love It To Death*, *Killer*, *School's Out*, *Billion Dollar Babies*, *Welcome To My Nightmare*, and *Trash*. He's continually punctured the balloons of pomposity and pretense—and pushed the envelope of rock 'n' roll—on the way to not only rock stardom but the status of a household name.

"In the '90s, there are certain words we avoid or think we've outgrown," Alice concludes. "Words like temptation, sin, redemption. These words are old words, but they're not dead. These are words that I wanted to explore with this new album."

Now, with the release of *The Last Temptation*, Alice Cooper adds yet another extraordinary chapter to a remarkable and timeless body of work.

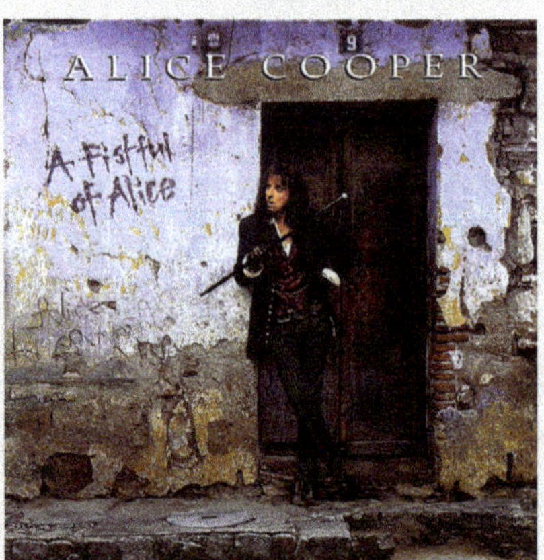

Exhibit #23
A FISTFUL OF ALICE
Acquired: 1997

When the promotional department at Hollywood Records learned that the aforesaid anonymous author—you know, the one with a penchant for repetition—had personally interviewed Alice to promote *The Last Temptation* for Epic Records, they thought that lightning would strike twice if he was hired to interview The Coop again, this time for *A Fistful Of Alice*. The good news is that lightning *did* strike. The bad news is that it got caught in a bottle.

*** *** ***

PART ONE: THE SETUP

Uh-uh. I know what you're thinkin'. "Does this album rate six stars or only five?" Well to tell you the truth, it's so exciting I've kinda lost track myself. But seeing as how this is *A Fistful Of Alice*, the most powerful live Alice Cooper album in the world and will blow your ears *clean* off, you've gotta ask yourself just one question: "*Do I like hard-edged, in-your-face, kick-ass rock 'n' roll?*"

Well, *do* ya, punk?

'Cause if you do, and I *know* you do, then Alice has got just what you're looking for—and it's located deep in the heart of Cabo San Lucas, Mexico, where tequila is cheap and audiences demand that their rock 'n' roll contains nothing less than raw extract of rattlesnake shake.

So if you're expecting a chance to doze off in a mid-day siesta, then you've *definitely* come to the wrong place because Alice has pulled into Sammy Hagar's legendary Cabo Wabo Cantina and pulled out all the stops to ensure that *A Fistful Of Alice* accurately captures the unadulterated, pure putrid adrenaline-addled essence of his senses-shattering live performances.

Face it: there are few trends in modern music that Alice Cooper didn't anticipate and even fewer still that haven't been incorporated by this innovative showman into one of the most bizarre and entertaining rock attractions of all time.

The audacious precedent-shattering and inspirational taboo-defiling hoodlum flamboyance of Alice Cooper did more than forever alter the face of rock 'n' roll as we now know it. For not only did Alice virtually invent rock as theatre, he created new fashion trends, sparked a new sexual revolution, established higher standards for teenage decadence, and found time on top of all this to write and record a library of classic rock 'n' roll albums tinged with black humor and tainted with a brilliant streak of satire.

Love It To Death. Killer. School's Out. Billion Dollar Babies. Muscle Of Love. Welcome To My Nightmare. Trash. The Last Temptation.

These are the Alice Cooper albums of legend, well renowned all around the world. But as anyone who's ever seen him in concert will easily attest, you haven't even *begun* to hear the songs on these albums performed until you've heard Alice Cooper perform them *live*.

The fact that Alice Cooper is rock music's first and foremost influential legendary statesman of outrage is far beyond reproach. Take a good look around you at what passes for rock 'n' roll these days and you'll agree that any act worth its weight in rock 'n' roll, makeup, theatrics, and hard-edged, in-your-face, kick-ass punk attitude owes more than just a passing nod of respect in the direction of Alice Cooper.

What's *that* you say? You want *proof?*

Y'know, Alice was kinda *hopin'* you'd say that 'cause he's got thirteen lucky reasons he'd like you to *listen* to—but you'd better get your doctor to sign this medical waver first. That's how life-threatening *A Fistful Of Alice* is.

But don't take *my* word for it, listen to what Alice *himself* has to say about *A Fistful Of Alice*. This is *Alice* speakin'...

PART TWO: THE PAYOFF

"Ignore the scorpions," Alice advises with a smile as we sit and talk in the back room of Sammy Hagar's Cabo Wabo Cantina. "*Sure* they're poisonous, but they add *character* to the place."

"Here." Alice uncorks another bottle of Primo 100% Rotgut with his teeth and places it in front of me, right next to my empty shot glass.

"Aren't *you* having any?" I ask.

"I never *drink*...anymore. Remember my first live album*? The Alice Cooper Show?* It's my least favorite album. I had such a bad time, I don't even remember recording it! It was the last thing I did during the alcoholic phase of my career—which is why, after twenty years, I decided it was time to record another live one and get it *right* this time."

"Is that why we're here?" I ask as I empty my shot glass again. "That's right," Alice replies. "I was about to start rehearsals for my next tour when Sammy Hagar suggested that I come and record the results here, in front of 200 people, instead of in a stadium situation. I've always liked Mexico, so I thought: why not make one big party out of it?

"Sammy played some guitar—hey, it's his place, right?—and I called up Rob Zombie and Slash and invited them to also come down and join in. Rob does a great job singing on 'Elected' and 'Feed My Frankenstein' and as for Slash, well, I don't need hammering or technique, and Slash is just like Joe Perry, my other favorite guitarist: a straight ahead, all the way, right down the middle, rock 'n' roll guitar player."

I steady my hand as Alice fills up my glass for the fourth time. "What about the song selection?" I manage to ask. Alice leans forward. "I *didn't* want to do 'Billion Dollar Babies.' Sure, I wanted to play some of the old songs, but I also wanted to do some different stuff instead, like 'Teenage Lament '74.' I wanted to give the *real* Alice Cooper fans something *new* to listen to—but that doesn't mean we modernized any of the songs. We still play them pretty faithfully to the original versions."

"What about the new studio song at the end of *A Fistful Of Alice?*" I slur.

"You mean 'Is Anyone Home'? It's the ultimate lonely song," Alice confides. "I am truly a rebel against computers—I *never* want to be able to work one! There are people so dependent on the Internet that they never go out! I picture the guy in 'Is Anyone Home' living in some apartment in a big city; a guy who's tired of going out to bars—tired of going out *anywhere*. Eventually, he ends up living all alone in his little cell, with the only thing connecting him to the outside world being his computer.

"Of course," Alice laughs, "it ends up that everyone *else* has gone out and he's the only one left inside, trying in vain to find someone to connect to!"

"Any last words before I go?" I ask, sliding off my chair.

"Last words? Yeah, I got some last words," says Alice menacingly as he stands up and dusts off his leather pants. "Tell everyone that Alice has more energy now than he did twenty years ago! Better yet, just play them *A Fistful Of Alice* and they'll get the message!"

"That's it?" I ask as I begin to pass out.

"No, there's one more thing," Alice says as he looks down at me. "You're cut off."

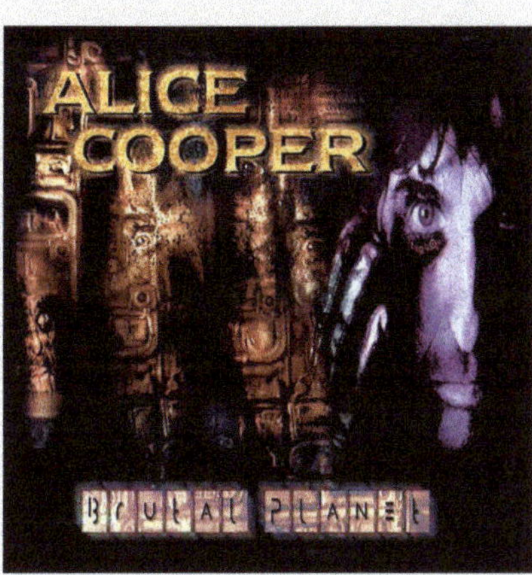

Exhibit #24

BRUTAL PLANET

Acquired: 2000

What we've got here is a triumph of communication and rumination in sonic sync, solidly ensconced within the album that many Alice fans were waiting for; one which accurately improved on the bludgeoning heavy rock sound of the day while adeptly addressing the pressing issues of time immemorial. For with the aptly-named *Brutal Planet*, not only did Alice show that he could be as industrially din 'n' dark as the rest of the new whippersnappers nipping at his heels, but that he could also be far more thoughtfully enlightening than any of them could ever hope to be. In fact, there are many reasons as to why this...

Hold on, just a second! That looks like... It is! Quick, over there to your left, coming out of the gift shop! It's legendary progressive rock keyboardist Rick Wakeman of Yes! Rick! Rick, over here! He's coming this way! Isn't this exciting? Rick, I didn't know you were an Alice Cooper fan!

"Alice, in fact, is a real good mate of mine. Apart from the non-drinking thing, or the straightening out, the other thing we have in common is that we're both huge fanatical golfers. In fact, we stood on the street last November in London—we were both staying at the same hotel, the Leonard, in London—and we were both leaving at the same time and it was really weird that we stood on the pavement discussing golf for about 45 minutes. Now, if anybody would have said to me years ago that Alice and me would be standing on the street in London discussing the merits of the PGA tour and how our golf game was... I mean, it was incredibly surreal. But that's what happens. What happens to old rock 'n' rollers? They stop drinking and they start playing golf!"

Rick, I was just saying that on *Brutal Planet*, Alice has been tackling some of the more serious issues going on in the world today, *vis-à-vis* good versus evil.

"I'm biased, I'm a big Alice Cooper fan. I have been all the time. I think one of the good things that Alice is doing... It's great when you can think clearly enough to express yourself musically on how your thought patterns change and how you think. And if you can do that in a way that's still entertaining, then you've succeeded. And Alice succeeds in doing that. There's a lot of artists who try to put over their thoughts and words in music and it's thunderingly boring. But Alice is one of those who can do it in a very entertaining way. Cheers!"

Thanks, Rick!

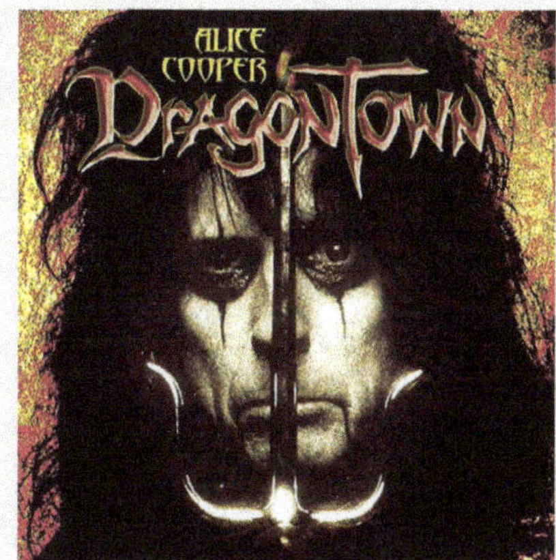

Exhibit #25

DRAGONTOWN

Acquired: 2001

Gosh, wasn't it great running into Rick Wakeman like that? What a swell guy! Now, for this next exhibit, you might want to put your headphones back on to hear this display properly translated.

Dragontown shì Alice Cooper de dì shíwǔ zhâng gèrén zhuânjí. Tâ yú nián zài Pçn huǒ jìlù shàng fâxíng. Yǔ *Brutal Planet* yîyàng, zhè zhâng zhuânjí zhǎnxiànle bǐ tâ zhîqián de xǔduô zhuânjí gèng zhòng de jînshǔ fçnggé. Tâ zài gônggào pái de "dǐngjí dúlì zhuânjí" páiháng bǎng shàng páimíng dì wèi, zài gônggào pái qiáng páiháng bǎng shàng páimíng dì wèi, zhè shì tâ zì nián de *DaDa* yǐlái de zuìdî zhuânjí páiháng bǎng biǎoxiàn, hòu zhě gçnběn méiyǒu shàng bǎng.

Zhè shì dì yî zhâng bù bâohán dân qû de Alice Cooper lùyîn shì zhuânjí. Jǐnguǎn kù pò zài nián hé nián de *Descent Into Dragontown* xúnyǎn zhông xúnyǎnle zhè zhâng zhuânjí, dàn zhǐyǒu sì shǒu *Dragontown* gçqǔ – "xìng, sǐwáng hé jînqián," "huànxiǎng nánrén," "měi gè nǚrén dôu yǒu yîgè míngzì," hé "Triggerman" – zài zhè cì zhîchí xúnyǎn zhông wánquán yǎnchû, zhǐyǒu "xìng, sǐwáng hé jînqián" hé "huànxiǎng rén" liú zàile zuìhòu. Chúle nián yuè zài xúnhuí yǎnchû qíjiân de wǔ chǎng "Disgraceland" yǎnchû wài, *Dragontown* méiyǒu zài zhuânjí de zhîchí xúnhuí yǎnchû jiéshù hòu xiànchǎng yǎnchû.

Yî jîdûji‡o yînyuË wÈi dǎoxi‡ng de z·zhǏ de biânjì jiâng k˘ pÚ bǐ zuÚ chçng tâ "zhuâ zh˘ mÛguǐ de m‡ikËfçng bǏng shǏt˙ xiËlÚu tâ de dǎnli‡ng bǏng jiçl˘ tâ de xié'Ë jǐhu‡.î JǏnyîb˘ zhǐchû ìZhË shǏ t‡i wǎnleî jiçl˘le ìw˙jûw˙sh˘ de zhçnxi‡ng," zhǐchû "tông wǎng dǏy˘ de d‡ol˘ sh‡ng d‡och˘ dôu shǏ hǎorÈn hÈ sh‡nyǏî bǏng jiâng "xǏng, sǐw·ng hÈ jînqi·nî bǐ zuÚ zhçny·n, Èr b˘shǏ zhçnzhËng guâny˙ ìxǏng, sǐw·ng hÈ jînqi·n, d‡n zhËngr˙ shËngjîng suǒ shuô dǏ n‡y‡ng fǎnduǏ tâ.

Qǔm˘ ìDisgracelandî k‡n d‡o k˘ pÚ z‡i mÛfǎng mâo w·n shì tǏgông shîj˘. ZhË shǒu gç yǔ pǔ léi sî lǏ de zuǏhÚu jǐ ni·n hÈ suìhÚu de sǐw·ng yǐjì zhË shǒu gç yǒuguân, k˘ pÚ shuô: ìWǒ yǒudiǎn z‡i pǏngl˘n tâ de huângmi˘ xǏng, shǏshì sh‡ng, yǒushǐ yǐl·i zuǏ wěid‡ de y·ogǔn yîngxióng sǐ y˙ cËsuǒ.î

Zǒngzhî, *Dragontown* shǏ guânk‡n *Urotsukidoji: Legend Of The Overfiend* shì tîng de wánměi zhuânjì!

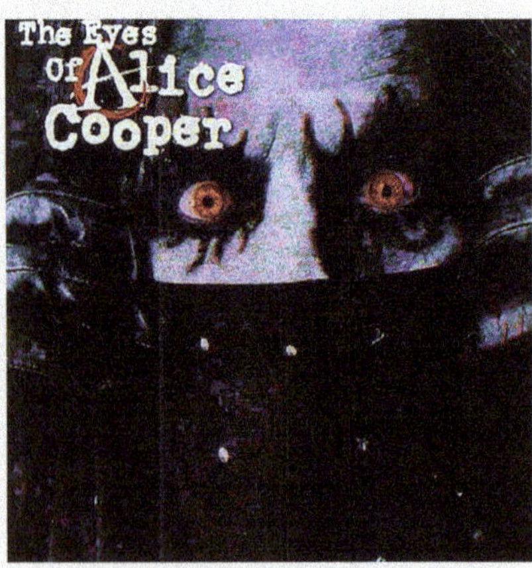

Exhibit #26
THE EYES OF ALICE COOPER
Acquired: 2003

Good evening. My fellow citizens, I come before you tonight not to bury Alice but to praise him.

Now, before the nattering nabobs of negativism start slinging incendiary phrases like "conflict of interest" around, just let me say this about that: The readers of *Alice Cooper Confidential* have a right to know whether their rock critic is taking payola. Well, let me make one thing perfectly clear: I am *not* taking payola. I've earned everything I've got.

And although I don't live high on the hog, as my good friend Jim "Dandy" Mangrum would say, I did manage to save up enough money once to buy my girl a coat. Not a fur coat, mind you, but a good cloth coat. She wanted a leather jacket, like those Ramones wear, however the price tag was too steep for my humble means. But she understood, and that's why I love her.

Now then, about this new Alice Cooper album.

The first thing you'll notice, as evidenced by the album's title and cover photo, is that Alice has changed his trademark eye makeup for the first time in more than 30 years. To fully understand the significance of this move, it must be remembered that the single most important factor determining Alice's image has been the evolution of his eye makeup from mincing to menacing.

The eerily disturbing, fem-demented, spider-eye design of *Pretties For You*, *Easy Action*, and *Love It To Death* evolved after *Killer* into two dark malevolent orbs of death which would instantly be known as Alice's trademark visage, cementing his new persona as chief atrocity exhibitor of a new brand of dementia: Evil as a commodity.

Thus, by reverting to a modified splatter design, Alice is consciously signifying a return to the snidely snarky and darkly droll humor of his earliest days; a maverick move which signals—as befitting the anarchy logo adorning Alice's name—that it's time to ditch the dire-warning diatribes and have some rebellious fun for a change, in lieu of yet another album crammed with cautionary warnings.

Because after the salvation-seeking, torn-from-today's-headlines trilogy of *The Last Temptation; Brutal Planet;* and *Dragontown*, Alice has opted to abjure those harrowing urban terror tales and take a break from trying to salvage the world. Having hammered home his moral point in spades, Alice has stepped down off his soapbox and removed his *The End Is Near* sandwich board to rock 'n' roll like there's no tomorrow. And starting with the very first track, he does just that.

In "What Do You Want From Me," the macho man who hated Oprah and opera in *Dragontown*'s "Fantasy Man" becomes the ultimate hussy-whipped protagonist who's forced to give up seeing his drinking buddies because his worst half demands to be escorted to the opera instead. Yet no matter what this poor pud does, it's never enough to sate her scabrous soul. "I burned all of my porno," he laments. "I disconnected my X-Box! Dumped all my girlfriends! Given you everything! What do you want from me, baby?"

Don't ask because, in "Man Of The Year," Alice does everything it takes to be a model citizen but, just like the harried organization man profiled in *Brutal Planet*'s "Sanctuary," he's doomed to an early demise from day one. There's literally an upside to this downer, however: "I lied in perfect state," Alice brags, breaking one of the seven deadlies even in death. "And later I will meet the Lord. I bet he can't wait to meet The Man Of The Year."

Then, as if suffering through yet another ignominious identity crisis in "Between High School And Old School" wasn't bad enough, Alice gets the deep freeze treatment in "Novocaine." Then, adding insult to injury, he gets the long distance cold shoulder in "Bye Bye, Baby" but what a way to go. I tell ya, there's nothing like a buncha horny horns bleating behind a wall of wailing guitars to generate that classic swaggering "Under My Wheels" feel. And in 2003, it doesn't get much better than that.

But it does get a lot worse. "Be With You Awhile" is the kind of wretched, mush-sodden, romantic ballad that only a submissive castrate could be forced to enjoy. But, hey, even The Coop's got a right to make a few bucks from all them snoozak soft-rock radio stations, right? Besides, that's why Philo Farnsworth invented the fast-forward button.

Luckily, it's at this point that the album kicks into nitro-fueled overdrive beginning, appropriately enough, with "Detroit City," a witty inner-city ditty which you all know about by now. Face it: any song that can namedrop Iggy Pop; David Bowie; MC5; Ted "Offensive" Nugent; Bob Seger; Kid Rock; and Eminem in a scant 30 seconds flat—thus leaving lots of primo space for Mr. Kramer to work his magic—is more than worthy of the Motor City moniker.

Keeping the revs into the red, "Spirits Rebellious" is as wildly raucous a raver as you're likely to hear these days. But it's not all fun and games, as "This House Is Haunted" ably attests. This theatrical contrapuntal centerpiece is the best aural delineation of Alice's inner demons since *Welcome To My Nightmare*'s "Steven." No, really. This diseased little jewel is a malignancy of the highest order.

And as for "Love Should Never Feel Like This," suffice to say that this is what a romantic song *should* sound like. Has any writer ever described the debilitating physical effects of love more accurately than Alice when he says that it makes you "look like a junkie who's been strung out on meth"? Nah, didn't think so.

Meanwhile, "The Song That Didn't Rhyme" is an ironic cautionary tale of woe which concerns the all-too-common malady of a studio session gone seriously wrong. It's all about "a three-minute waste of your time, with no redeeming value of any kind," Alice warns. "But thanks for the $12.99."

Then, in the best "I'm Your Gun" curtain-closing tradition, the final two tracks ("I'm So Angry" and "Backyard Brawl") roar toward the finish line like a mobile WMD lab with acid-severed brakes, steered by Slim Pickens. Make no mistake, *The Eyes Of Alice Cooper* is a much better rock 'n' roll album than *Trash* ever was.

Maybe it's that painting stashed in the attic but, amazingly, for whatever the reason, the trademarked tough-as-nails timbre in Alice's voice is as strong as ever. Stop me if you've heard this one before but, hard as it may be for you to believe—and, truth be told, sometimes I can't believe it myself—Alice Cooper is still here, rocking out like all get-out.

Which is why, even though Alice hasn't attended a political convention since the last time he ran for President, there's no doubt in my mind whatsoever that Wild Party delegates the world over will unanimously nominate this album on the very first ballot.

In other words, *The Eyes* have it.

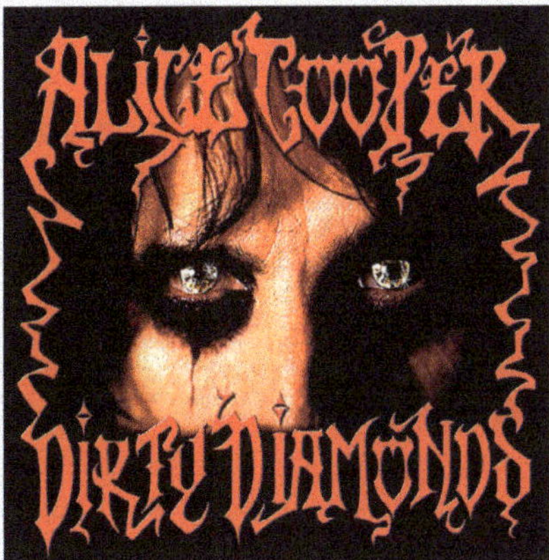

Exhibit #27

DIRTY DIAMONDS

Acquired: 2005

Whatever you do, don't let the psychedelic cover lettering fool ya 'cause, although there ain't nothin' dopey about this hep 'n' heavy hard rocker, it *is* trippy as all get out. F'rinstance, willya just dig that crazy Kyuss sound on the title track? And how about the buffeting butane brawls-to-the-wall supersonics of… Oh, gosh, it's getting late and close to closing time so we'd better get a move on.

HPTJ01 OR1L C 1 COMP EHPTJ01
0.00 LEFT ORCHESTRA 0.00 09:33
CN 41520
OR1L ALICE COOPER OR1L
IN CONCERT
C 1 HAMILTON PLACE GREAT HALL C
CIE/GST.INCL
1OCT04 FRI OCT 1 2004 - 8:00PM

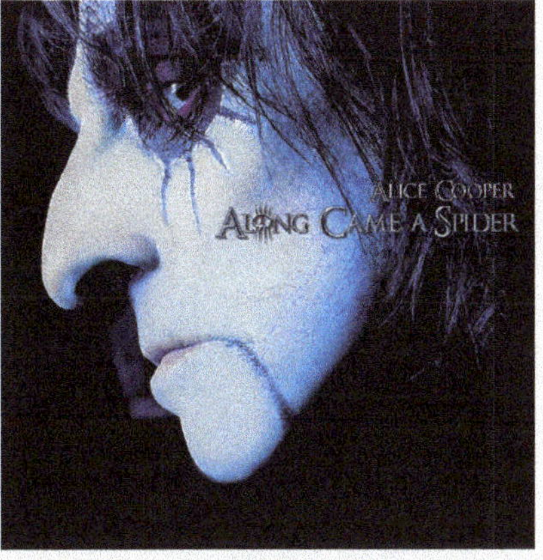

Exhibit #28

ALONG CAME A SPIDER

Acquired: 2008

Please hurry, it's getting late and we have to… Yes, this is the album about Steven from *Welcome To My Nightmare*, but we don't have *time* for that right now. Yes, yes, S-T-E-V-E-N and S-P-I-D-E-R both start with the letter S and both have six letters with two of them aligning, very good. No, I don't know *why* the color in the video was drained to make everything green, maybe it's a *bile* thing. Now will you *please* hurry along?

Exhibit #29

WELCOME 2 MY NIGHTMARE

Acquired: 2011

Yes, yes, I *know* I said that *Along Came A Spider* was about Steven from *Welcome To My Nightmare*, but so is *this* one. No, it's *not* a trilogy. No, "The Underture" is *not* the same song from *Tommy*. No, "Disco Bloodbath Boogie Fever" is *not* a previously unreleased outtake from the *Alice Cooper Goes To Hell* recording sessions. Will you *please* stop asking so many questions and move along?

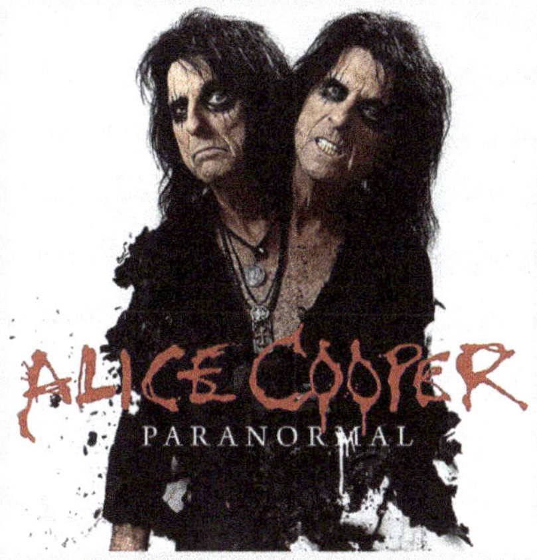

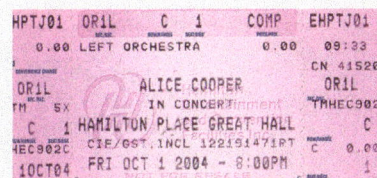

Exhibit #30

PARANORMAL

Acquired: 2017

I'm sorry, but I simply *refuse* to talk about this record. Why? It's none of your *business* why. I *know* I brought up the subject but… Well, all right. If *that's* how you feel about it, I'll *tell* you why. The reason why I won't talk about this record is because I wrote a message to Alice Cooper through his website. That's right. I wrote a message to him. And do you know when that was? It was back in 2002, that's when it was.

Yes, I *know* it's a long time ago. Reply? What makes you think I received a reply? I *never* received a reply! Not even a simple automated boilerplate thank you. You'd think that the person in charge…

Of *course* somebody got my message! You don't think that they just *disappear* into thin air, do you? I mean, why ask for messages when you don't even have the common decency to… *What?* Of *course* I still remember what I wrote. Because my lawyer insists that I keep a copy right here in my saddle bag, *that's* why. Here, *here* it is.

"Dear Alice, I was just watching the X-FILES and it occurred to me that you should make a record about UFOs and aliens. I think this is a great idea and I even have a title for you to use PARABNORMAL which is a combination of paranormal and abnormal. Please let me know what you think."

Yes, well, we *have* sent a cease and desist letter to everyone, even though I *still* think that *Parabnormal* is a *much* better album title than… Well, I certainly *hope* to get something from them. After all, you don't think I want to spend the rest of my life in this *mausoleum* doing this *docent* work, *do* you? What do you *mean* I sound prissy?

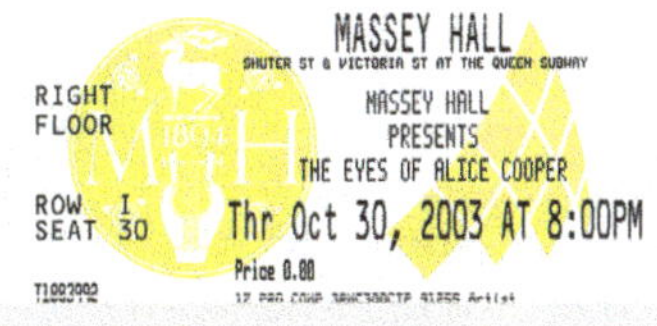

Photograph ©
Phillip Solomonson
Philamonjaro.com

Photograph ©
Phillip Solomonson
Philamonjaro.com

Photograph ©
Phillip Solomonson
Philamonjaro.com

All photographs ©
Robert Matheu

Exhibit #31

DETROIT STORIES

Acquired: 2021

Those flickering lights mean it's last call to leave the hall before they lock the doors. I'm sorry we ran out of time, but don't worry. Anyone interested in hearing about stories from Detroit is invited to read the exclusive previously unpublished interview with Alice that can be found near the back of your guide. Oh, and make sure you don't forget to buy a copy of *Rock Critic Confidential* by Jeffrey Morgan on your way out. All proceeds go to… Oh, there go those flickering *lights* again! Well, thank you for coming and I *do* hope you enjoyed the tour. This way to the egress.

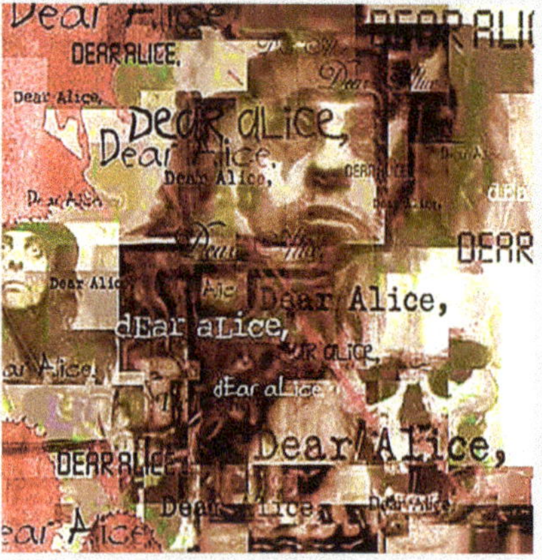

Exhibit X

DEAR ALICE

Acquired: ?

Oh, you're still here? Got locked in for the night, did you? Well, I *warned* you. And to think that it's a long weekend, too. Now you're stuck until… Oh, I live upstairs so I'm not going anywhere.

This? Oh, this is a very *special* exhibit. So special, in fact, that it's permanently closed off to the public. But since you're going to *be* here for a while, I don't suppose there's any harm in you listening.

You see, these are rare recordings of Alice Cooper reading his fan mail. You know, the messages that his fans write to him on his website? They're printed out so Alice can record them during his protracted stays in the Renfield Nelson Asylum. We keep them all archived on these water-cooled exabyte drives.

Now hold still while I wrap this gaffer tape around your ears so the headphones won't fall off. After all, you don't want to miss a single minute of… There, that's nice and snug. How about a little more here around your wrists so you can't lower the volume or turn off the… There, that should do it.

Okay, let the show begin, now you're ready. I'll come back in a few hours and check up on you.

Photograph © Ted Kutyla

SECTION 1969

PHOTOGRAPHED BY NASH THE SLASH

Photograph ©
Nash The Slash

Photograph ©
Nash The Slash

Photograph ©
Nash The Slash

18

SECTION FIVE

THE COOP CONVERSATION

Photograph © Alan Gibson

Photograph © Shawn Cook

THE COOP CONVERSATION

We close with this previously unpublished *tête-à-tête* from 2009, wherein the authorized biographer of two (count 'em) two Hall Of Fame rockers talks to one inductee about the other inductee. So sit back and relax as the stars of our show have a casual chit-chat about how things were, way back at the very beginning. No, really, *do* stop me if you've heard this one before but, the telephone is ringing...

> ***Thank you for calling so we can talk about The Stooges***

JEFFREY MORGAN: Hello.

BRIAN NELSON: Horrible.

JEFFREY: Horrible?

BRIAN: Horrible.

JEFFREY: *What's* horrible?

BRIAN: *Everything's* horrible.

JEFFREY: Wait a minute, who *is* this?

BRIAN: Oh, puh-*lease*. It's… *horrible*.

JEFFREY: You've got the wrong number. I'm expecting a *very* important phone call from Iggy Pop and you're tying up the line, my friend.

BRIAN: [*laughs*] Let me put Mr. Alice Cooper on the phone for you.

ALICE: Hi Jeffrey, this is Alice. [*laughs*] How *are* ya?

JEFFREY: I'm doing good, how are *you* doing?

ALICE: Horrible.

JEFFREY: [*laughing*] Well, join the party—and thank you for calling so we can talk about The Stooges.

ALICE: Oh, yeah, no problem at all. I mean, you know, it's the kinda thing where I kinda came up at the same time as Iggy and so, you know, I was watching this guy. When you're from L.A. or Phoenix and you go to Detroit and you're playing a big pop festival for the first time… I'd never heard of the MC5 before. I had never heard of Iggy and The Stooges and so those were the bands that were on this festival. And I'm watching the MC5 and I said: "Oh, these guys do a *show*. This is *great!*" I was so unused to seeing bands do shows. Y'know, Detroit bands did *shows*. And then I saw Iggy and I thought: "*What the hell…?*"

JEFFREY: Well, that's what I was gonna ask because 2009 marks the 40th anniversary of Alice Cooper.

ALICE: Right.

JEFFREY: And it also marks the 40th anniversary of The Stooges. In 1969, anyone who saw the Alice Cooper Group knew that they were seeing something that they'd literally never seen before.

ALICE: Right. And that's the kind of thing that *this* was. *I* was even surprised!

JEFFREY: So that's your first memory of seeing The Stooges.

ALICE: Yeah, I saw them and I went… *Immediately*, you know, my competition gene rose up in me and I went: "*Oh*, here's an entity to be *dealt* with." You know, *this* guy is… This, you know, very few… You know, I'd look at other bands and I'd go: Okay, lead singer, so what, so what, so what, so what. Y'know, 'cause I was pretty used to getting the audience *totally shocked* by what *we* were doing and, you know, nobody had ever seen anything like *me* before. And then I saw somebody that *I* had never seen anything like before.

JEFFREY: So you knew, finally, what it was like for people to see *your* act.

ALICE: Yeah, and the best compliment I think I ever gave anybody was: Iggy's one of the only guys I wouldn't want to go on *after*.

JEFFREY: Well, that's what you always say. When you wrote the liner notes to the reissue of the first Stooges album, you wrote that they made a permanent impression on you, but in what *way* did they make a permanent—

ALICE: I had never seen anybody… You know, first of all, there was no punk—or at least it wasn't *called* punk. I'd seen bands that were kind of raw bands before, that were kind of, you know, just *down*, and I'd just kinda look at them and go: "Ah, they're not very good." 'Cause I'm always looking for how good the guitar player is, and how good the songs are, and I could always just write them off as being crummy garage bands.

But then I heard this band that was *so basic*…and *knew it* to the point where they used it as a theatrical piece. The fact that they just stood there and just played those chords, those three chords…*with an attitude*. And then this guy, this lead singer, who was sort of like Mick Jagger's illegitimate love child, you know, was up there and he was *a total show* unto himself. So I said: It *looks* like an accident…but I know it's *not* an accident. These guys had really created something that is *really* unique to anything that I had ever seen before.

JEFFREY: Well, like you were saying, you saw a lot of bands perform when you were just starting out.

ALICE: Yeah!

JEFFREY: Now how long did it take for you, and at what point, did you realize that The Stooges just weren't just another faceless band, but musicians who were operating *on the same level* as The Alice Cooper Group?

ALICE: It was…it was *totally different*. It was sorta like… To get the audience back after Iggy got on… This was back when he'd go in the audience, get in a fight with a Marine, get knocked out, they'd carry him back up on stage *bleeding*, he'd finish the song, he'd put peanut butter on himself—and still…no props! *He was the prop!* He was the theatrical prop of the band.

JEFFREY: So you knew *immediately* that—

ALICE: This guy was *really good* at what he did, and I just wondered if *he* knew how good he was. You know, *he* was not a magnificent singer and the *songs* were not magnificent songs, but they were *perfect* for that band. And I just got to the point where… I mean, I got addicted to "Loose" and "TV Eye" and "I Wanna Be Your Dog" to the point where—we did so many shows with them—that they were one of the only bands where I would say: "Hey, listen, we're going to see these dudes. I wanna see a couple of these songs." Generally I would just go: "Hey, I'm gonna stay in my dressing room and, you know, get ready for the show" 'cause I just didn't care. But with The Stooges [*laughs*] I wanted to actually see the show!

JEFFREY: Because you never knew what might happen!

ALICE: Yeah, I was… Well, we worked with The Doors before and The Doors were like that, too. Y'know, The Doors had a thing for a while where you went there 'cause you didn't know what Jim was gonna do. You didn't know if Jim was gonna fall off the stage, you didn't know if he was gonna take twenty-five minutes to start the song or.. And honestly, most bands back then were a pretty much formulated thing. So when something came along new like that, you *really* wanted to see it. So working with The Doors was different, but working with The Stooges was *entirely* different.

Right, now we're at Brian Wilson's house, this is amazing!

JEFFREY: What are your thoughts on the fact that you and Iggy both knew and were influenced by Jim Morrison, and the different directions that you both *took* from that?

ALICE: Yeah, I think that… I mean, when I first saw Morrison… The first time I heard him, I went: "This guy's an *opera* singer." You know… [*singing*] "When the mu-sic's o-vah…" I'm going: What kind of voice is *that?* I'm used to Mick Jagger. And then when I *saw* The Doors, I started listening to them and then, all of a sudden, this guy was not just the lead singer, he was, like… [*pauses*] He was like a *poet*. He was sort of, like a… He was almost like a Victorian *poet*. But he was this guy that was just… He was James Dean… He was all these guys rolled up into one. And *totally* unpredictable. There was nothing where you… You really couldn't put a moniker on the guy. He didn't do anything like anybody else.

The rest of the band, Robbie and the rest of the guys, were just great musicians and great players but they were smart enough, when it came to the show, to get out of the way of Jim. Let Jim be the show. Well, that's the same thing with Iggy. Get out of the way, let Iggy do the show.

JEFFREY: And basically, to me, it seems that you took the *cerebral* aspects of The Doors' performance and Morrison's psyche, and Iggy took the *physical* part.

ALICE: I think so, too. I see it as… That's exactly it. Iggy was *always* much more sexual than Alice Cooper when it came to, just, raw sex and down and dirty… Almost sort of like the ultimate hippie. You know: barefoot, torn up Levis, and no shirt—and has no problem with taking his pants off. Whereas Alice was sort of this elegant vampire. I wanted Alice to be the thing that was indescribable. Alice was sort of a surrealistic… He was a lead singer, but he was totally surrealistic. And again, I didn't want you to be able to *compare* me with anybody 'cause really, at that time, there really *wasn't* anybody to compare me with.

So when I saw a kindred spirit in Iggy, I just kind of smiled and went: Okay, this is gonna be fun because… It was a *challenge!* And everybody *always* wanted there to be a feud. Everybody always wanted there to be: Who's crazier? Alice or Iggy? Who did this and who did that? And then they started *combining* 'em, okay. Alice took a crap on stage and Iggy ate it. Or Iggy took a crap on stage and Alice ate it. Then they started combining the urban legends. [*laughs*]

JEFFREY: Didn't you and Iggy once go to Brian Wilson's house?

ALICE: Yeah!

JEFFREY: Iggy says he has *no* recollection of this. What do *you* remember of it?

I'm serious, this is… the greatest song ever written

ALICE: That was after the Grammy awards, and not only… I remember this *so specifically* because we were sitting there and he says: "I want you guys to come over." And it was me and Iggy and, I think, one of the guys from Three Dog Night, Danny Hutton. I think he was there, and somebody else. And we went there—it might have been Bernie Taupin, I'm not sure—but we went there and we kept looking at each other going: "Right, now we're at Brian Wilson's house, this is amazing!"

And…he couldn't get the door open and he said: "Be very quiet, my kids are all asleep." And he couldn't get his key out, so he *broke* the window with a big rock. Then, of course, he went in and he brought his kid out, he was holding his [*laughs*] the baby by one leg, saying: "Look, this is my baby." It was *totally* crazy. And then he went down in the basement and he sits down at the piano and he says: "I'm gonna play you guys the greatest song ever written." And we sat there thinking: Well, that'll be good if Brian Wilson says... And then he starts playin'

Photograph ©
Jeffrey Morgan

Photograph © James Pappaconstantine

Photograph © James Pappaconstantine

Photograph © Jeffrey Morgan

Photograph © James Pappaconstantine

Photograph ©
Shawn Cook

Photograph ©
Shawn Cook

Photograph © Shawn Cook

"Mammy's Little Baby Loves Short'nin' Bread." And he says: "I'm serious. This is technically the greatest song ever written." And you know, we sat there and went: "Okay."

And the cool thing was, he had in his basement a seventy-two track studio and he kept the master tapes of *Pet Sounds* on the board so you could *mix* it anyway you wanted to mix it.

JEFFREY: Just like they do now on the Internet.

ALICE: Yeah! So Iggy was on one… I had five or six faders down on one set, I had another one down here. Danny Hutton had a few down here. And we were mixing it the way *we* wanted to hear it. I pushed my fader up and all of a sudden you heard *dogs* barking and I said: "Where did *that* come from?" But that was the toy. Everybody who came up there could mix *Pet Sounds*.

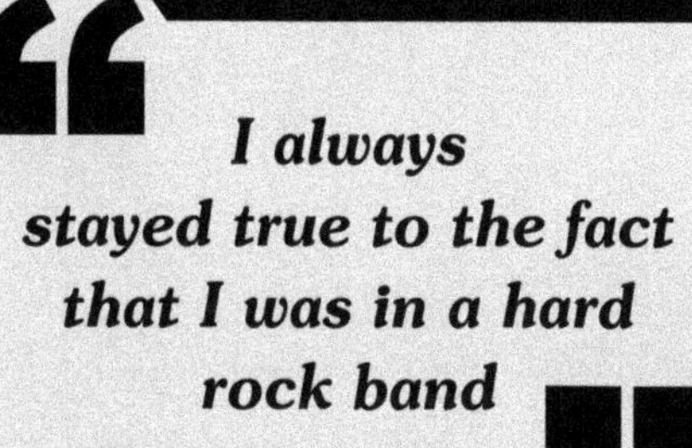
I always stayed true to the fact that I was in a hard rock band

JEFFREY: I once asked Ted Nugent if he thought that his music would have been different in some way if he'd grown up in Chicago or New York as opposed to Detroit and he said he didn't think it would've mattered. He said that no matter where he'd grown up, what you saw now was probably what you would've got. Do *you* think The Stooges would've been the same had they been from another state other than Michigan?

ALICE: I honestly *don't* think so, unless... I think if it was from a Midwest state like Cincinnati, St. Louis, Chicago, Detroit, yeah. *But*… Detroit had that added sense of *danger* to it. Detroit had that, you know… We were all Detroit kids, we all grew up in Detroit. I mean, *I* grew up and it was always a very *dangerous* town. But it was also… The one thing about Detroit that was *very* unusual was that, *even now*, if you were from Detroit, you were *fraternity*. In other words, I can walk into a house full of rappers, who were the most dangerous guys in the world, and they'd look at me and I'd go: "Detroit" and they'd go: "Oh, okay." And it *was* okay. In fact, they'd probably *protect* you. Because you're a Detroit guy. There was always this fraternity of: *If you're from Detroit, you're okay*. You could walk into… My guys in my band, with hair down to their waist, could walk into the…probably the most dangerous bar in Detroit, where there's nothing but black guys that kill people for a living, and we would be fine. Because we're musicians and we're from Detroit. So you're okay.

JEFFREY: How do you feel about The Stooges now receiving the overwhelming recognition that they now enjoy, given the ups and downs that both you and Iggy have suffered through over the past four decades?

ALICE: I think the one thing that stayed consistent is that *we* stayed consistent. We might have gone through a lot with what happened in our lives, but I go see Iggy now and I think of what Alice does now, and it's *not that much different* from what we did in the beginning. I always stayed true to my theatrics and I always stayed true to the fact that I was in a hard rock band: two guitars, bass, drums.

The first thing that we would do, ninety percent of our show, was we would rehearse the music. Ninety percent. The other ten percent was the show. To me, you've got to be a *killer* rock band before you're a theatrical band. And I think The Stooges were the same kind of thing. They believed in that kind of music *so much*, that that's what they did. And if they ever started doing things other than what they do, I would be disappointed. I say the same thing about AC/DC. If they ever learn, like, three or four more chords, they wouldn't be AC/DC. [*laughs*]

JEFFREY: You spoke earlier about always looking for how good the guitar player is. How does Ron Asheton fit into that line of thought?

ALICE: Ron Asheton was not easy to know. Ron Asheton was sorta like Glen Buxton. He was very similar to Glen Buxton, in the fact that he *wasn't* the life of the party. He was the guy that stood in the corner with his drink with his sunglasses on and his white boots, whatever he was wearing. He had a look that was very, very cool and he didn't say a lot and when he played, he played *within himself*, is what I like to say. He never tried to play something that he couldn't play. So he played totally within himself and he was *very satisfied* with what he played. I don't think we ever heard how *good* Ronnie could be, because the music didn't really go to that, it never really asked for him to be a great guitar player. I mean, as far as a lead player.

But, when you talk about keeping that thing…keeping that music down right to point…right to the *guts* of it, *that's* what he did. I just don't think that he was in the type of band where… If he was a *great* guitar player, probably… I mean, I'm talking about like a Steve Vai or a Jeff Beck, he really wouldn't have fitted in that band. I think he needed to be a *real punk* "I just like to play this kind of music" guitar player. He might… On his own, he might've been really, really good. I never heard him really just let out and play. But he never let me down, he never disappointed me when I saw him on stage.

JEFFREY: When I spoke with Lou Reed and Ron Mael back in the '70s, both of them bemoaned the fact that their audiences often didn't see the humor in what they were

> **“*I think a lot of people at that time missed the sense of humor in Alice Cooper and missed the sense of humor in Iggy*”**

doing. Do you feel the same way?

ALICE: Yeah. I think a lot of people at that time missed the sense of humor in Alice Cooper and missed the sense of humor in Iggy. I think there definitely was a sense of humor to both bands that a lot of people missed. They saw us as being something that their *parents* hated and they saw us as being something they would like to *be* like…

We were almost like characters that really didn't *belong* in this world. It was one of those things where… It was sort of like you were witnessing a couple of *monsters*, really. Iggy was unreal, I was unreal—and even *Ted Nugent* was unreal. When Ted would get on stage he was this unreal kind of *thing* up there. [*laughs*] And I think that was the thing about us that was great: the fact that we didn't *relate* to a lot of people.

JEFFREY: And a lot of people *still* can't relate to the three of you.

ALICE: Yeah, I *love* that!

Photograph © Robert Matheu

Photograph ©
Shawn Cook

AFTERWORD
by Dennis Dunaway

Ironic that a guy that knows how to structure a sentence together is writing a book about the kids in the back of the class.

Dennis Dunaway

Photograph © Robert Matheu

Photograph ©
Robert Matheu

All Photographs © James Pappaconstantine

Photograph ©
Philip Solomonson
Philamonjaro.com

Photograph ©
Philip Solomonson
Philamonjaro.com

THANK YOU KINDLY

Thanks be to **God**, first and foremost.

***

I'm eternally and deeply indebted to my parents, **Anne Morgan** and **Joe Morgan**, for a lifetime of unconditional love and lenience.

***

This book would not exist were it not for the incessant insistence of **Teddie Dahlin**, the visionary CEO and Publisher of New Haven, who commissioned it on the grounds that I had more to say about Alice Cooper. Believe me when I tell you that, having already said everything I had to say about him, a book about Alice was the absolute last thing in the world that I'd ever want to write - but she was right.

***

Needless to say, both **Alice Cooper** and **Toby Mamis** deserve credit for their friendship and support over the many decades, far above and beyond whatever thanks I could ever possibly hope to say or repay.

***

My sincere thanks to **Dennis Dunaway** for writing the Afterword.

***

A long-overdue word of recognition goes to **Steve "Mac" McLennan** who, in addition to using his Coop contacts to acquire most of the photos in this book, also provided some much-needed encouragement and timely advice along the way. Thanks, Mac.

***

Thanks also to **Trevor Dare**, who worked with Mac to patiently and painstakingly take the time to upgrade and tag a vast majority of the photos in this book, thus making my job as editor all the more easier.

***

My thanks, as always, to **Sheryl Matheu** for graciously allowing me to use in my books the photographs taken by her late husband and my good friend, **Robert Matheu**.

***

I am indeed indebted to **Trevor Norris** for letting me use the historic photographs that our good friend **Nash The Slash** took of the Alice Cooper Group performing here in Toronto at the Galaxi Youth Pavilion in the Canadian National Exhibition on August 31st 1969. For years, Nash and I talked about putting out a book of our photographs, but his death prevented that plan from coming to fruition. That's why I know that Nash would be just as pleased as I am that some of our photographs are finally appearing together in this book. Trevor, I thank you for enabling that to happen.

***

Once again I give another big collective thank you to all of the photographers who generously donated their images to the cause. You know how I hate to repeat myself, so please turn back to the second page and take another good long gander at their names because, without them, all you'd have to look at are my words—and what fun would *that* be?

***

And speaking of fun, where would I be without **Pete Cunliffe**, the absolute best designer a rock critic could have? Pete *gets it* like nobody else does; that's why he's always able to make my books look so visually vital.

***

My thanks and a tip of the Howdy! hat to **Ric Root** for his adept typography skills which help make the *Rock Critic Confidential* advert on the last page so retro reminiscent.

***

What else can I say about **Brian "Renfield" Nelson** that I haven't already said? Plenty. And I deeply regret that I no longer have the opportunity to say it to him. I wish I could have done more to help you. I knew about the darkness, but I didn't know how pervasive it was. Nevertheless, you were still able to provide more than enough laughter and light to ignite what I write, alright? So thanks, pally.

***

And a sincere heartfelt thanks to *you* for buying and reading *Alice Cooper Confidential*, regardless of whether you purchased it because you're an avid obsessive completist or because you thought that it might be worth your hard-earned money. I appreciate your support and I thank you once again.

*** *** ***

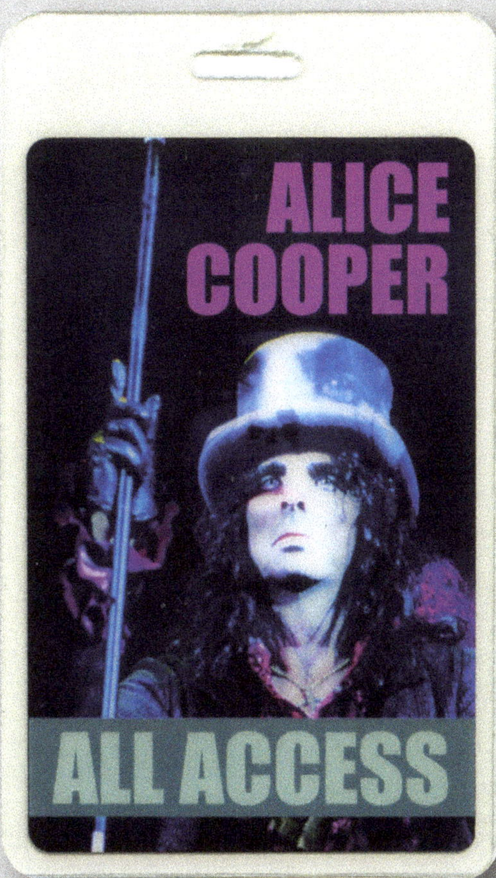

***

A final word about being a fan which, at its heart, is what *Alice Cooper Confidential* is all about. Toby once told me: "We're lucky to know him." These words he speaks are true, because that "we're" includes everyone who ever bought one of his records; attended one of his concerts; or tapped one of their toes whenever "School's Out" came on the radio.
We're *all* not worthy.

***

So what better way to conclude *Alice Cooper Confidential* than by repeating what I wrote at the end of that much-mentioned authorized biography. Words which, thankfully, still remain as true today as they did when I first wrote them, back at the end of the last century:

***

There can be no denying that this is nothing less than the gripping story of one of rock 'n' roll's most exciting heroes. The chronicle of Alice Cooper's vastly influential career is as sensationally spellbinding as the very life it depicts.

***

His accomplishments herald Alice Cooper as a true original in an era where originality is disdained. The triumphs and tribulations heard on Alice Cooper's albums continue to thrill millions all over the world to this day, with his name and image remaining an inextricable part of our language and culture, as familiar as they are enduring.

***

Indeed, no better example of Alice Cooper's timelessness can be found than in the fact that he still sings "I'm Eighteen" with all the passionate fervor and belief that he first brought to the song. For as long as there is a part of us that will always remain 18, we will all have far more in common with Alice Cooper than we might realize—or dare to publicly admit.

***

After all, you're still here, and so is Alice.
Rocking out like all get out.
And ain't that what it's all about?

***

Remember The Coop, huh?

Major funding for *Alice Cooper Confidential* provided by

The National Endowment for Rock Criticism

Additional funding provided by

16 Magazine

Rock Critics Without Borders

The Wisenheimer Arts Council

The Alfred P. Fakakta Foundation

The Alan Freedmason Charitable Trust

Pansy Smiff and Mrs. Abagail Flusser

The Illuminati Investment Group

Nance Feigele Fund

Payola Suisse

and taxpayers like you

Thank you!

Photograph ©
Philip Solomonson
Philamonjaro.com

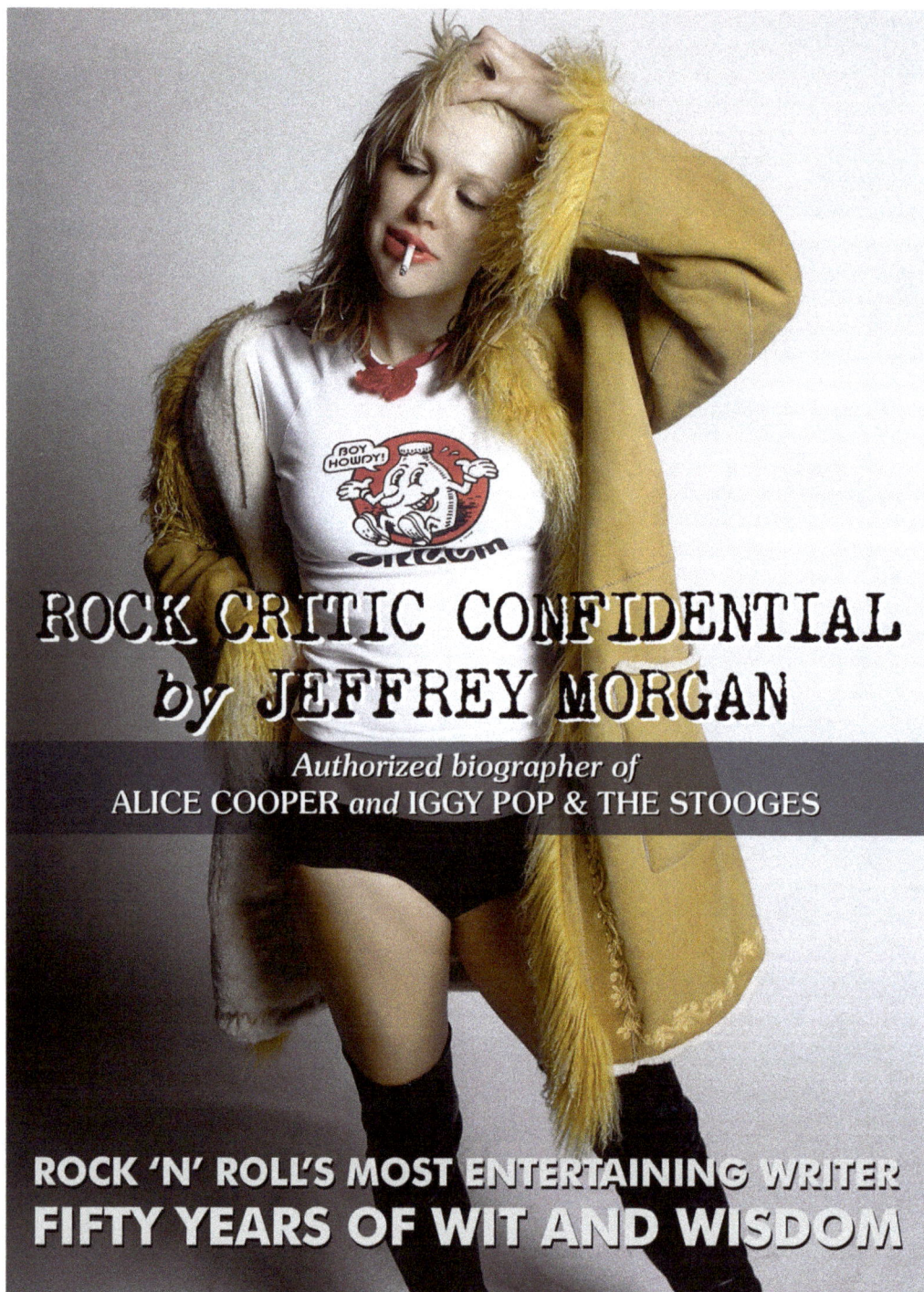

www.ingramcontent.com/pod-product-compliance
Lightning Source LLC
Chambersburg PA
CBHW062009150426
42812CB00013BA/2583
9781949515442